U.S. Marine Corps
SCOUT-SNIPER

U.S. Marine Corps
SCOUT-SNIPER

World War II
and
Korea

Peter R. Senich

PALADIN PRESS
BOULDER, COLORADO

Also by Peter R. Senich:

The Complete Book of U.S. Sniping
The German Assault Rifle: 1935-1945
The German Sniper: 1914-1945

U.S. Marine Corps Scout-Sniper:
World War II and Korea
by Peter R. Senich

Copyright © 1993 by Peter R. Senich

ISBN 0-87364-710-6
Printed in the United States of America

Published by Paladin Press, a division of
Paladin Enterprises, Inc., P.O. Box 1307,
Boulder, Colorado 80306, USA.
(303) 443-7250

Direct inquires and/or orders to the above address.

All rights reserved. Except for use in a review, no
portion of this book may be reproduced in any form
without the express written permission of the publisher.

Neither the author nor the publisher assumes
any responsibility for the use or misuse of
information contained in this book.

The use of the U.S. Marine Corps emblem on the cover
of this book in no way constitutes an endorsement by the
U.S. Marine Corps or the Department of Defense.

Dust jacket photo credit: U.S. Marine Corps.
Front flap illustration by Max Crace.

Contents

Chapter 1	Sharpshooter: The Time between Wars	1
Chapter 2	Sniper Equipment: The Rifle Team Influence	23
Chapter 3	A Target Scope for Snipers	39
Chapter 4	Sniper Issue: A Match Grade System	57
Chapter 5	The Riflescope in Combat: Problems in the Field	71
Chapter 6	The Bolt-Action Sniper Rifle: The End of an Era	87
Chapter 7	The Target Telescope	103
Chapter 8	Telescopic Sights: The M1 Rifles	117
Chapter 9	Scout-Sniper: Training the Specialist	155
Chapter 10	Sniper: The Japanese Approach	177
Chapter 11	Scout-Sniper: Combat Experiences	195
Chapter 12	Special Equipment: The Combat Edge	217

Preface and Acknowledgments

An innovative sharpshooting concept developed during the First World War in Europe. The general principles, organization, and methods employed by the highly successful scouts, observers, and snipers against the Imperial German Army would serve American military forces for more than 20 years.

An extension of the state of the art as it existed in 1918, the United States Marine Corps (USMC) view of training scouts and snipers after 1920 was based on trench warfare and the tactics developed by the British during the "Great War."

As the General Staff (British Expeditionary Force) had stated in "Scouting and Patrolling" (December 1917), an early treatise dealing with the training and employment of snipers:

> The distinction between Scouting and Sniping is clear: the primary object of a Scout is to obtain information; of a Sniper, to kill.

Many of the precepts established during World War I would serve as the foundation for training Marine Corps snipers during the war with Japan. Yet with the advent of jungle warfare in the South Pacific in 1942, an entirely new chapter in the art of fieldcraft and marksmanship as it related to the Marine sniper would necessitate formulating new and more efficient tactics necessary to effectively eliminate the enemy and remain alive in the process.

As a part of the overall effort to field satisfactory sniper equipment beginning in late 1940, in addition to evaluating sniping rifles, telescopic sights, and related hardware, the Marine Corps set about to determine the best course of action for training and fielding a new breed of combat specialist: the scouts and snipers, or simply "scout-snipers," as they would be known in the Corps.

It is a topic of considerable interest among military history buffs and small arms enthusiasts. And while a fair amount of information has been published concerning the USMC scout-sniper, until now, the historical continuity of this fascinating subject has never been satisfactorily summarized in one publication.

Unfortunately, amidst the general apathy that followed World War II, untold quantities of significant documents and records were either destroyed or so completely dispersed that a concise determination of this unique facet of Marine Corps history has required painstaking research.

This work is the culmination of a veritable odyssey through Marine Corps archives that began more than 20 years ago. The material presented herein consists of information obtained from documents, reports, letters, intelligence sources, direct observations, and the firsthand recollections of knowledgeable individuals who served within, or in close proximity to, the Marine Corps as it then existed.

A delicate balance between what was actually employed by combat personnel at the field level as opposed to what the "official" Marine Corps position was in many cases, this volume provides a thorough presentation of the circumstances surrounding the training, equipment, and combat experiences of the United States Marine Corps scout-snipers during the war in the Pacific and the Korean conflict.

The following organizations rendered invaluable assistance in the form of documents, technical information, photographs, and other pertinent material. For this help I wish to thank:

American Rifleman magazine
Brookfield Precision Tool
John Unertl Optical Company
Leatherneck magazine
Library of Congress
Lyman Products Corporation
Marine Corps Air-Ground Museum
Marine Corps Gazette
Marine Corps Historical Center
Marine Raider Museum
National Archives and Records Service
Parsons Riflescope Service
Rock Island Arsenal Museum
Springfield Armory NHS
U.S. Army
U.S. Patent Office
West Point Museum

In addition, the following gentlemen provided me with photographs, vital data, first-person accounts, and, in many cases, their encouragement:

J.B. Anderhub
Maxwell G. Atchisson
Robert Bell
Michael Buchman
Clark S. Campbell
Bruce N. Canfield
Francis B. Conway
Allan D. Cors
G.A. Costner
Daniel J. Crawford
Richard Culver
Stan Deka
William Douglas
Chris Doumis
Scott A. Duff
Garry Fellers
Stephen M. Fleischman
Kent J. Goff

John G. Griffiths
Kenneth Haney
William D. Harris
Carlos Hathcock
Albert Hauser
Otto Hebel
Fred L. Honeycutt, Jr.
Eric Johnson
Harold E. Johnson
Chris Marsh
Mitchell E. Mateiko
John C. McPherson
George Niewenhous
Hayes Otoupalik
Gil Parsons
William J. Ricca
Craig Roberts
R.G. Rosenquist
Elroy Sanford
Win Scott
Paul M. Senich
Thomas Shannon
K.L. Smith-Christmas
Thomas F. Swearengen
John Unertl, Jr.
Donald Urtz
Stuart G. Vogt
Walter R. Walsh
Joseph T. Ward
Dean H. Whitaker
Doss H. White
Daniel T. Whiteman
William H. Woodin

A very special expression of thanks to:

Max Crace	Kenneth Kogan
Mark K. Edmondson	Elliott R. Laine, Jr.
Blair M. Gluba	Donald G. Thomas

Although these organizations and individuals deserve all due credit for helping me locate and piece together the myriad informational odds and ends, any error in putting these pieces in their final form properly falls to me.

Preface and Acknowledgments

Scout-Sniper

"An especially trained RIFLEMAN (SSN745) who engages in scouting and patrolling activities to obtain information concerning strength, disposition, and probable intentions of enemy forces; disrupts enemy communications; destroys enemy personnel by rifle fire. May perform supervisory duties involving the control, coordination, and tactical employment of other SCOUT-SNIPERS. Must possess all the qualifications of SSN745 (Rifleman). Must be particularly skilled in employing the principles of camouflage to conceal himself. Must know how to move over various kinds of terrain without being detected. Must be skilled in the use of the rifle, with and without telescope sight. Must know techniques of searching terrain for signs of enemy activity. Must be able to read maps, make sketches, and use compass and field glass."

—United States Marine Corps, June 1945

Sharpshooter: The Time between Wars

CHAPTER 1

The A5 telescopic sight (style A, 5 power) manufactured by the Winchester Repeating Arms Company at its New Haven, Connecticut, works, was considered to be one of the best commercial sights available in the United States when introduced in 1910. Despite its efficiency for target shooting under controlled conditions, and its rather extensive use by British and Canadian snipers during the early stages of the First World War, the A5 rifle scope proved entirely too fragile for sustained combat use. Nevertheless, the Winchester device was the only rifle scope to see unilateral use by British, Canadian, and, to a limited extent, American snipers following their involvement in the European war.

As discussed in early Winchester technical data, in original form the A5 scope was unique in that the tube was not drawn, but bored and turned from a solid piece of steel. Although a variety of reticle patterns were available and interchangeable, the standard, single cross-hair pattern appears to have seen the most use in sights employed by the military.

The nickel-steel front mount, designed to prevent indentation of the tube, had a spring-loaded, bevel-nosed plunger engaging in a long corresponding groove in the underside of the tube to keep it from rotating, and to permit longitudinal movement. This ensured that the axis of the tube remained constant once adjusted.

The standard commercial rear mount, shaped to allow clearance for elevation and windage adjustments, had two springs to hold the tube in contact with the elevation and windage adjustment screws (drums). The tube was constantly thrust upward toward the top of the mount by a "grasshopper" type of flat-wire spring with a coil or turn in it near its lower end. Standard procedure with the Winchester sight was for the tube to be pressed downward gently after a shot was fired to ensure that it was seated properly. Lateral thrust was provided by a spring-loaded plunger located in a housing in the left side of the mount. Elevation and windage adjustment, set by micrometer dials with divisions (markings) enameled in red at the factory, were near impossible to read in anything but optimum light. The vast majority of A5 sights that saw military use have the division markings redone in white for obvious reasons.

World War I Marine Corps sharpshooter with an M1903 Springfield rifle and 5-power Winchester A5 telescopic sight. Though few in actual number, USMC combat personnel were trained as scouts, observers, and snipers during the Great War in Europe. (Max Crace illustration.)

U.S. Marine Corps Scout-Sniper: World War II and Korea

Winchester A5 telescopic rifle sight (Style A, 5-power) in standard commercial form, as introduced to the American market in 1910. A popular target scope prior to World War I, the Winchester sight saw extensive use by military rifle teams for match shooting purposes. (Peter R. Senich.)

Standard commercial Winchester A5 sight bases as mounted to an M1903 Springfield (474180). In this case, the rear scope base was attached to the standard sight base in order to place both scope bases on the barrel (6-inch spacing), as deemed desirable in some quarters for this type of scope. So far as some of the early match shooters were concerned, "7.2 inches between block centers is predicated on the scope being at least 18 inches long. If it is shorter then the blocks must be closer together—6 inches for the Winchester A5." (Springfield Armory NHS.)

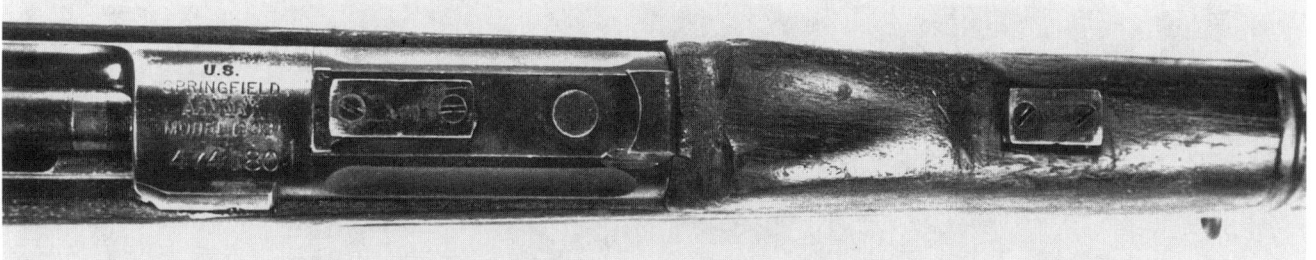

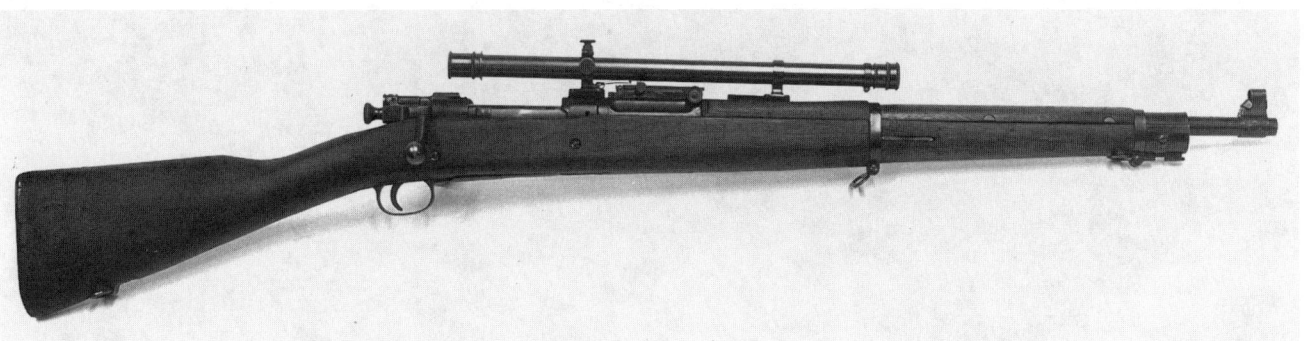

Winchester B5 telescopic rifle sight (Style B, 5-power) mounted to an '03 Springfield (454040) with early Marine Corps service to its credit. According to early Winchester data, "The Style B–5 power telescope has the same magnification as the Style A–5 power, but a smaller field of view." A limited number of B5 sights were provided for training purposes during World War I. (Douglas Collection.)

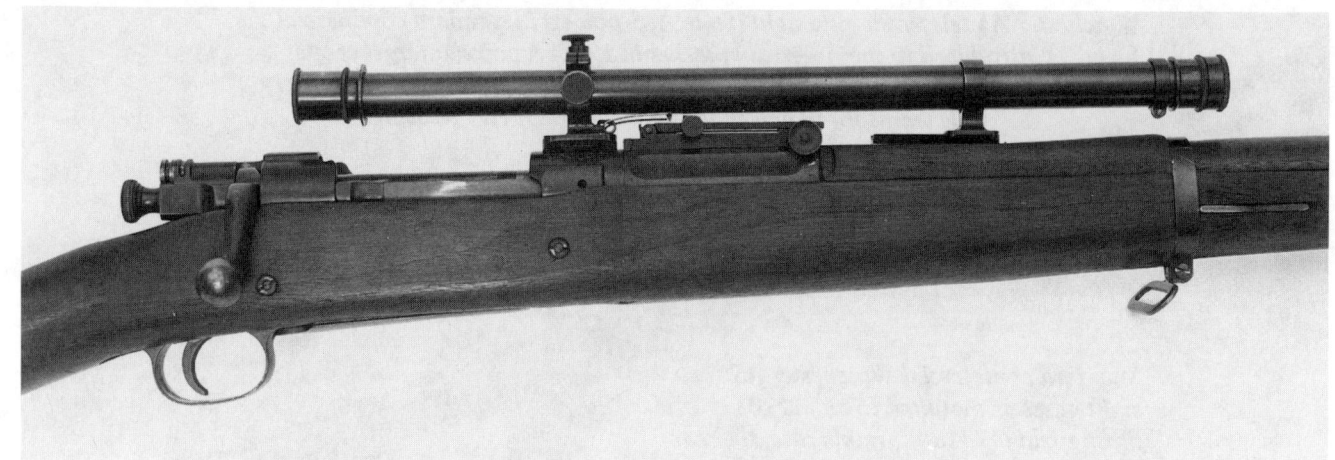

A close-up view of the USMC M1903 rifle with the Winchester B5 telescopic sight. Though virtually the same as the Style A, the Style B was available in 3, 4, and 5 power. The No. 1 rear mount (shown) did not have micrometer markings. The front mount was used with both the No. 1 and No. 2 rear target mounting. Marine Corps markings (USMC) and the rifle serial number appear beneath the stock behind the trigger guard. (Douglas Collection.)

A Marine Corps sergeant circa World War I, sighting a Winchester A5-equipped M1903 Springfield rifle. Despite some combat exposure, the Winchester sight served the Marine Corps primarily as a target scope. (U.S. Marine Corps.)

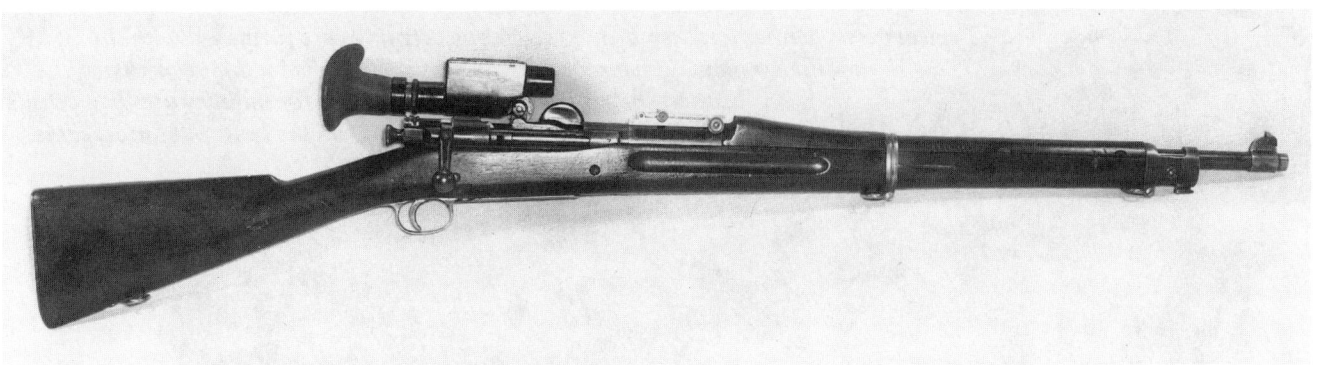

A unique First World War Springfield Armory M1903 sniper rifle (1917) with a Warner & Swasey 5.2-power M1913 Telescopic Musket Sight. Whenever Army and Marine Corps combat personnel were billeted in the same area, enterprising individuals often made off with a weapon of their choice from one camp or the other. A documented example of this practice was an original Army sharpshooting rifle employed by a Marine marksman during World War I. A number of "notches" were added to the handguard in the process. (Cors Collection.)

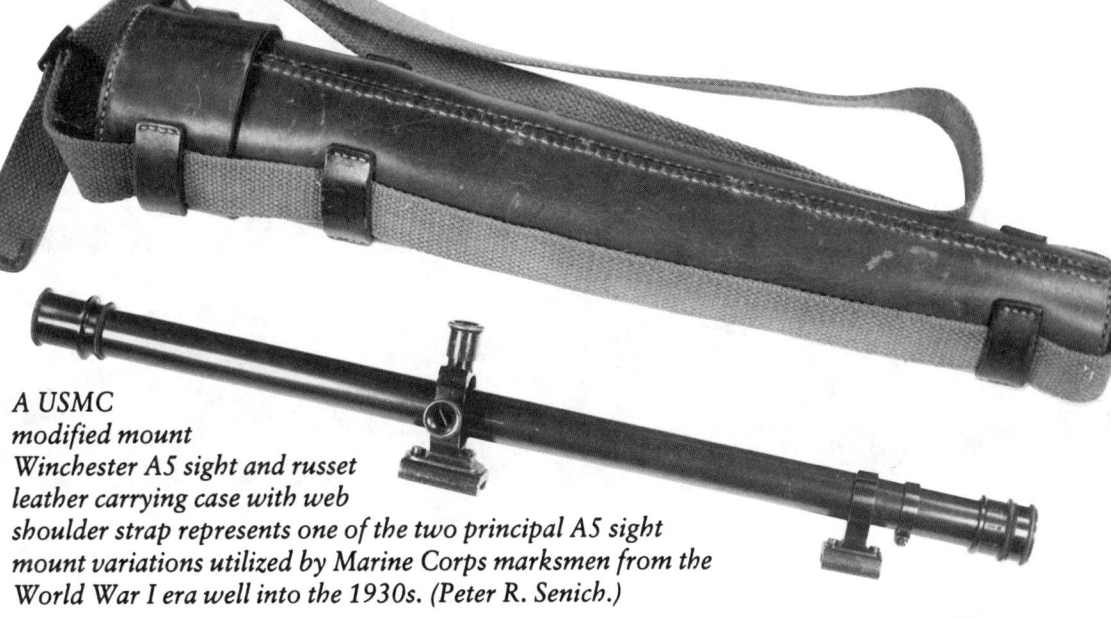

A USMC modified mount Winchester A5 sight and russet leather carrying case with web shoulder strap represents one of the two principal A5 sight mount variations utilized by Marine Corps marksmen from the World War I era well into the 1930s. (Peter R. Senich.)

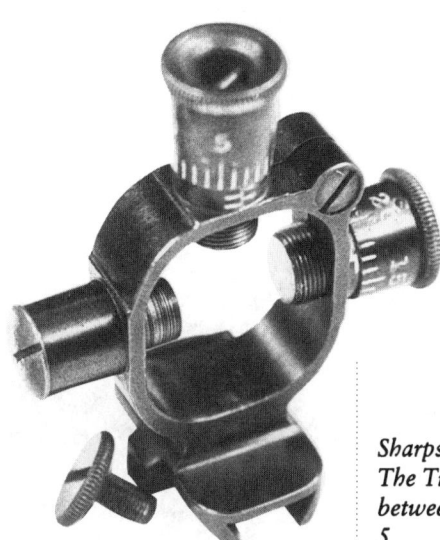

Comparative view of a standard commercial Winchester A5, No. 2 rear mount (right) and the same type of mount as modified for USMC service. In addition to the "Mann-type" taper dovetail mounting, a spring-loaded plunger replaced the standard "grasshopper" spring. The elevation and windage adjustment drums and values remained the same. (Peter R. Senich.)

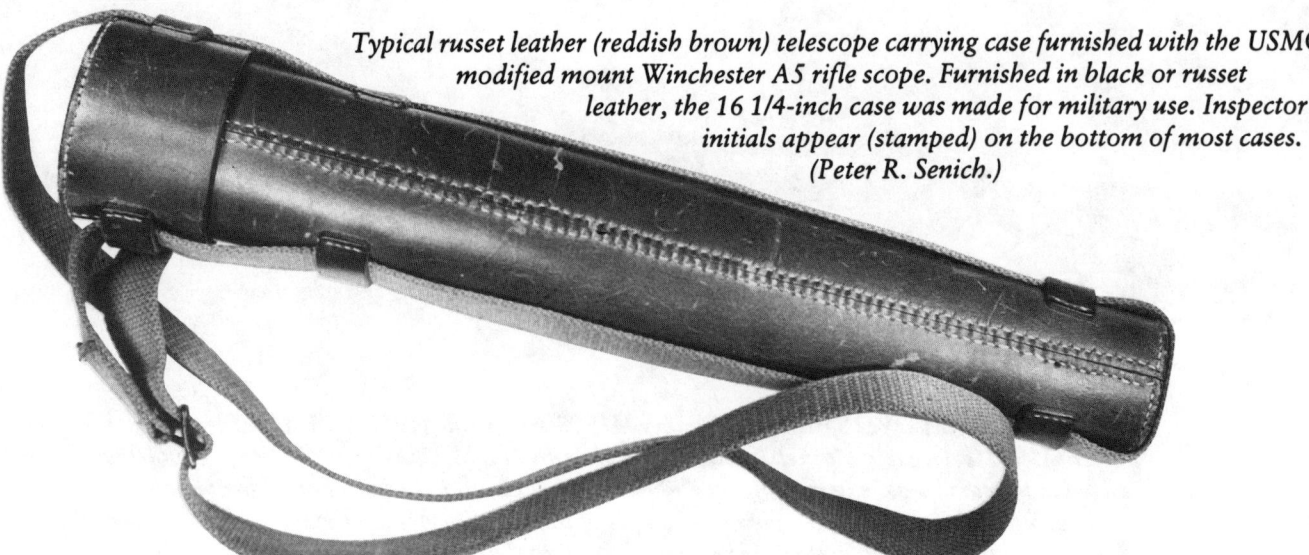

Typical russet leather (reddish brown) telescope carrying case furnished with the USMC modified mount Winchester A5 rifle scope. Furnished in black or russet leather, the 16 1/4-inch case was made for military use. Inspector's initials appear (stamped) on the bottom of most cases. (Peter R. Senich.)

Model 1903 rifle and USMC modified mount Winchester A5 sight with bases attached to the barrel and receiver ring for 7.2-inch spacing between mount centers as an alternate to 6-inch spacing. Each provided different adjustment values at the target at various ranges with a given mount. For some, the longer spacing was considered optimum for "long-range rifles." (Peter R. Senich.)

A close-up view of the typical tapered sight bases as employed with the M1903 Springfield rifle for Marine Corps A5 scope mountings. Even though their function remained the same, various tapered dovetail scope mounting blocks were used with the Winchester sight. (Peter R. Senich.)

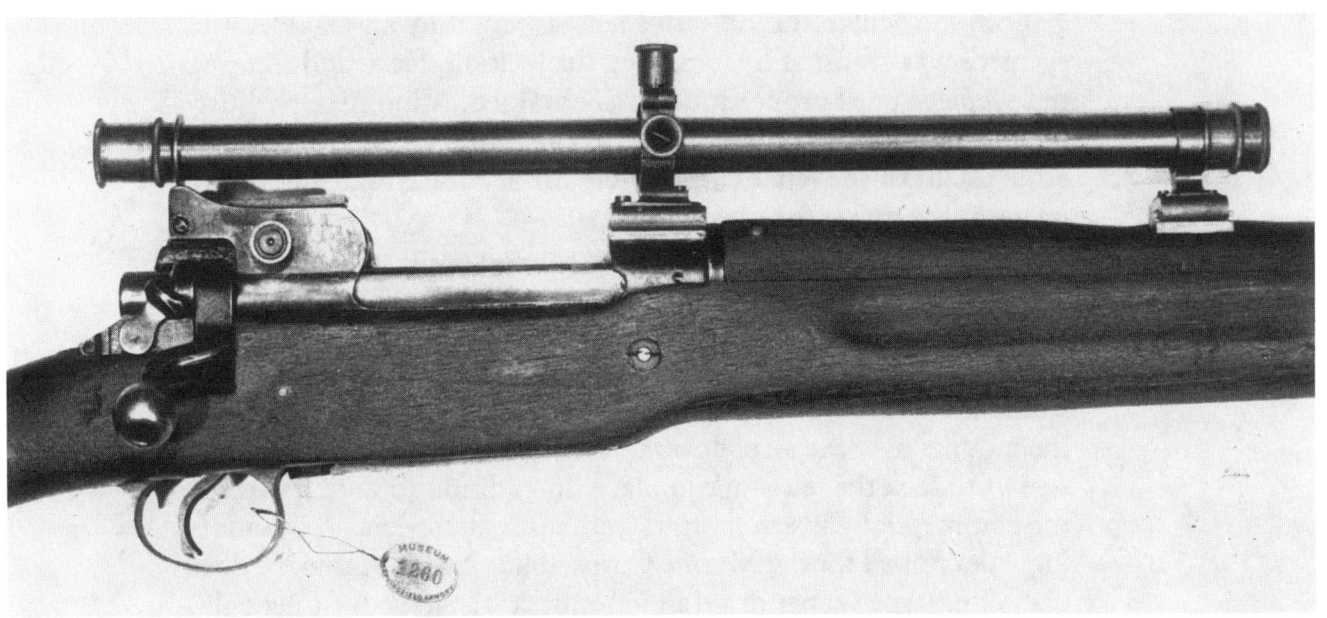

Model 1917 (Enfield) rifle with a USMC modified mount (tapered base) Winchester A5 telescopic sight, and experimental Elder rear sight (adjustable windage) once considered for Marine Corps use. (Springfield Armory NHS.)

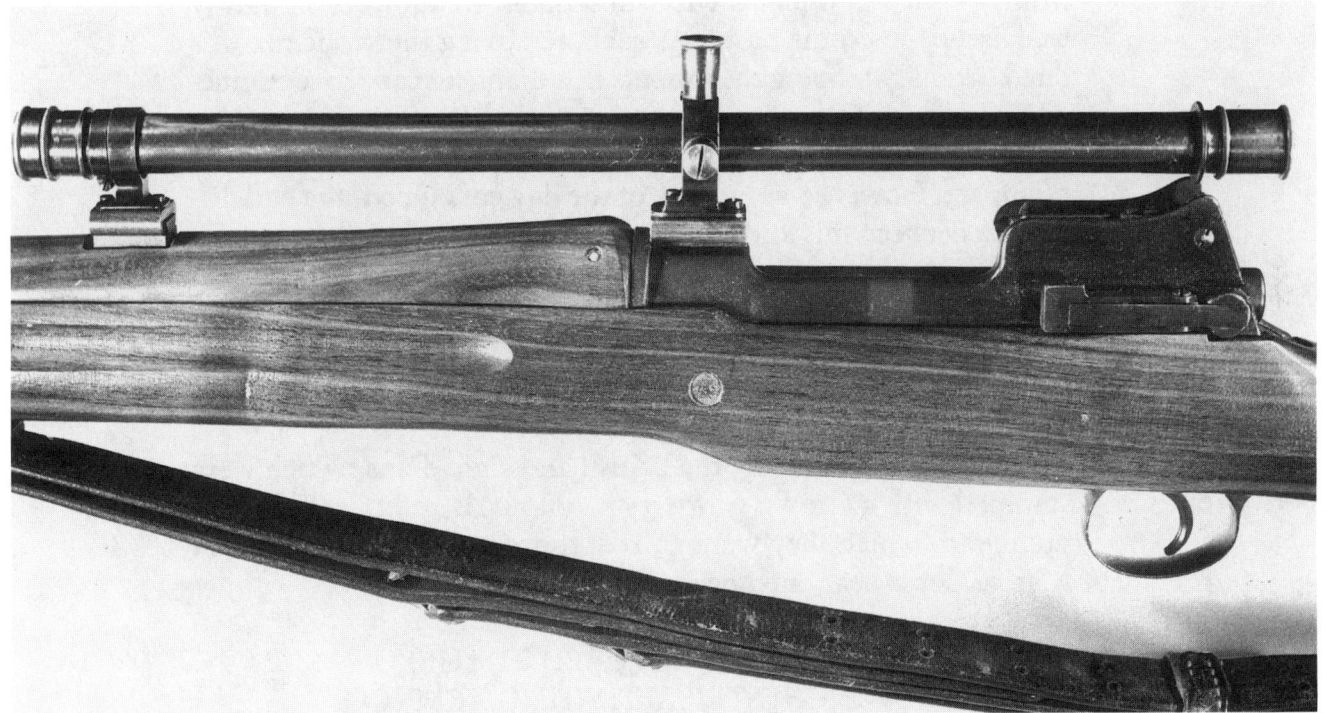

A standard Model 1917 (Enfield) rifle with a USMC modified mount Winchester A5 telescopic sight. Although Marine marksmanship and the Enfield rifle are rarely connected, according to M.D. Waite (American Rifleman, Sept. 1976), "In 1918, the Model 1917 rifle was prescribed for use at the National Matches to be held that year at Camp Perry, Ohio. In these competitions Corporal F.L. Branson, USMC, won the 1,000-yard Wimbledon Cup Match and gold medal award with a score of 92. He fired standard Model 1906 ball ammunition in his rifle." By all accounts, a substantial number of Model 1917 rifles were placed in USMC ordnance depots following World War I. (Conway Collection.)

Both the ocular and objective lenses were fully adjustable. The eyepiece was adjusted by loosening the locking sleeve and rotating the eyepiece until proper focus was obtained. Micrometer adjustment of the objective lens provided a simple means for minute adjustment of the lenses and reticle for accurate focusing of the image at the reticle for various ranges.

A locking stop ring located between the front mount and the objective end of the scope positioned the sight for correct eye relief (approximately 2 inches) when pulled back into battery after firing.

Placing the scope on the weapon entailed turning out both the front and rear mount clamping screws as far as necessary, slipping the mounts over the steel dovetail bases, and firmly tightening the screws to lock the telescope in place. In addition to military use of the commercial pattern mounts and bases, a "special A5 mounting," developed for the Marine Corps, made use of Mann-Neidner or "Mann-type" taper dovetail bases, special click adjustment elevation and windage drums, and a spring-loaded plunger directly beneath the tube in place of the regular "grasshopper" spring.

The mounts in this case, without clamping screws and corresponding to the configuration of the taper dovetail bases, were firmly pushed into place, with subsequent weapon recoil tightly wedging them on the bases. As such, removing the scope necessitated carefully tapping the mounts in a manner that proved somewhat difficult. The primary purpose of this system was to ensure that removing and replacing the sight would not change the point of impact. However, as experts of the day concluded, the end difference between this and the standard A5 mounts was not enough to justify the increased cost and trouble.

Although Winchester mounts with regular elevation and windage drums were also modified for use with Mann-type bases, the A5 telescopic sights employed by the military were standard commercial scopes.

Unlike those issued by the British and Canadians, which were stamped with a Crown property proof mark and the rifle serial number to which they were paired, those used by the Army and Marine Corps bear only the manufacturer's legend:

MANUFACTURED BY THE
WINCHESTER REPEATING ARMS CO.
-A5
NEW HAVEN, CONN. U.S.A.
PATENTED FEBRUARY 9, 1909

A method of mounting the Winchester scope on the Model 1903 Springfield service rifle had been devised and noted in the "Report of the Chief of Ordnance" as early as 1912. In 1915, however, comprehensive evaluations of various telescopic sights by the Army School of Musketry, including both top- and side-mounted A5 sights, found the following objections to the Winchester sight, as recorded in a report dated 19 December 1915:

(A) The field of view is so small on account of the excessive power as to seriously affect its usefulness, except for slow fire at fixed targets for which work it was considered excellent.

(B) The spacing of the brackets only 6 inches apart on such a long telescope is considered a source of weakness.

(C) The bolt of the rifle cannot be operated unless the telescope is pushed forward about 2-1/2 inches from its firing position. This fact and the necessity of drawing the sight back to the firing position after each shot materially increases the time of firing.

(D) The exit pupil is so small that the sight is of no use in poor light.

For these reasons, the Army School of Musketry reports that the Winchester A5 sight is not suitable for general military use.

Concurrent with the Army's rejection of the A5 rifle scope, the British and Canadians, desperately attempting to match the German sniping effort, obtained a considerable number of readily available A5 sights, adapting them to both specially modified Ross sporting rifles and to the British S.M.L.E., Mark III service arm for sniping purposes.

After the United States was drawn into the European conflict, as an expediency, the A5 sight was pressed into service as cited by the *Handbook of Ordnance Data*, dated 15 November 1918: "Five hundred of these sights were purchased by the United States Army, Ordnance Department, for emergency training use."

While serving primarily in a supplementary capacity with the Army, the Marine Corps adopted the Winchester A5 scope as its sniper standard:

The Winchester telescopic sight, model A5, produced by the Winchester Repeating Arms Co., with a special Marine Corps mounting, was found satisfactory in use by the Marine Corps and adopted as Marine Corps standard.

In the case of either the Army or USMC, however, extremely few A5 sights were employed by American snipers in European combat zones during the First World War.

A combat sketch by W.J. Aylward depicts a Marine Corps sniper sighting his mark from a rooftop at Chateau Thierry, 1918. Telescopic sights were considered of marginal value by some riflemen, and according to various accounts, many Army and USMC marksmen actually preferred using conventional sights for sharpshooting purposes during World War I. The rifle is a Model 1917 Enfield. (U.S. Marine Corps.)

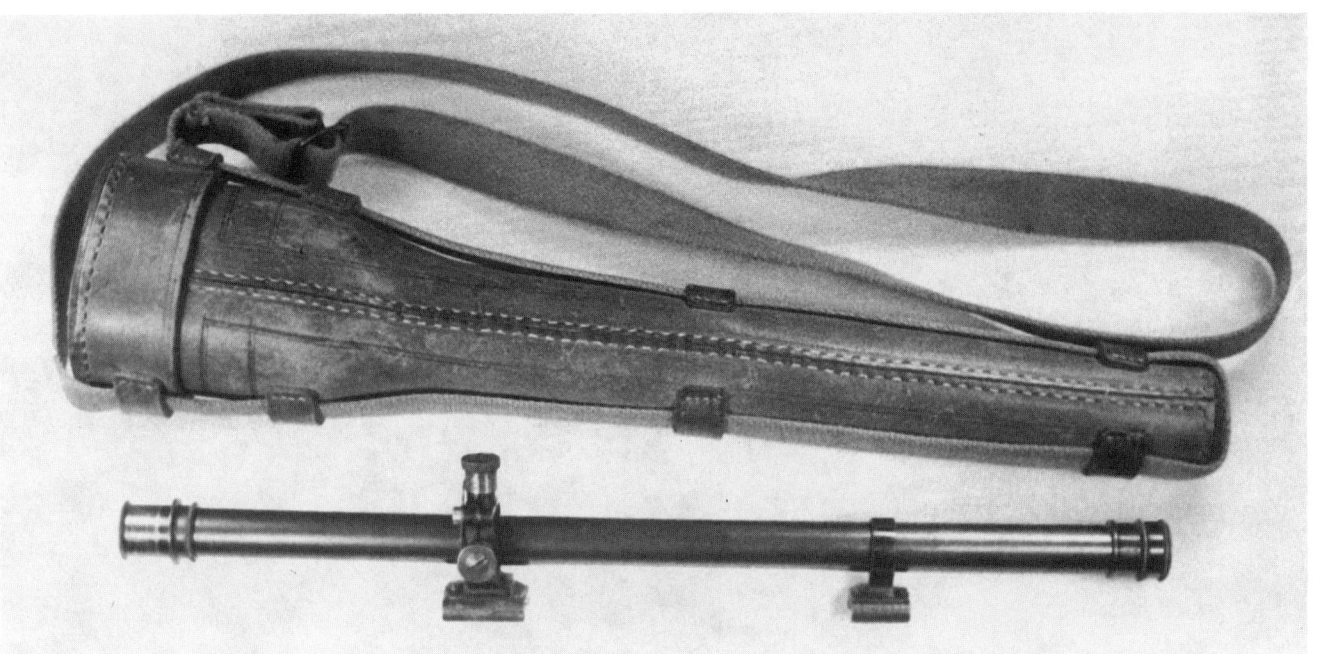

Believed to be the "Marine Corps standard" referenced in the Handbook of Ordnance Data *(No. 1861) dated 15 November 1918, this is a Winchester A5 telescopic sight with "special USMC mounting" and commercial carrying case adapted for military use by the addition of a shoulder strap and loops for the same. With the exception of the mounts, the 15 7/8-inch long, .750-inch tube diameter, and 10-ounce sights were standard commercial models with a "single cross-hair reticle pattern." Though believed to have been procured directly from the Winchester firm, the sights are not known to bear USMC markings. (Peter R. Senich.)*

Special Winchester A5 sight mounting developed for the Marine Corps made use of Mann-type tapered dovetail bases, special click adjustment elevation and windage drums, and a spring-loaded plunger directly beneath the tube. In addition to scale pointers for the adjustment drums, the elevation micrometer graduations were changed from "minutes" to "yards." The adjustment drums (.500-inch diameter) were left unfinished in bright metal. In this form, a limited number of Winchester telescopic sights were employed by Marine riflemen during early combat in the Solomon Islands in 1942. (Peter R. Senich.)

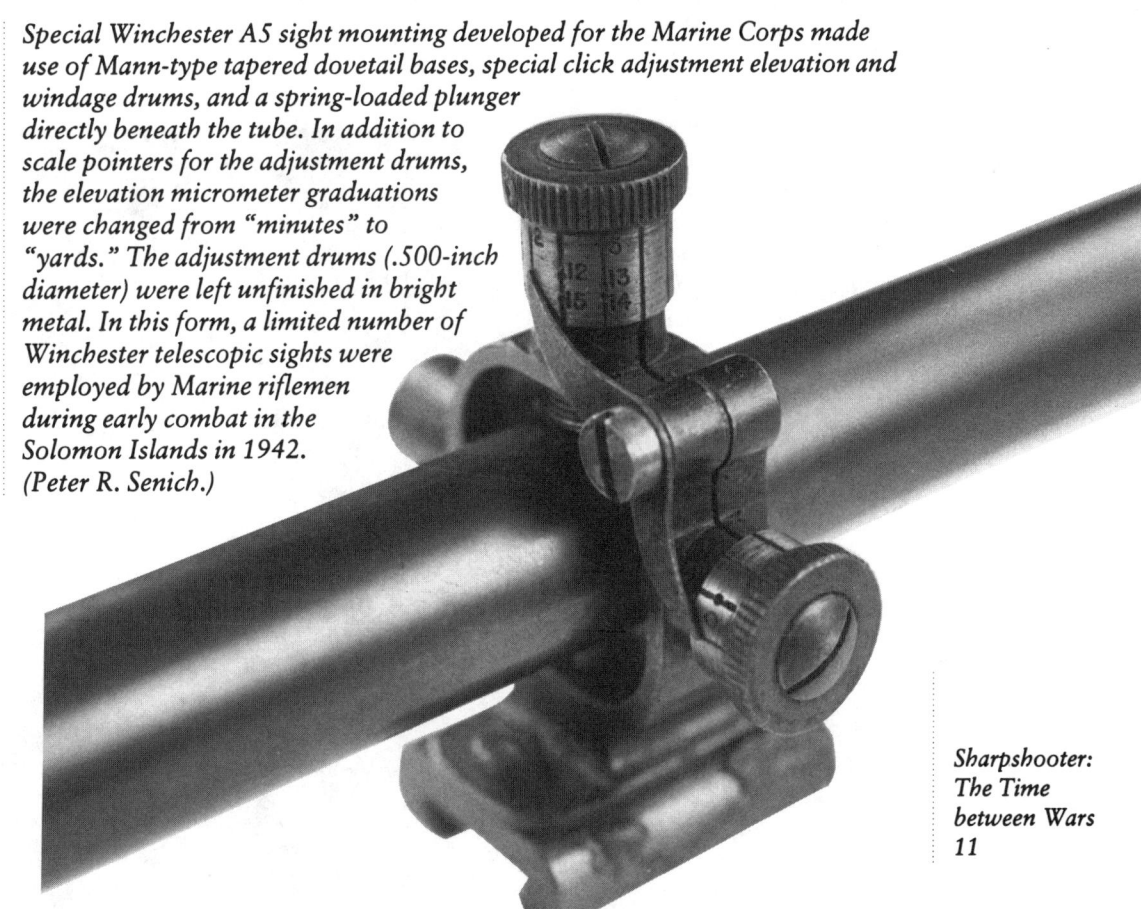

Top view of the Marine Corps-issue Winchester A5 scope carrying case lid with rifle number, marksman's name, and USMC in ink faded with the passing of years. Similar cases with names and rifle serial numbers have also been reported. In one instance, the name "Damerow," rifle number "673181," along with "Scout Sniper" and the year "1918" were duly noted. (Peter R. Senich.)

The underside of the USMC A5 scope case lid with the marksman's name, G.C. Chandler, M1903 rifle serial number originally paired with this sight (No. 672932) and range table. (Peter R. Senich.)

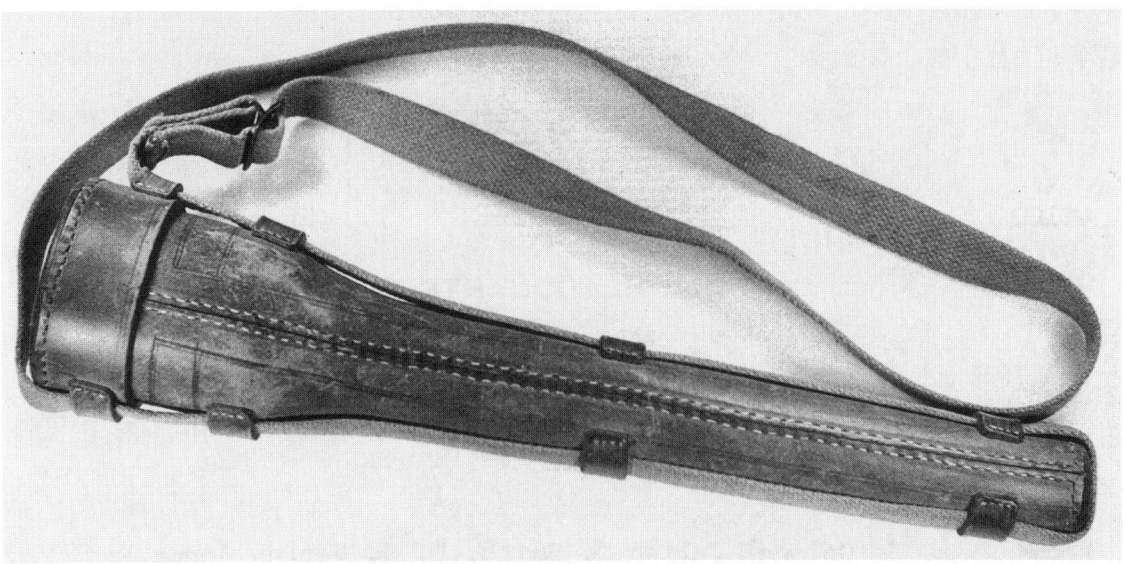

An adaptation of the standard "Winchester telescope sight case" originally furnished with a "strap lock" for the lid and a carrying handle in commercial form. The 17 1/2-inch case was made of heavy tan or russet leather. As a matter of interest, in addition to telescope carrying cases made of black and russet leather, Winchester A5 sights with the "special USMC mounting" and the "USMC modified mount," along with appropriate mounting blocks and leather dust caps, were offered for sale to the general public some years ago by a dealer (L. Bender) in northwestern Ohio. Obtained as surplus directly from the Marine Corps, this unique lot of telescopic sights and related hardware is believed to have been the bulk of the remaining USMC Winchester target scope inventory. (Peter R. Senich.)

Production of A5 sights continued until the telescope operations and manufacturing rights were purchased from Winchester by the Lyman Gunsight Corporation in 1928, thus marking the end of the A5 scope as such. Nevertheless, this rifle scope remained in quasi-military use with Army and Marine Corps rifle teams and was retained on USMC sniping equipment until its tacit replacement with the improved Lyman 5A telescopic sight, referred to for a time as the "Lyman-Winchester sight." So far as the average marksman was concerned, there was little actual difference between the Winchester A5 and the Lyman 5A target scopes. Even though the Lyman scope had, by all accounts, performed reasonably well in Marine Corps service, this was peacetime and the principal use of the Lyman device had been as a target sight for competitive match shooting.

Recognizing that continued use of the early target scopes had passed the point of practicality, in late 1940, with the clouds of war gathering on the horizon, Col. Julian C. Smith, USMC (a leading proponent of Marine Corps marksmanship, who, during his career, would serve as commander of the Second Marine Division in the Pacific theatre), in a proposal viewed by some historians as the actual impetus for the Marine Corps sniping program as it then evolved, focused attention on the fact that German snipers

00100

HEADQUARTERS
MARINE BARRACKS, QUANTICO, VIRGINIA

22 October, 1940

From: Colonel Julian C. Smith, U. S. Marine Corps.
To: The Major General Commandant.
Via: The Commanding General, Post.

Subject: Recommendation for telescopic snipers' sights.

1. In the last war it is understood that the Germans used a great number of light hunting telescopic sights of from 2½ to 4 power, which proved very effective in the hands of snipers. Further, that the American Army experimented with target-type sights for the same purpose, but which proved unsatisfactory for rough work on the battlefield.

2. A number of American firms today make telescopic sights for big game hunting which have proven very effective. A typical big game hunting telescopic sight has a wide field of view, at least 30 feet at 100 yards. The eye relief is long so there is no danger of the eye piece striking the eye on the recoil of heavily charged rifles. The tube is short and sturdy, and the instrument requires no more care than a pair of binoculars. These sights and mounts can be used under every condition where any iron sights can be used effectively, and under many conditions of light, target and background where iron sights would be entirely ineffective. Three typical sights of this type made in the United States are the Lyman, Alaska, Noske 2½ power field scope, and the Weaver 330 and 440. With these scopes the full field of view may be seen with the eye anywhere between 2½ and 5 inches in rear of the eye piece. It enables them to be mounted close to the barrel with the eye piece in front of the bolt handle, so they can be used on the Springfield 30-03 without modification of the bolt handle or safety. With proper mounts they can be removed from the rifle and replaced in a few seconds in perfect alignment. All of them have internal adjustments in minutes for both elevation and windage.

had made effective use of "hunting sights" in a combat environment during the First World War, while experience "had proved target-sights unsatisfactory for rough work on the battlefield."

In the form of a recommendation to the Major General Commandant, Headquarters, USMC (22 October 1940), Colonel Smith proposed that the Marine Corps give due consideration to certain types of American big-game hunting sights which, in his

2000-40-40

Subject: Recommendation for telescopic snipers' sights.

3.   The general characteristics of these sights are as follows:

	Power	Weight	Length	Field of view at 100 yds.	Eye Relief	Price	Mount
Lyman Alaskan	2½	8 oz.	10½"	40 ft.	2½ to 5"	$45.00	Griffin and Howe..........$25.00
Noske Type A	2½	9 oz.	9½"	38 ft.	Long	52.00	Noske No. 2....16.00
Type A	4	9½ oz.	10¼"	22 ft.	Long	54.00	Noske No. 2....16.00
Weaver 330	2-3/4	10-1/8 oz.	10½"	35 ft.	3 to 5½"	27.50	Weaver Type B.. 5.00
440	4	10½ oz.	11¼"	27 ft.	3¼"	32.50	Weaver Type B.. 5.00

4.   It is recommended that at least one each of these sights be purchased with a view to determining their value as snipers' telescopic sights.

JULIAN C. SMITH

00100   1st endorsement   22 October, 1940.
HEADQUARTERS, MARINE BARRACKS, QUANTICO, VIRGINIA.

From: The Commanding General.
To: The Major General Commandant.

1.   Forwarded.

L. McCARTY LITTLE

10-23-40 10-29-40 djb

opinion, had proven very effective. These were the Lyman Alaskan (2.5 power), Noske field scopes (2.5 and 4 power), and the Weaver Model 330 and 440 (2.75 and 4 power). As Colonel Smith recommended that "at least one each of these sights be purchased with a view to determining their value as snipers' telescopic sights."

The "Recommendation for Telescopic sniper's sights" from Col. Julian C. Smith to the Commandant, USMC 22 October 1940. Considered to be the impetus for the Marine Corps sniper program during World War II. (U.S. Marine Corps.)

In response to Smith's proposal, Adjutant and Inspector (Target Practice Section) Merritt A. Edson, the officer then in charge of all Marine Corps target practice and range activities, stated in part (28 October 1940):

> Present Marine Corps organization and equipment tables make no provision for the designation of snipers or for telescopic sight equipment. There would appear to be no valid reason for the procurement of sights as recommended in the basic letter unless the present organization tables are modified to establish a necessity therefor.
>
> There are 887 sights, telescopic, accessory, M1903 rifle, now on hand at the Depot of Supplies, Philadelphia, Pa. These sights are Lyman 5A type which were procured during the last war. They have never proved satisfactory and it is considered that any of the sights mentioned in the basic letter are superior for use as a sniper's sight. It is believed that the various manufacturers would agree to furnish sample sights without cost to the Marine Corps for experimental purposes, in comparison with the Lyman 5A sight, if the need for such equipment is apparent.
>
> It is recommended that the basic letter be referred to the Division of Plans and Policies to determine whether there is a need for snipers equipment in the Marine Corps and that tables of organization be modified, if necessary, in accordance with their decision.
>
> That, if snipers equipment is required, the manufacturers mentioned in the basic letter be asked to furnish sample sights for experimental purposes by the Marine Corps Equipment Board to determine which sight, if any, shall be procured.

Note: Merritt A. Edson's service during World War II is well known. In the first American offensive in the Pacific, Edson commanded the First Marine Raider Battalion and received the Congressional Medal of Honor for his action at the Battle of Bloody Ridge on Guadalcanal (Solomon Islands).

As then followed in mid-November 1940, Headquarters, USMC authorized the "Test of Lyman 5A type telescopic sights," whereby:

> The Quartermaster is requested to make the necessary arrangements with the manufacturers to have one (1) each of the Lyman, Noske and Weaver sights recommended in the reference (a) submitted to the Marine Corps Equipment Board for comparative test with the Lyman 5A type sight. The Quartermaster is further requested to make the neces-

IN REPLYING ADDRESS
THE MAJOR GENERAL COMMANDANT
AND REFER TO NO.
2000-40-40
AO-263-fop

HEADQUARTERS U. S. MARINE CORPS
WASHINGTON

13 November, 1940.

From: The Major General Commandant.
To: The Quartermaster.

Subject: Test of Lyman 5A type telescopic sights.

References: (a) Ltr Col.J.C.Smith,USMC., to MGC, file 00100, dated 22 Oct 40. (Copy attached)
(b) Memo, Director, Div.of Plans & Policies to MGC, file AO-283-njp, dated 7 Nov 40.

    1.   Reference (a) recommended that several types of telescopic sights now available commercially be purchased and tested for possible use by snipers.

    2.   Reference (b) approves the recommendation contained in reference (a) and further approves having the Marine Corps Equipment Board make comparative tests of the several types now available commercially with the Lyman 5A type now on hand at the Depot of Supplies, Philadelphia, Pa.

    3.   The Quartermaster is requested to make the necessary arrangements with the manufacturers to have one (1) each of the Lyman, Noske and Weaver sights recommended in reference (a) submitted to the Marine Corps Equipment Board for comparative test with the Lyman 5A type sight. The Quartermaster is further requested to make the necessary arrangements to have five (5) of the Lyman 5A type sights delivered to the Marine Corps Equipment Board.

    4.   By copy of this letter The Marine Corps Equipment Board is requested to make the necessary comparative test and advise this Headquarters of the results; make recommendations regarding the suitability of the types submitted; and if the Lyman 5A type should be retained, modified, or discarded.

T. HOLCOMB.

Copy to: A&I (Target Practice)
M.C.E.B.
Col. J. C. Smith, USMC.

Correspondence from the Commandant, USMC, (13 November 1940) authorizing "comparative tests" of telescopic rifle sights for possible sniper use. (U.S. Marine Corps.)

sary arrangements to have five (5) of the Lyman 5A type sights delivered to the Marine Corps Equipment Board.

By copy of this letter the Marine Corps Equipment Board is requested to make the necessary comparative test and advise this Headquarters of the results; make recommendations regarding the suitability of the types submitted; and if the Lyman 5A type should be retained, modified, or discarded.

In due course, the Marine Corps Equipment Board (MCEB), Marine Barracks, Quantico, Virginia, under date of 27 March 1941, responded to the Commandant, USMC as follows:

The Board has conducted a thorough test of telescopic sights within the past few months. During the test, it was apparent that telescopic sights must be developed in conjunction with the proper type of rifle and that to complete the equipment for snipers, spotting telescopes must be available to enable the sniper-observer-scout teams to work in pairs. All tests were conducted by personnel of the Rifle Range Detachment, Marine Barracks, Quantico, Virginia under immediate supervision of Captain George O. Van Orden, U.S. Marine Corps. During the test period, Captain Van Orden and Chief Marine Gunner Lloyd compiled a comprehensive treatise on the art of sniping, two copies of which are enclosed. These officers deserve the highest commendation for their effective and painstaking research.

Ironically, even though the report "Equipment for the American Sniper," by Van Orden and Lloyd, was unquestionably the most comprehensive study of sniper use and equipment ever compiled for the military, it did not settle the simple question as to which telescopic hunting sight would serve the Marine Corps best—the original intent of the evaluations. To the consternation of many, in addition to recommending that a commercial target rifle (Winchester Model 70) be introduced to the supply system, it recommended another target scope (Unertl Snipers' Telescope) as well.

While there can be little doubt that the hardware selected was perhaps the best then available to the Marine Corps, the Director, Division of Plans and Policies, USMC, challenged the Equipment Board in a memorandum to the Commandant dated 8 April 1941:

The President of the Equipment Board recommends the procurement of one thousand (1,000) sets of telescopic sight equipment for the use of snipers estimated at five hundred (500). The estimated cost of such a purchase would amount to approximately $200,000. Present or proposed tables of organization do not provide for special personnel for such duty.

No special training program for snipers is contemplated by the Army and no steps are being taken to procure special equipment. Training of snipers and their employment is covered briefly in FM 7-5, Section 288, in which this responsibility is placed on company commanders.

Special equipment is costly and requires specially trained personnel to maintain and use it. Procurement problems at this time and supply problems in case of active operations would be difficult.

It is believed, therefore, that sniper training should be conducted within combat units using such equipment as is available at least initially. It is proposed, therefore, to equip forty rifles M-1903 with the Lyman 5A sights in stock and send twenty to each Division for training purposes.

That the Commanding Generals, First and Second Marine Divisions be directed to initiate a training program for snipers and to make recommendations after a suitable period as to the type of equipment required and as to a suitable training program.

Viewed as a compromise at Marine Headquarters, it is important to note that the Adjutant and Inspector and the Quartermaster were to concur with this alternative.

At this juncture, however, as correspondence dated 25 June 1941 from the Detachment Quartermaster (Quantico) to the Quartermaster (Headquarters) indicates, there were not any rifles available for training snipers in accordance with the alternative recommendation:

It is requested that authority be granted to equip thirty (30) rifles, U.S. cal. .22, M-2 with scope blocks for the Winchester 5-A telescopic sight (or other standard telescopic mounts) and with the Lyman Model 17-A (aperture) front sight with inserts, the installation of these parts to be made at the Depot of Supplies, Philadelphia, Pa.

In view of the fact that neither .30-caliber rifles or ammunition is available at the present time it is desired to conduct practice firing for the snipers school with .22 caliber rifles.

In an apparent move to counter any further dilution of what he regarded as the best equipment for the emerging sniper program, Capt. George O. Van Orden, USMC, directed a memorandum to the Detachment Quartermaster (Quantico), under date of 7 July 1941:

There is increasing evidence of the need for precision rifle fire in landing operations, defense installations and open warfare of the type now being conducted in the Near East. It is well that a number of officers and men become acquainted with the possibilities, characteristics and limitations of the fine equipment necessary to the delivery of accurate fire. In this connection, on request of the First Marine Division, this detachment recently conducted a course for Sniper-Observer-Scouts during which an effort was made to demonstrate to the thirty one officers and enlisted students the correct technique of employment of Snipers. The effectiveness of the instruction was materially decreased through shortage of satisfactory equipment. The procurement of the Sighting Telescopes will, when combined with the caliber .22 rifles now being modified for use with telescopic sights, make possible effective instruction in precision shooting.

Presupposing a demand for precision equipment in the near future, instrument repairmen should become familiar with the equipment that will unquestionably be procured. The procurement of the "Unertl Sniper," the only completely satisfactory sighting telescope available in the United States, will provide the means by which the instrument repairmen in the Ordnance School may become familiar with the characteristics and care of first class sighting telescopes.

The designer of the "Unertl Sniper" has gone to considerable personal expense to build a model now on loan to me for comparative study and for use as a standard. Mr. Unertl has asked no compensation for his work, but it is known that he could not well afford the expense of building the pilot model and bringing it to Quantico for test as he did. Since the Marine Corps Equipment Board recommended the adoption of the "Unertl Sniper" as the standard sighting telescope and the immediate purchase of one thousand telescopes for training and for reserve, it is thought that the purchase of twenty telescopes will be a material recognition of the excellence of his work.

The requisition should include in the specifications the statement: Each of these telescopes, in every particular, is to be, optically and mechanically, the equal of or superior to the "Unertl 8 Power Sniper" now in the hands of the Commanding Officer, Rifle Range Detachment, Quantico, Va., and which is hereafter to be known as the standard reference telescope.

Resultantly, an order for "20 Telescopes, sighting, Unertl Sniper" was "forwarded approved" via the Post Quartermaster (Quantico) to the Quartermaster (Headquarters).

Acceptance at Quantico notwithstanding, the Quartermaster (Headquarters), responding to the request for 20 Unertl sights, replied on 15 July 1941:

World War I-era Winchester A5 USMC "special mount" sight in use by a Marine Corps sniper on Guadalcanal. In addition to Lyman 5A target sights, a small number of Winchester A5-equipped M1903 rifles were also pressed into service during early phases of the Solomon Islands campaign in 1942. (U.S. Marine Corps.)

The recommendation of the Marine Corps Equipment Board that one thousand telescopic sights, "Unertl Sniper," be procured was not approved, but in lieu thereof the Major General Commandant directed that 40 M1903 rifles be equipped for employment of Lyman 5A sights and that 20 rifles with serviceable telescopic sights be furnished each Marine division for test and training.

The supply of 20 telescopes, sighting, "Unertl Sniper," is not approved in view of the foregoing.

While not clearly defined, from all indications, procurement of the Unertl telescopic sight in any quantity would be delayed until after the war in the Pacific had actually begun.

Consequently, when the Marine Corps began the Pacific campaign in the summer of 1942 with large-scale amphibious operations in the Solomon Island group, the Model 1903 Springfield Rifle mounting the Lyman 5A, as well as some of the early Winchester scopes with the USMC mounting, though small in actual number, were brought to bear against the Japanese on Guadalcanal.

Sniper Equipment: The Rifle Team Influence

CHAPTER 2

The treatise "Equipment for the American Sniper" (1941), though largely rhetoric, would influence the course of the Marine Corps sniping program through World War II and beyond.

A 72-page report with equipment photographs and an addendum dealing with telescopic sights, it contained the results of a three-month test involving "every type of rifle, telescopic sight, and spotting telescope available in the United States in quantities sufficient for the requirements of the Marine Corps." Evaluations were conducted by personnel of the Rifle Range Detachment,

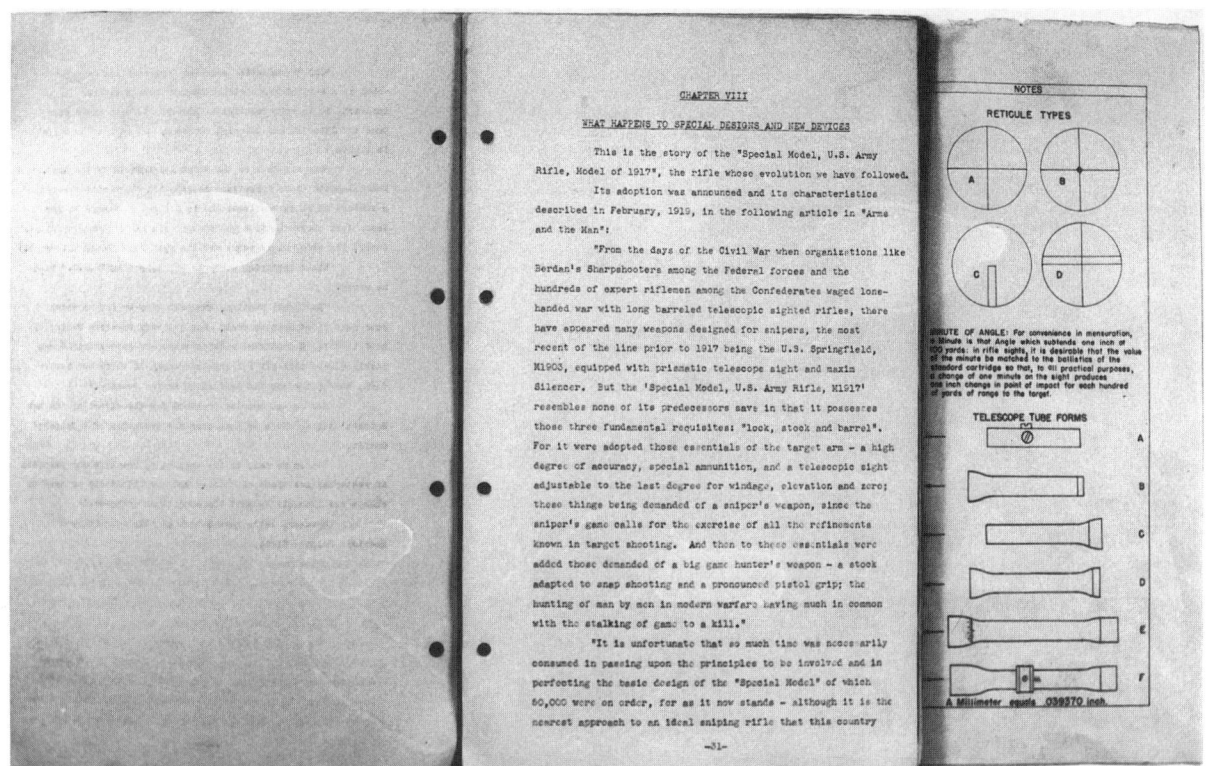

Marine Barracks, Quantico, Virginia, under the supervision of Capt. George O. Van Orden and Chief Marine Gunner Calvin A. Lloyd.

An original copy of "Equipment for the American Sniper," by Van Orden and Lloyd, a 72-page report with equipment photographs and an addendum dealing with telescopic sights. The Marine Corps published and circulated 1,000 copies of the "Van Orden Treatise" in early 1941. (Peter R. Senich.)

The test was originally intended to determine the best telescopic sight for Marine Corps sniper use, with a variation of the Unertl target scope selected over the Lyman Super Targetspot or Fecker target scopes, for example. In some quarters, however, the results of the "Van Orden Treatise" came down to a matter of personal preferences rather than objective conclusions. Apart from recommending that a commercial rifle be adopted (a topic of some controversy by itself), it chose a target scope over a proven hunting scope, such as the Noske field sight or, in particular, the Lyman Alaskan, a superb rifle scope for its time. The "rifle team influence" was unquestionably a deciding factor in the ultimate selection process.

Referenced by Van Orden and Lloyd as "A Selection of Equipment for the American Sniper," the culmination of their three-month equipment study is presented as originally stated in 1941:

Q *What is the most efficient Snipers' Rifle available in America today?*

A It is the Winchester Model G7044C Rifle.

Q *Is this rifle practical?*

A Yes: it is a Military-Target type, bolt action, 5-shot magazine rifle, chambered for the standard military cartridges. It weighs 10 1/2 pounds, and is fitted with a medium weight barrel 24 inches in length, with a super-accuracy life in excess of 3,000 rounds. It is mounted in a "four-position" sporting-type stock having a high comb especially suited for telescopic sighting, a broad fore-end, a fully developed pistol grip, and it is fitted with a sling swivel adjustable for position. Its bolt handle is so designed that the bolt may be actuated with the telescopic sight in its firing position.

It is equipped with a hinged floor plate which is easily released by pressing a button so that the magazine may be emptied with one operation. The rifle, which is durable beyond reasonable expectations and in this respect is superior to the U.S. Rifle, caliber 30, M1903, is easy to repair and adjust and has parts interchangeable with those of any rifle of the Model 70 series. It may be procured in other barrel weights and lengths for special situations, and may be chambered for the caliber 30 Magnum cartridge. Any type of sight, metallic or telescopic, may be fitted to this rifle. The high standards of the Model 70 series have produced the most accurate long-range rifle in the world, as has been demonstrated by many years of competitive success. The selected rifle meets, in every important particular, the requirements of the Sniper.

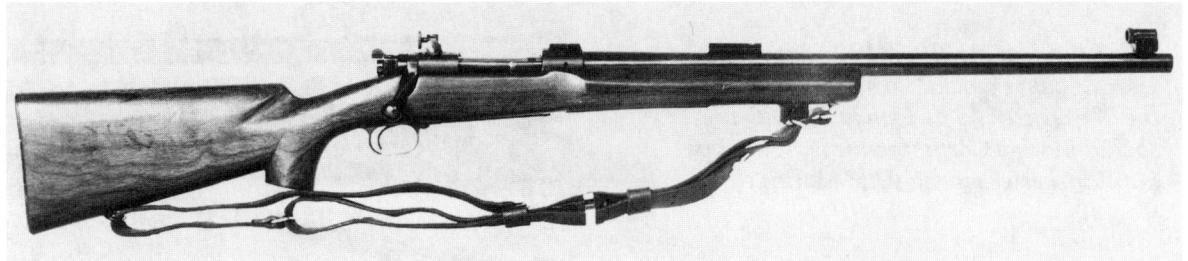

Winchester Model 70 (G7044C) selected by Van Orden and Lloyd as the optimum rifle for Marine Corps sniper use in 1941. As the weapon was then described: "A military-target type, bolt action, 5-shot magazine, chambered for the standard military cartridge (.30-06). It weighs 10 1/2 pounds and is fitted with a medium-weight barrel 24 inches in length, with an accuracy life in excess of 3,000 rounds. It is mounted in a 'four-position' sporting-type stock having a high comb especially suited for telescopic sighting, a broad fore-end, a fully developed pistol grip, and is fitted with a sling swivel adjustable for position. Its bolt handle is so designed that the bolt may be actuated with the telescopic sight in its firing position." The rifle was also fitted with a Lyman No. 77 detachable front sight with interchangeable inserts, Lyman No. 48WH rear sight graduated in quarter minutes of angle, and standard telescopic sight bases. (U.S. Marine Corps.)

Q *Is this rifle procurable?*

A Yes: it is a standard production model of the Winchester Repeating Arms Company.

Q *Is there a substitute rifle obtainable?*

A Yes: we suggest two rifles, both highly procurable and practical. The first is described as follows:

To the "U.S. Rifle, caliber 30, M1903A1, National Match," less barrel and stock and their attached parts, is assembled a high pressure barrel similar to that of the "U.S. Rifle, caliber 30, M1903, Style 'T,' 30 inch Heavy Service Barrel," but reduced in length to 24 inches. The rifle is mounted in the Stock Assembly, complete with band, sling swivels and sling, of the U.S. Rifle, caliber 22, M2, or similar, which has been modified to bed the heavy barrel. In addition, a recess for cleaning gear is drilled in the base of the stock and the stock fitted with the Butt Plate Assembly of the U.S. Rifle, caliber 30, M1903. This rifle may be made up of parts standardized for years and is easily assembled by small arms mechanics without special tools. The barrel length of the type of barrel selected is sound, as proven by the several World Record runs of bulls-eyes made at ranges from 100 to 1,000 yards, with rifles of similar weight and barrel length. The rifle is chambered for the standard military cartridges and has the advantages that its

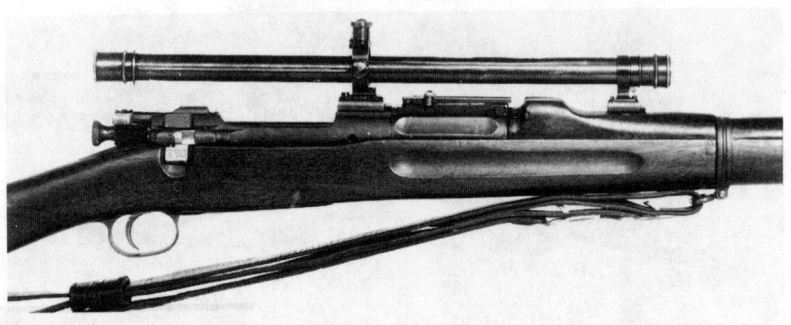

U.S. Rifle, Caliber .30, M1903 with USMC "taper blocks" to accommodate the Winchester A5 or Lyman 5A with the special Marine Corps mounting. The scope is a Winchester model. (U.S. Marine Corps.)

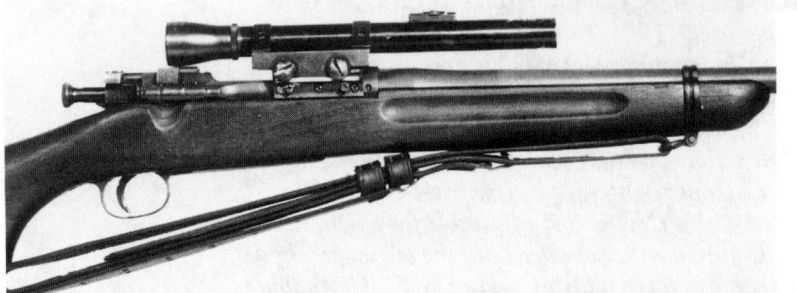

M1903 Springfield "Sporter Model" fitted with a Lyman Alaskan 2.5-power hunting sight in a Neidner side-bracket mount. (U.S. Marine Corps.)

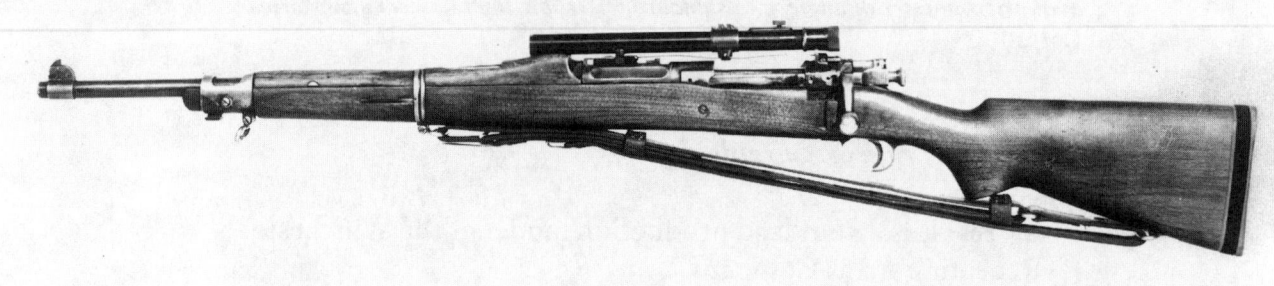

A "slightly modified" M1903A1 rifle fitted with a Weaver 330 telescope in a G.K. Turner "Instant-Detachable" scope mount. Referenced as "useful in jungle fighting," the Springfield rifle was fitted with a "folding battle-type sight" for use when the scope was removed. (U.S. Marine Corps.)

repair parts are carried in the Standard Nomenclature Lists. This substitute will well satisfy the snipers who may be armed with it.

The second type, which, while having a limited usefulness, would prove valuable in special situations such as operations against bush-whackers, guerrillas, and in jungle fighting, is the Sporter-Type rifle in 30 caliber. Several fine models are commercially available, including one of the Model 70 series, but a satisfactory Sporter type may be made up by small arms mechanics by assembling the U.S. Rifle, caliber 30, M1903, less fixed base, to the stock assembly of the U.S. Rifle, caliber 22, M2, or similar. Fitted with fast sights, both telescopic and metallic, it would be most effective for short range combat: for open warfare and general sniping, it would be disappointing when compared with our selected Snipers' Rifle because of its light weight barrel and its less precise performance.

Q *What is the most efficient Snipers' Cartridge available in America today?*

A It is the Cartridge, ball, caliber 30, Palma, or equivalent grade, as manufactured by the Frankford Arsenal Remington Arms Company, Western Cartridge Company Winchester Repeating Arms Company, or the Peters Cartridge Co.

Q *Is this ammunition practical?*

A Yes: it is interchangeable with the standard military cartridges and all experienced riflemen are familiar with the characteristics of the target cartridges. The selected cartridge has high velocity, flat trajectory and superb accuracy. It will be necessary, in some cases, to specify that the bullets be so seated in assembling as to permit the loading of the cartridges into the magazines from clips of five rounds each.

Q *Is this ammunition procurable?*

A Yes: such cartridges are in regular production in the plants of Remington, Western and Winchester.

Q *Is there a substitute ammunition available?*

A Yes: the M1-type military cartridges are ballistically interchangeable with the super-accurate target cartridges up to medium ranges. It would not be too difficult a problem to provide lots of Armor Piercing and Tracer Cartridges with characteristics reasonably similar to those of the Super Cartridge and the M1 substitute. The Cartridge, ball, caliber 30, M2, would be useful at short ranges.

Q *What are the most efficient Snipers' Metallic Sights available in America today?*

A The rear sight is the Lyman No. 48WH Receiver Sight. The front sight is the Lyman No. 77 Detachable Front Sight.

Q *Are these sights practical?*

A Yes: both sights are designed for quick removal or attachment to the rifle *in zero*. The 48WH sight is designed for the Winchester 70, and in precision of adjustment in elevation and deflection, more than meets the requirements of the sniper. The front sight is hooded, and is furnished with nine interchangeable inserts, including posts and apertures, from which the sniper may select the sighting aid best suited to the situation. The sights are familiar to all experienced riflemen and an understanding of them is easily acquired by the tens of thousands of men who have been taught to shoot with the several U.S. Rifles, caliber 22, equipped with the Lyman 48-C Receiver Sight.

Q. Are these sights procurable?

A. Yes: they are standard production models of the Lyman Gunsight Corporation.

Q. Are there substitute sights available?

A. Yes: the Redfield Olympic, the Parker Skylight Sight, the Lyman 17A and several other fine front sights of similar design adaptable to the Winchester Model 70 are in production and available in large quantities. The Lyman 48WJS and the 57W are Receiver Sights suitable for the Snipers' Rifle, and in addition, many production models by Pacific, Marble, Redfield and Vaver are available.

If the suggested M1903 Modification is furnished the Sniper, the correct sight combination is the Lyman No. 48-C Receiver Sight and the Lyman No. 77 front sight. The rear sight fits into the recesses of the stock of the modified rifle, and has micrometer adjustments in 1/2 minute steps with adjustable indices. In addition to meeting nearly all the requirements of the Sniper, the Lyman 48-C is an item of issue and its parts are carried on the Standard Nomenclature Lists. Substitute sights are available in models by Vaver, Redfield and Pacific.

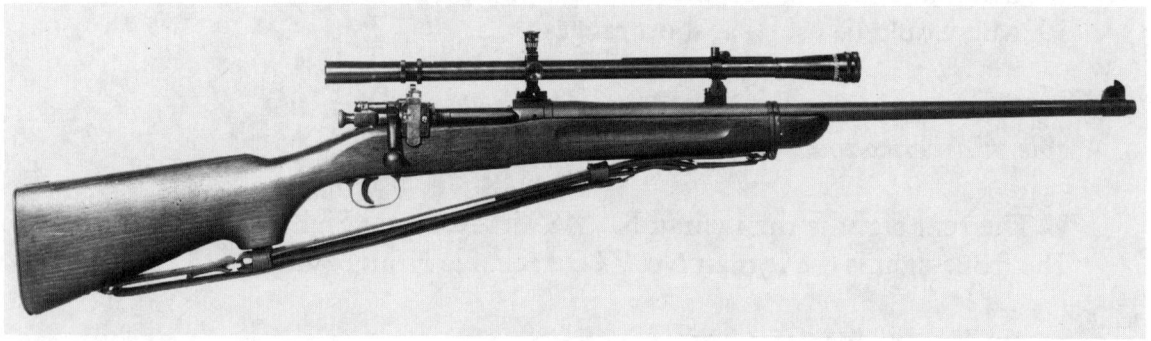

A "mid-range" Model 1903 USMC test rifle with an M2 stock, Lyman 48 rear sight, and Lyman 8-power Junior Targetspot scope in standard target mounts. (U.S. Marine Corps.)

Q. What are the most efficient Observers' Telescopes available in America today?

There are two models of similar efficiency for the purpose: the Bausch and Lomb 50 Millimeter Spotting Scope, with interchangeable eyepieces at 12.8, 19.5 and 26 power, equipped with a retractable sunshade, and, the Argus 55 millimeter Spotting Scope, with interchangeable eyepieces at 12.8, 20 and 26 power, and equipped with a fixed sunshade.

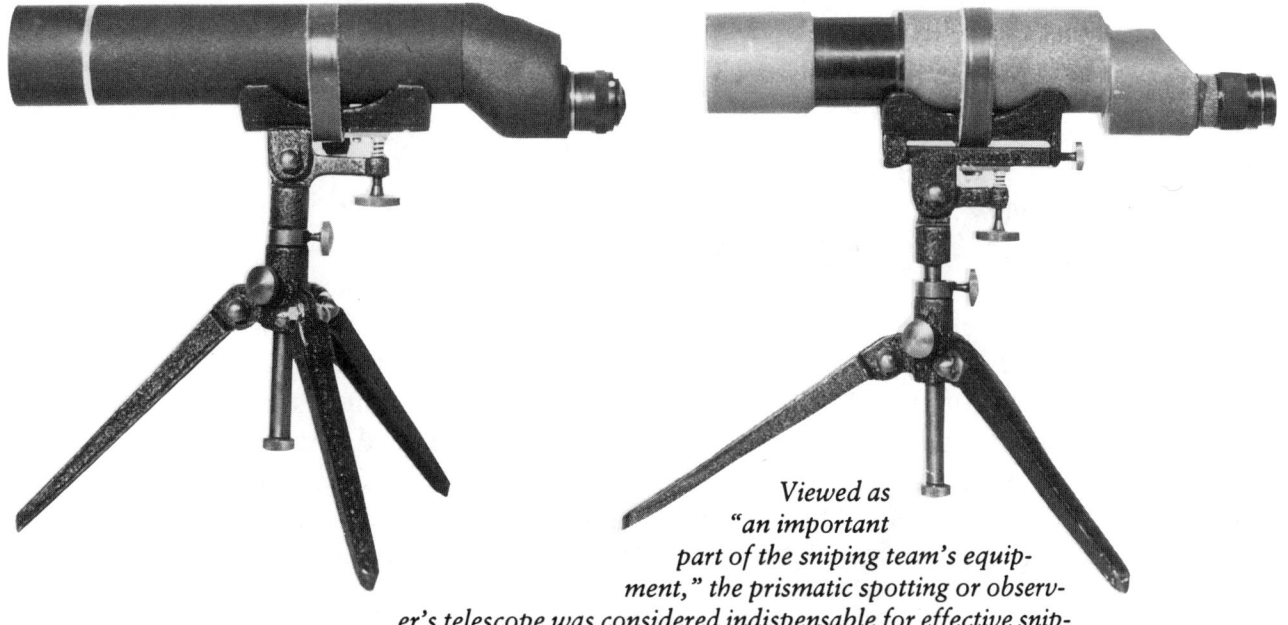

Viewed as "an important part of the sniping team's equipment," the prismatic spotting or observer's telescope was considered indispensable for effective sniping. Selected as the "best available," the Argus 55mm (left) and Bausch & Lomb 50mm spotting scopes were noted as "two models of similar efficiency." (U.S. Marine Corps.)

Are these Observers' Telescopes practical?

Yes: they are short, prismatic telescopes of similar characteristics and quality, and meet the requirements of the Observer.

The Argus weighs 43 ounces and is 16 inches in length, sunshade in position. At 20 power, it has an exit pupil of 2.8 millimeters, a luminosity of 7.9, a field of 14.5 feet at 100 yards and an eye relief of 14 millimeters. The Bausch and Lomb, similar though having an Objective 5 millimeters smaller than the Argus, weighs 38 ounces and is 13 inches long, sunshade retracted, and has a field at 19.5 power of 14 feet at 100 yards.

Are these telescopes procurable?

Yes: both are standard production models of large optical manufacturing companies.

Q: Are there substitutes available?

A: Yes: the One Extension Draw Tube Telescopes in 20 power by Mossberg and Bausch and Lomb, which fold to 10 and 13 inches respectively, are useful though limited by small field. The Fecker and Unertl Variable Power Prismatic Spotting Scopes have limited usefulness, having restricted fields and being primarily designed for target spotting.

Q: What is the most efficient Observers' Telescope Mount available in America today?

A: It is the Mossberg "Spotshot" Stand.

Q: Is this mount practical?

A: Yes: it is unique in design, sturdily built of aluminum alloy and steel, finished in black crinkle, and adaptable to all types of Observers' Telescopes. It has screw adjustments for horizontal and vertical motion of the cradle, and stays in position when adjusted. It is compact when folded, presents the minimum of profile when in position for use; its height is adjustable from 9 1/2 to 14 1/2 inches, and it weighs 2 1/4 pounds.

This stand, incidentally, when combined with the Mossberg "Spotshot" Telescope, is furnished with a two-compartment leather case to fit the telescope and stand.

Q: Is this mount procurable?

A: Yes: it is a standard production model of O.F. Mossberg and Sons.

Q: Are there substitutes available?

A: Yes: there are several Tripod-Type telescope mounts in production. Among the finest are the Freeland mounts with precision screw adjustments, the Wollensak and the Westchester Trading Company models.

Q: What are the most efficient Snipers' Telescopic Sight Mounts available in America today?

A: They are the Snipers' Telescopic Sight Mounts as manufactured by John Unertl.

Q: Are these mounts practical?

A Yes: they are similar to the Unertl Target-Type Mounts, Pat. No. 2208913, of Dural, blackened by the Anodizing Process. Elevation and Deflection Scales in graduations of 1/2 minute are illuminated with white lines and figures. Changes in elevation and deflection are made by turning large knobs: a movement of 1/4 minute is indicated by a sharp, easily felt and audible click. One click in elevation or deflection, with the center of the mounts positioned 7.2 inches apart, will produce a 1/4-inch change in impact for each 100 yards of range to the target.

The Adjusting Knobs are fitted with a reference arrow to assist in quickly locating a mean range and deflection, and may be adjusted to a zero reading. A stop is provided to indicate minimum elevation as an additional aid to sight setting in poor light and to provide a zero check point. The mounts are of the height to which target shooters are accustomed and will permit the metallic sights to remain mounted in position on the rifle while the telescope sight is in place. 125 minutes of adjustment may be made in elevation and 100 in deflection, or 50 minutes each way from zero. The mounts are quickly attached to their bases by sliding them into place: they are then positioned *in zero* by tightening Clamp Locking Screws with large wing-nut and coin slotted heads, which enter indents in the bases, bringing the mounts into precise and secure alignment. In addition to the Snipers' Telescope, any Target-Type telescope having a standard tube diameter of 3/4 inch may be mounted in the Snipers' Mounts. The mounts are furnished with heavy, case-hardened steel bases for the M1903 Modification Snipers' Rifle and are equally suited to the bases furnished with the Winchester Model 70 Rifle.

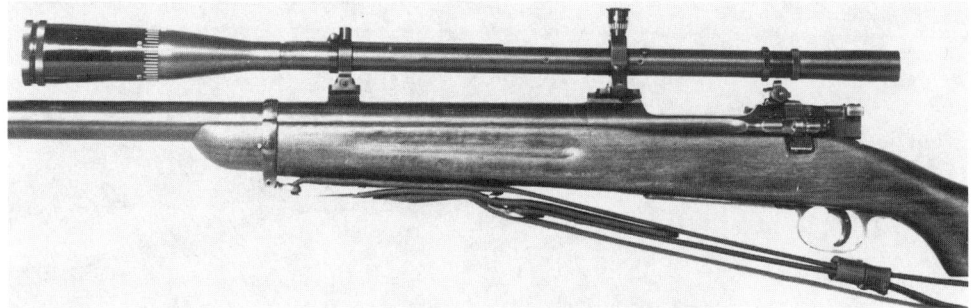

The M1903 Modification Snipers' Rifle (left), a Springfield '03 receiver fitted with a free high pressure barrel (heavy barrel) mounted in an altered M2 stock. The target scope is a 12-power Lyman Super Targetspot in standard mounts. (U.S. Marine Corps.)

An alternate view of the M1903 Modification Snipers' Rifle (above). Regarded as "highly efficient," the 12 1/2-pound rifle made use of a Lyman 48C rear right with an '03 front sight fitted to the 24-inch heavy barrel. The M2 stock was modified "to bed the heavy barrel." (U.S. Marine Corps.)

Are these mounts procurable?

Yes: in form they are similar to all standard Target-Type Mounts and are manufacturable in several factories in the United States.

Are there substitute mounts available?

Yes: the Mounts manufactured by J.W. Fecker and the Lyman Gunsight Corporation and other mounts of similar design are satisfactory.

If a Sporting Rifle is to be made available for jungle fighting, the most efficient side mount for the required Hunting-Type telescope is the side-bracket mount manufactured by the Niedner Rifle Corporation. The base and clamp screws, of case hardened steel, are secured to the side of the receiver by three screws and two taper pins. The bracket, of special alloy steel, which carries the telescope, is quickly detached from the rifle or remounted *in zero*. The telescope is held centrally over the bore and at a sufficient height to permit the permanent attachment of auxiliary metallic sights.

It may be noted here that the objection to off-set mounts for telescopic sights may preclude any consideration of charger-loading and top ejecting rifles as satisfactory weapons for sniping in any situation requiring the assistance of a telescopic sight. A U.S. Rifle, caliber 30, M1, with a telescope mounted in target-type mounts, has been tested and the over-the-receiver mounting was found to have introduced problems in loading and ejecting and in the positioning of the tele-

Winchester Model 70, Caliber 300 Magnum with target stock, Lyman No. 77 front and No. 48WH rear rights, 28-inch barrel and Fecker 10-power target scope in Fecker target mounts. According to the test report, the 14-pound, 300 Magnum Model 70 was noted as "particularly adapted to long-range sniping." (U.S. Marine Corps.)

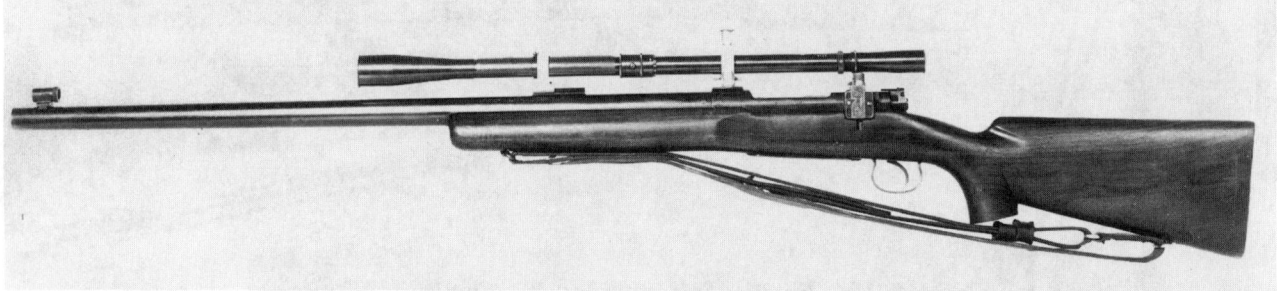

scope which make it unsuitable for sniping. Further test is being made of a bracket arrangement to be mounted on the left side of the receiver of this rifle, which is designed to carry a hunting-type telescope in a mount similar to the G.K. Turner Instant Detachable Scope Mount: this mounting will permit charger loading and will not interfere with free ejection, and will permit the sniper to use the metallic or telescopic sight at will. However, because of the off-set, the mounting will not be satisfactory to the sniper.

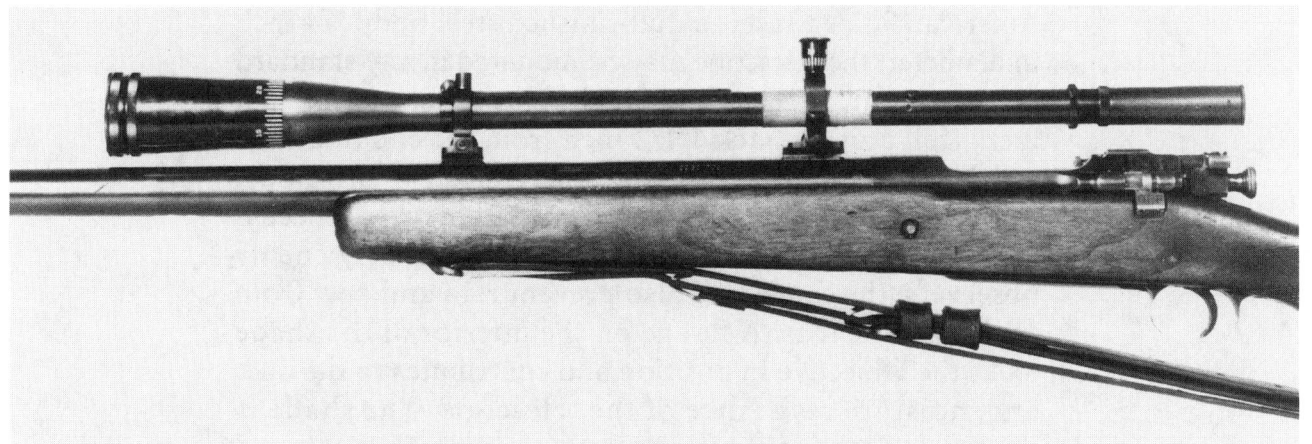

Also deemed suitable for long-range sniping: a .30-caliber M1903 rifle with heavy barrel (free high pressure barrel), special stock, Lyman No. 77 front and No. 48WH rear sights (rear sight detached), and a Lyman 10-power Super Targetspot in Lyman target mounts. (U.S. Marine Corps.)

Q What is the most efficient Snipers' Telescopic Sight available in America today?

A It is the Unertl 8 Power "SNIPER."

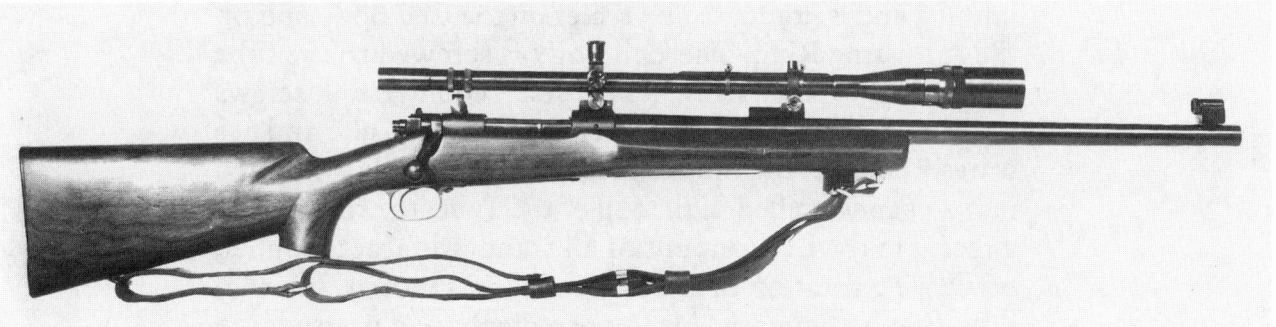

Winchester Model 70 (G7044C) with the Unertl 8-power Sniper scope as tested by the Marine Corps beginning in late 1940. The Model 70/Unertl combination was considered suitable for sniping at any range up to at least 1,000 yards. (U.S. Marine Corps.)

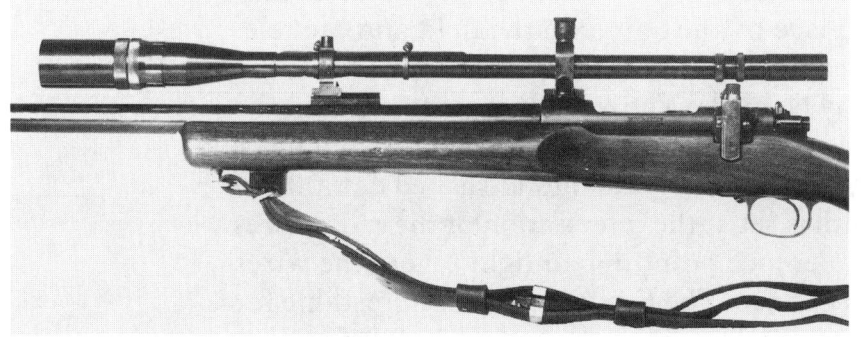

Winchester Model 70 (G7044C) with Unertl 8-power Sniper scope (left view). Though considered a "super-accurate snipers' rifle," the highly regarded Model 70/Unertl combination was not adopted by the Marine Corps. (U.S. Marine Corps.)

Q *Is this sight practical?*

A Yes: the "SNIPER" was designed especially for the American Sniper. It has a dull-finished steel body 3/4 inch in diameter: the telescope may be mounted in any standard target mount. It has a 1 1/4 inch Objective, carried in a metal cell unit set back 1 1/2 inch from the end of a steel sunshade screwed to the end of the Objective Cell Body. The length of the sunshade is designed to prevent reflected rays of light from the Objective being viewed by enemy observers: the shade will also prevent rain and dew from falling on the lens. A flange on the interior of the shade locks the Objective in position and contributes to the dust and moisture resistance of the telescope. The shade is threaded to receive a steel protecting cap which is screwed into position when the scope is not in use. While the shade adds 1 1/2 inches to the length, its benefits are obvious and it is a feature not included in any other production telescope. When the shade is removed from the Objective Cell Body, the Objective Cell, grooved to provide positioning by a key in the Objective Cell Body, may be removed to permit cleaning, drying, or replacement of components. A Range Adjustment, locked in position by the shade, permits the positive elimination of parallax from thirty five feet to infinity, and is graduated by scales on the Cell Body and on the Adjusting Ring. The Cell Body is screwed to the tube and locked by a set screw. Three small countersunk screws position the Erector Cell in the center of the Tube and are waterproofed at the time of assembly. A steel rib is sweated into a channel milled in the top of the Tube: the rib engages a recess in the front mount of all standard target mounts, preventing rotation of the telescope in its mount. Internal reflection is eliminated by an open diaphragm pressed into position in the Tube. The Reticule, a long brass cell, fitted with Tungsten Steel Cross Wires, .0009 of an inch in width, is easily removed for repair by removing the Eye Piece Cell and two positioning screws. The Cross Wires are held in the cell by small screws: in case of breakage, a human hair may be set in place by the Sniper in the field and the telescope continued in service until a replacement or repair by an armorer may be made. The reticule is set forward in the Tube so that the wires will not be damaged in assembling or disassembling the telescope. A diamond-shaped dot .002 of an inch in width is set at the intersection of the cross wires to provide a reference point in bad light where the wires may be difficult to see. The Eye Piece Cell is adjustable for the individual eye and is retained in position after focusing by a locking ring. The end of the Cell is threaded to receive a steel protecting cap. The length of the scope proper is 21 3/4 inches; with the sunshade in position the overall length is 24 inches. The total weight of the telescope, with mounts and steel protecting caps in position, is 24 ounces.

The lenses are fully Achromatic, corrected for flatness of field and with freedom from objectionable colors, and are ground from a stable glass unaffected by the sun's rays and saltwater.

The diameter of the Exit Pupil is 4.2 millimeters, giving a relative luminosity of 17.64, which is 144% of the light gathering power of other eight power telescopes tested. Its resolution and luminosity are such that the rungs of a ladder observed at a range of 550 yards were defined thirty minutes after sunset on an overcast day; a man in a khaki uniform could be defined at 150 yards, and a man in a green uniform at 75 yards, in the night when visibility with the unaided eye was less than 25 yards, and, when assisted by the light of a Lake Erie Chemical Company 37 millimeter Star Shell fired from a point 100 yards in front of the sight, a number of "E-kneeling" Silhouette Targets were sharply defined at ranges of from 650 to 700 yards.

Considering available lens systems, it provides the maximum power, luminosity and resolution compatible with wide field, small objective and the other requirements brought out in our studies.

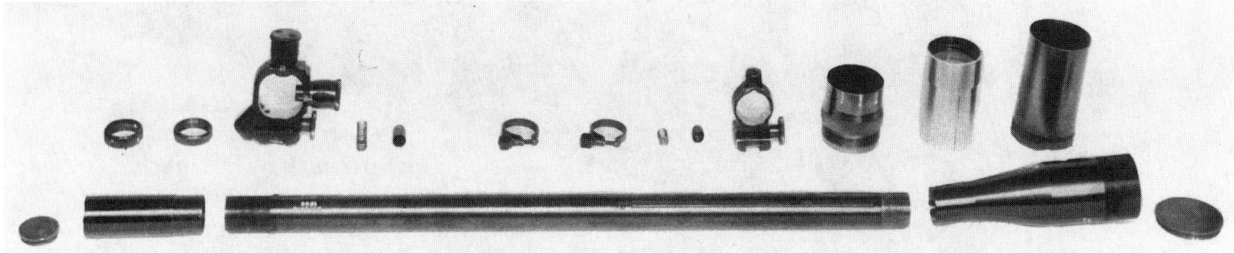

An early Unertl Sniper scope disassembled to show simplicity of design. The 8-power sniper model was based on the 1 1/4-inch objective Unertl target scope popular among match shooters before the war. The scope bears a prewar commercial serial number (1573). (U.S. Marine Corps.)

As part of the overall equipment evaluations, a comparative table (the addendum) classified the available "American Sighting Telescopes" according to their adaptability for military purposes.

The rifle scopes were tested and rated on the basis of their value for general sniping, long range, training, jungle warfare, etc. A total of 29 telescopic rifle sights manufactured by Lyman, Noske, Belding & Mull, Weaver, Carolyn, Unertl, Malcolm, Pechar, Fecker, and Winchester were included in the evaluations held at Quantico.

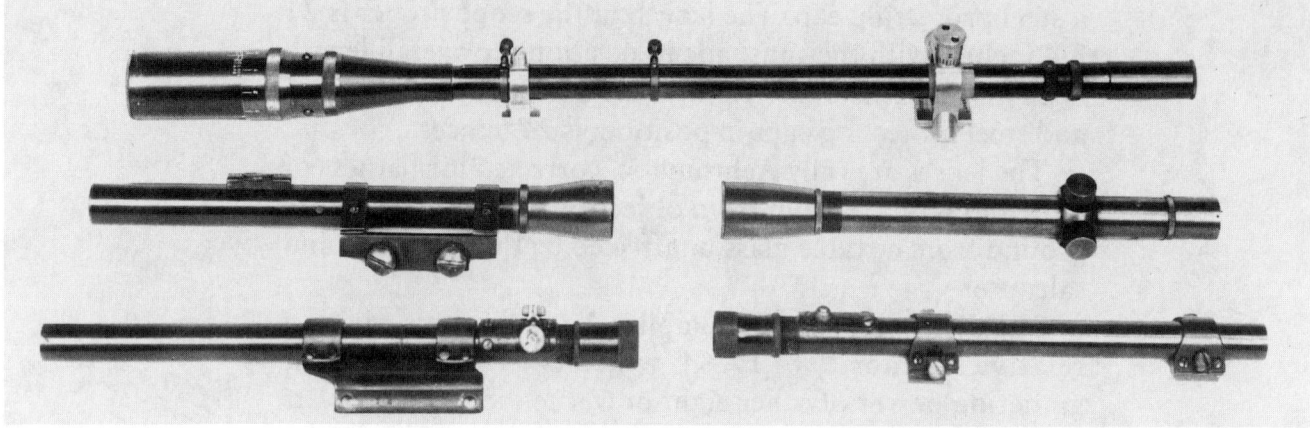

A small sampling of the 29 rifle scopes evaluated by the Marine Corps. A transitional 8-power Unertl Sniper scope is shown with a Lyman Alaskan in a Neidner side-bracket mount, a 3-power Unertl hunting sight, a Weaver Model 440 with a T-2 mount, and a Weaver 330 scope with a B-2 mounting. (U.S. Marine Corps.)

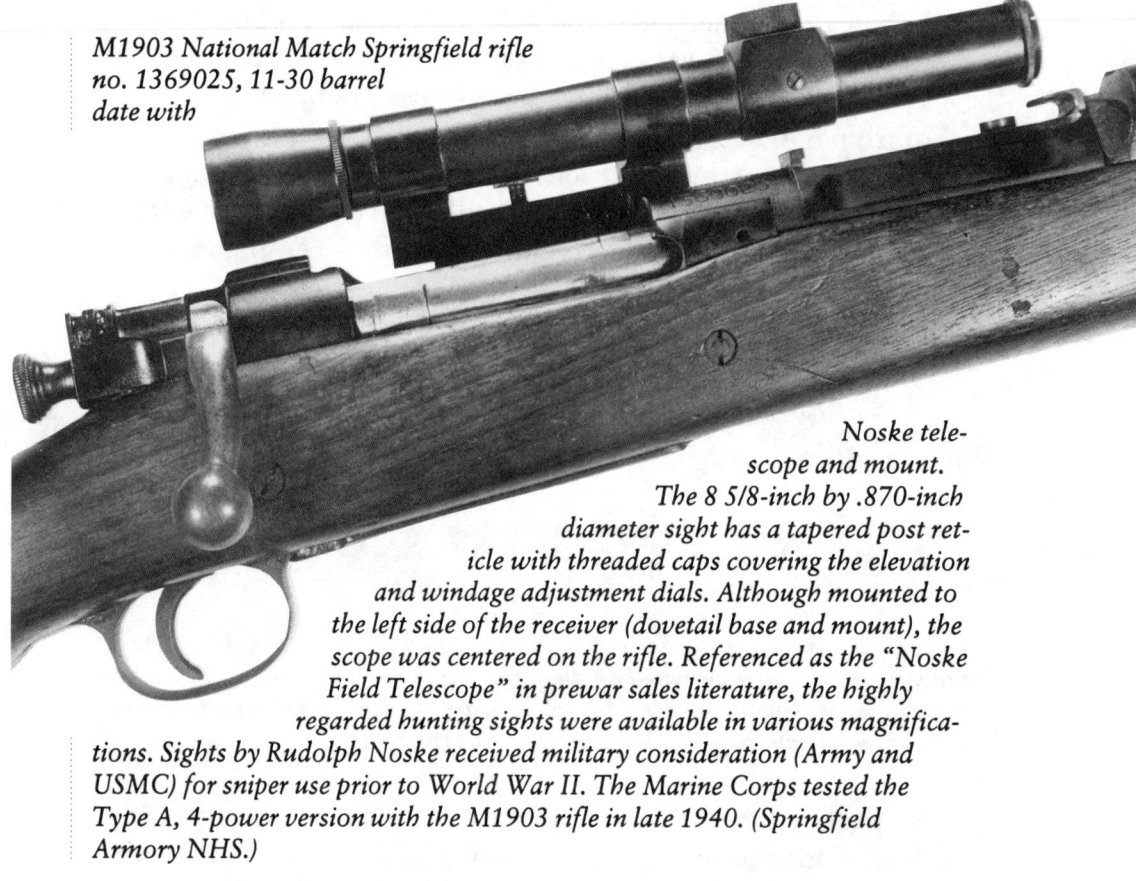

M1903 National Match Springfield rifle no. 1369025, 11-30 barrel date with Noske telescope and mount. The 8 5/8-inch by .870-inch diameter sight has a tapered post reticle with threaded caps covering the elevation and windage adjustment dials. Although mounted to the left side of the receiver (dovetail base and mount), the scope was centered on the rifle. Referenced as the "Noske Field Telescope" in prewar sales literature, the highly regarded hunting sights were available in various magnifications. Sights by Rudolph Noske received military consideration (Army and USMC) for sniper use prior to World War II. The Marine Corps tested the Type A, 4-power version with the M1903 rifle in late 1940. (Springfield Armory NHS.)

As the report continued:

> In making comparative tests of the telescopes, one fact stood out: considering selling price, and, therefore, its to-be-expected quality and the purpose for which it was designed, each of the American Sighting Telescopes is, without exception, of fine quality and good performance. Some limitation,

such as a non-standard tube diameter requiring a special mount, too limited field for the purpose, too high a power in bright light, insufficient resolution, or too low luminosity may have precluded the selection of a given telescope for military employment; but, in every case, it is satisfactory for the purpose for which it was intended.

As the Van Orden and Lloyd report concluded:

> In summation, the items that are available in America today, procurable in sufficient quantities within a reasonable time, and efficient to the extent that the Sniper can hit any target he can see at any range up to at least one thousand yards and which will be generally satisfactory in every situation are:
>
> *The Rifle*: The Winchester Model 70, caliber 30, G7044C.
>
> *The Ammunition*: The Western Cartridge, ball, caliber 30, "Match," or equal.
>
> *The Metallic Sights:* The Lyman No. 48WH Receiver Sight, or equal, and the Lyman No. 77 Front Sight, or equal.
>
> *The Sighting Telescope:* The Unertl "Sniper" Telescopic Sight or equal, mounted on the Unertl Snipers' Mounts, or equal.
>
> *The Observers' Telescope*: The Argus 55 millimeter Spotting Scope, or equal, mounted on the Mossberg "Spotshot" Stand, or equal.

As a matter of interest, though the Model 70 Winchester would not serve the Marine Corps as an "official" sniper rifle during World War II, in one form or another, the Model 70 would serve the Marine Corps rifle teams and snipers for the next 30 years.

Ironically, a Model 70 Winchester mounting a "USMC marked" 8-power Unertl scope would eventually stand as a symbol of sniper effectiveness in the hands of the legendary Marine marksman Carlos Hathcock. Considered by many to be one of the foremost soldiers of the Vietnam War era, Hathcock was credited with 93 confirmed kills.

14.26/EPM/cwh

THE MARINE CORPS EQUIPMENT BOARD
MARINE BARRACKS, QUANTICO, VIRGINIA

3 April, 1941

From: President, Marine Corps Equipment Board.
To :   Captain George O. Van Orden, U.S. Marine Corps,
        Rifle Range, Marine Barracks, Quantico, Va.
Via :   The Commanding General, Marine Barracks,
        Quantico, Virginia.

Subject: Letter of Appreciation.

1. In November, 1940, the Marine Corps Equipment Board received a directive to conduct comparative tests of the several types of telescopic sights available commercially in conjunction with the Lyman 5A telescopic sight. During the period 1 December, 1940, to 25 March, 1941, the supervision of all experimentation has been under your charge.

2. As a result of the comprehensive and detailed experimentation carried out by you, it was found that telescopic sights and rifles were available commercially to supply ideal equipment for arming snipers in the Marine Corps. Based upon your recommendation, the Marine Corps Equipment Board has recently recommended the acquisition of one thousand units for equipping snipers.

3. The treatise "Equipment for the American Sniper" compiled by you and Chief Marine Gunner Calvin A. Lloyd, U.S. Marine Corps, is a valuable contribution to military knowledge and in particular, that knowledge required for a complete understanding of the sniper's problem. This treatise is obviously the result of detailed research and it is apparent that every effort was expended in the solution of the problem.

4. Your work as a member of the Marine Corps Equipment Board is highly appreciated by its President.

E. P. MOSES.

A letter of appreciation from E.P. Moses, President, Marine Corps Equipment Board (MCEB) to Capt. George O. Van Orden, USMC (3 April 1941). (U.S. Marine Corps.)

CHAPTER 3

A Target Scope for Snipers

In the first six months of 1942, the United States' commitment to the "Europe First" policy had limited the men and materiel available for large-scale operations against the Japanese in the Pacific theater of operations.

Even though the rapid expansion of American military forces followed the attack on Pearl Harbor, with few exceptions, Marine combat personnel were raw recruits with no experience beyond basic drill and weapons training. There had not been any combined services large-scale exercises, and most units had no experience in amphibious landings. While this would change quickly, amidst the confusion of preparing for total war, any consideration at that point for selecting suitable sniping equipment was, at best, relegated to minimum-priority status.

A close-up view of the USMC Model 70 Winchester (47262) and Unertl telescopic sight with standard 1/4-minute click target mount, clamp ring, recoil spring, and dust caps in place on both ends of the scope. The Unertl Combination Target Scope was essentially the same as the USMC contract sight. When introduced, the commercial model was available in 8, 10, 12, and 14 power. According to early Unertl sales literature, the "Combination Target Scope" was so-named because the "1 1/4-inch clear aperture objective" enabled the shooter to use the sight for shooting and spotting targets as well, "thus eliminating the need for a separate spotting scope." (Peter R. Senich.)

A combat-weary veteran of the Solomon Islands campaign (1942) is shown with a Model 70 Winchester rifle mounting a Lyman Alaskan telescopic sight. Even though Model 70 rifles with target scopes were reportedly used against the Japanese in the South Pacific, the Model 70 in "hunting trim" is believed to have seen the most combat use. In any case, the field use of such weapons was usually limited to officers and NCOs. Few enlisted men had the opportunity to carry a Model 70 Winchester into combat during World War II. (Max Crace illustration.)

USMC Model 70 (47262). The double-micrometer "split-frame" rear mounting is typical of those furnished with commercial target scopes. A three-point suspension mount, the steel micrometer screws were milled, hardened, and lapped in their own bearings to ensure accuracy; all steel parts and mounting screws were hardened accordingly. The dovetail was designed to fit all standard target bases. With few exceptions, .30-caliber (.30-06) Model 70 rifles produced during World War II were procured by the Army or the Marine Corps. Of parallel interest, a "museum grade" .30-06 Model 70 Winchester "Standard Rifle" (serial no. 47029) in original prewar hunting trim (Lyman Alaskan/Stith Mounts) bearing Rock Island Arsenal markings (RIA-FK3) has been duly noted as well. Although World War II-era Model 70 rifles in the 40,000-50,000 serial number range have been categorized by some as "USMC serial block Model 70s," from all indications the U.S. Army procured a considerable number of .30-06 Model 70 rifles from this same serial number range. (Peter R. Senich.)

A World War II manufacture (1942) "Army" Model 70 Winchester serial no. 51734 with Lyman receiver sight and Rock Island Arsenal markings (RIA-FK3). Even though the Marine Corps also procured a number of .30-06 Model 70 rifles during the war, their intended use remains unconfirmed and subject to debate. Although Winchester experts tend to disagree on the total number produced, Model 70 rifles continued in production during the war years. (Dean H. Whitaker.)

WINCHESTER REPEATING ARMS COMPANY
DIVISION OF WESTERN CARTRIDGE COMPANY
NEW HAVEN, CONNECTICUT, U.S.A.
WINCHESTER

United States Marine Corps
Quartermaster's Department
Depot of Supplies
Philadelphia, Pa.

July 20, 1942

Attention: Lt-Colonel M. L. Shively

Sirs:-

On May 29th this year we shipped United States Marine Corps a total of 373 Winchester Model 70 .30 Government 06 Rifles. All .30 Government 06 Rifles are now frozen under War Production Board Limitation Orders.

We have the following stock of Model 70 .30 Government 06 Rifles on hand which we can offer you subject to prior sale.

G7004C M/70	30 Govt. M/06 24" Rd.	1666
G7014C M/70	30 Govt. M/06 24" Rd. - #48WJS	173
G7024C M/70	30 Govt. M/06 20" Rd.	31
G7034C M/70	30 Govt. M/06 20" Rd. - #48WJS	27
G7074C M/70	30 Govt. M/06 20" Rd. - #57W	4
G7084C M/70	30 Govt. M/06 24" Rd. - #57W	43

It occurs to us that the Marine Corp may be interested in an additional quantity of the above rifles at this time and shall be glad to submit quotation if you will advise us what styles and quantities you may be interested in.

Respectfully,

WINCHESTER REPEATING ARMS COMPANY
Division of Western Cartridge Co.

Edwin Pugsley
Assistant Secretary

EP:D:vn/86

Winchester Repeating Arms Co. offer (20 July 1942) to sell additional Model 70 rifles to the Marine Corps. (U.S. Marine Corps.)

By mid-1942, however, in addition to serious efforts to choose the best telescopic sight, the question of adopting the Winchester Model 70, as recommended by Van Orden and Lloyd, became part of the overall problem—in effect, something more to consider.

While it appears that certain factions within the Corps would have preferred the Model 70/Unertl combination (if for no other reason than as an expedient at that point), as events transpired, by 4 July 1942, discussion between the Quartermaster (Headquarters), the Depot Quartermaster (Philadelphia), and duly concerned factions at Quantico brought about a proposal that "M1903 Rifles, national match and special target," as had been employed or intended for use by Marine Corps Rifle Teams, "be taken up as rifles, cal. .30, M1903 and issued as may be directed."

However, as the match and target rifles "had bright bolts" by design (polished and not parkerized), instructions for appropriate measures then followed on 10 July 1942: "It is requested that the bolts of the rifles mentioned be put through a blueing process and that rifles be taken up as rifles, caliber .30 'Snipers Equipment,' and held in stores pending instructions."

Concurrent with moves to have the USMC Team rifles "stand ready" for conversion to or use as sniping equipment, correspondence dated 20 July 1942 from the Winchester Repeating Arms Company to the Quartermaster's Department, Depot of Supplies (Philadelphia), stated in part:

> On May 29th this year we shipped United States Marine Corps a total of 373 Winchester Model 70 .30 Government 06 Rifles . . . . It occurs to us that the Marine Corps may be interested in an additional quantity of the above rifles at this time and shall be glad to submit quotation if you will advise us what styles and quantity you may be interested in.

Even though some experts contend that the aforementioned Model 70 rifles were earmarked for USMC sharpshooter use in the South Pacific, Marine Corps archives have not yielded the specific reasons for the acquisition of 373 Model 70 rifles at that time.

Of parallel interest, correspondence dated 29 July 1942, from the Depot Quartermaster (Philadelphia) to the Quartermaster (Headquarters) concerning the Winchester proposal did apparently seal the fate of the Model 70 as a sniper rifle for the duration of the war. As the letter related:

> The subject rifles are not considered suitable for general service use for the following reasons:
>
> (a) Not sufficiently sturdy.
> (b) Parts are not interchangeable with M1903 and M1 rifle parts.
> (c) Replacement parts will be difficult to procure.
> (d) Not fitted with sling swivels.
>
> These rifles are not considered suitable for use as sniper rifles. The 1047 rifles, U.S., caliber .30, M1903, "Snipers

UNITED STATES MARINE CORPS
QUARTERMASTER'S DEPARTMENT
DEPOT OF SUPPLIES
PHILADELPHIA, PA.

IN REPLYING
REFER TO No.
340-O

29 July, 1942.

From: Depot Quartermaster.
To: The Quartermaster.

Subject: Rifles, Winchester, Model 70, .30
             Government 06.

References: (a) DQP ltr 441-O to QM dated 4 July 1942.
             (b) QM ltr 215-12 to DQP dated 10 July 1942.

Enclosure: (A). Ltr Winchester Repeating Arms Co. to
             DQP, attention Lt-Col. M.L. Shively,
             dated 20 July, 1942.

    1.   The enclosure is forwarded for the information of the Quartermaster.

    2.   The subject rifles are not considered suitable for general service use for the following reasons:

    (a) Not sufficiently sturdy
    (b) Parts are not interchangeable with
        M1903 and M1 rifle parts.
    (c) Replacement parts will be difficult to
        procure.
    (d) Not fitted with sling swivels.

    3.   These rifles are not considered suitable for use as sniper rifles. The 1047 rifles, U.S., caliber .30, M1903, "Snipers Equipment" on hand at this Depot (references (a) and (b)) are believed to be superior to the subject rifles both in accuracy and durability. The parts for these rifles are interchangeable with those of the standard M1903 rifle.

M. C. GREGORY.

Marine Corps response to Winchester Repeating Arms Co., dated 29 July 1942. (U.S. Marine Corps.)

Equipment" on hand at this Depot are believed to be superior to the subject rifles both in accuracy and durability. The parts for these rifles are interchangeable with those of the standard M1903 rifle.

As a matter of interest, the small-arms collection of the Marine Corps Museum (Quantico, Virginia) includes a number of Winchester Model 70 match and sporting rifles bearing serial numbers consistent with World War II Winchester manufacture.

Though unsubstantiated at present, the acquisition of .30-caliber (.30-06) Winchester rifles by the Marine Corps may have been a part of the general emergency small-arms procurement taking place at that time.

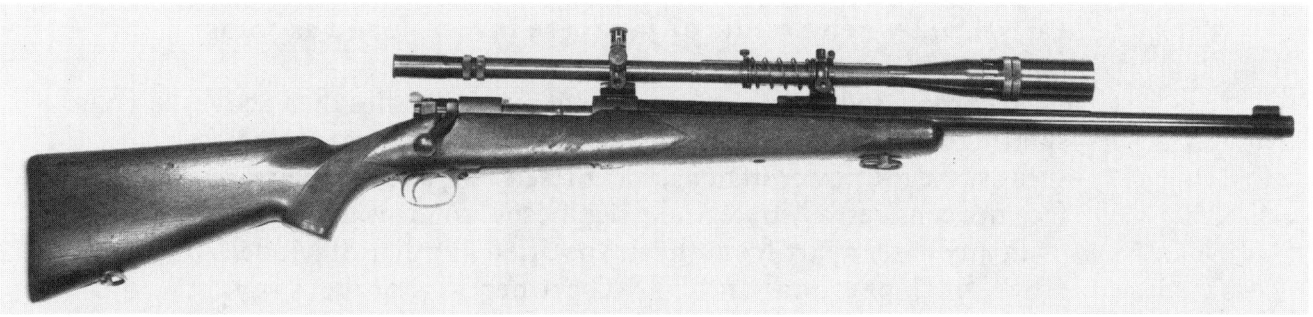

Winchester Model 70 (serial no. 47262) manufactured in 1941 with a commercial Unertl 8-power 1 1/4-inch objective "Combination Target Scope." A Marine Corps modification, the rifle was rebarreled in the years following the war. In this form (24-inch medium-heavy target barrel, .790-inch muzzle diameter), the rifle was similar to the Winchester (G7044C) Model 70 variation recommended for USMC sniper use by Van Orden and Lloyd in 1941. Rifle no. 47262 is part of the Marine Corps small-arms collection. (Peter R. Senich.)

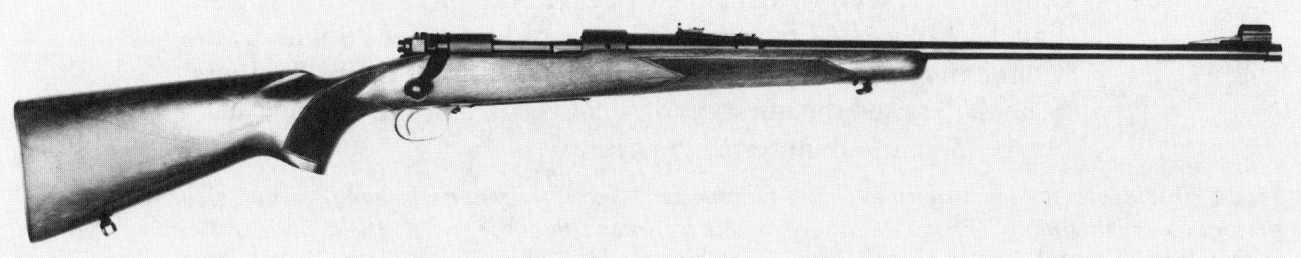

Korean War-era .30-caliber (.30-06) Model 70 Winchester Rifle. Referenced by many as a "sporting" or "hunting" rifle, the Winchester M70 "Standard Rifle" was furnished with a hand-checkered, walnut pistol-grip stock (straight-comb); hinged steel floorplate; clip-feeding slot; 5-round box magazine; sling swivels; leaf sights; front sight hood; and a steel trigger guard, magazine follower, and butt plate. The 24-inch standard barrel had a .600-inch muzzle diameter (nominal). In this form, the Model 70 was 44 5/8 inches in length with the 24-inch barrel and weighed 7 3/4 pounds without a sling. The most common Model 70 apart from the early target variations, .30-06 M70 Standard Rifles had been procured by the Marine Corps as a matter of course before and during World War II. Various USMC armorers recall prewar Model 70 rifles with serial numbers going back to original Winchester production in 1936. Despite some unofficial combat duty as sniper equipment in the Pacific theater, the USMC Model 70 rifles were not procured with sniper use in mind. Rather than a form of "emergency procurement," as practiced by the Army, Winchester experts have advanced the theory, though unconfirmed, that many of the World War II-era Model 70 rifles were originally procured by the Marine Corps for target shooting and hunting purposes by base personnel at the larger USMC installations. Though it is speculative, the rifles are believed to have been allocated to "Base Special Services," or simply "Special Services," to be checked out for recreational purposes. In some cases, the rifles were reportedly marked to indicate this use. (Donald G. Thomas.)

In what is referenced by some official World War II-era documents as "emergency procurement" due to the short supply of service rifles available for stateside military use, the Armed Forces purchased commercial rifles firing the .30-06 cartridge and 12-gauge shotguns from civilian arms manufacturers in early 1942 when threats of Japanese invasion and sabotage appeared imminent.

According to both military and civilian authorities then active, sporting rifles and shotguns were used in standing guard at places such as bridges, power stations, water reservoirs, and manufacturing facilities considered "strategically significant" to the war effort.

In any case, apart from the unspecified number of Model 70 rifles, both personal and USMC property, that were in fact employed for sniping purposes in the Pacific, such weapons were not authorized or considered part of the overall Marine Corps sniping effort at any level of command. The Model 1903 Springfield Rifle, in one form or another, would serve as the principal USMC sniping arm during World War II.

Interestingly, even though 40 M1903 rifles equipped with Lyman 5A target sights had been authorized months earlier in April 1941, well in advance of Pearl Harbor, a memorandum dated 19 July 1942 from the Division of Plans and Policies to the Commandant, in discussing the need for Marine Corps "Snipers' Schools," raised the question of what became of the "forty rifles." As the memorandum stated in part:

Model 70 Winchester (Standard Rifle) with a commercial 2.5-power Lyman Alaskan telescopic sight in a Redfield Junior military mounting. The .30-06 Model 70 with a Lyman rifle scope and Redfield, Stith, or Griffin & Howe mountings was considered "state of the art" in 1943 by many knowledgeable riflemen. By all accounts, a number of Model 70 Winchester rifles saw combat duty in this form. (Robert Bell.)

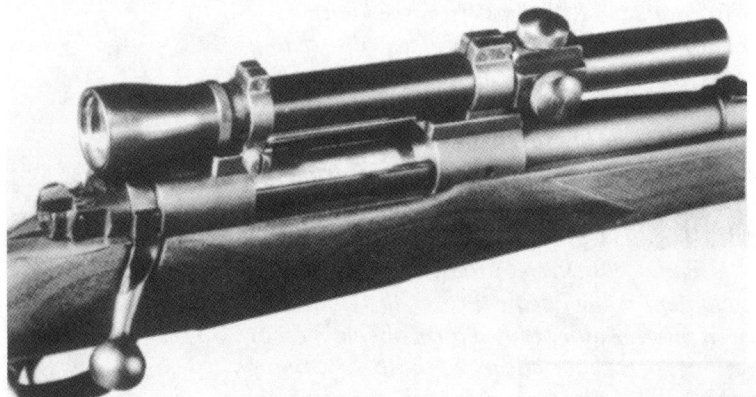

Model 70 Winchester (Standard Rifle) with a Lyman Alaskan rifle scope in a prewar Griffin & Howe double-lever (locking) side mount. According to Lyman records, the elevation and windage adjustment covers were added in 1942. As such, the Popular Lyman hunting scope became the Lyman Alaskan "All Weather" model. (Robert Bell.)

The forty (40) rifles equipped with telescopic sights were shipped to the 1st and 2nd Marine Divisions about May 1941. No reply has yet been received.

However unsuited the Lyman target sights may have been for combat and jungle warfare in particular, when the United States Marine Corps went to war in 1942, the Model 1903/Lyman combination would serve as the USMC sniping rifle.

Contrary to the fact that the Marine Corps had, perhaps arbitrarily, rejected the Winchester Model 70 in favor of the Model 1903 Springfield Rifle as the platform for its sniper issue, there was absolutely no question that the Lyman 5A telescopic sights then in use would have to be replaced.

Unfortunately, neither official archives nor Unertl company records have yielded specific information as to when the initial order for Unertl telescopic sights was placed. However, the Commandant of the Marine Corps received a request dated 23 December 1942 from the First Marine Amphibious Corps (FMAC), then engaged in combat with Japanese forces in the Solomon Islands, that a "scope-fitted sniper's rifle be adopted." From all indications, he responded as soon as possible.

As noted in a part of an abbreviated USMC "Chronological History of the Sniper Rifle" dated 27 April 1945, the Commandant approved the recommendation, and made vague reference to "a procurement program" in official correspondence dated 6 January 1943.

Consequently, experts believe that with the Unertl firm in a position to produce the 8-power "Sniper" telescopic sight in quantity, the initial order was placed in late December 1942, or perhaps during the early part of January 1943.

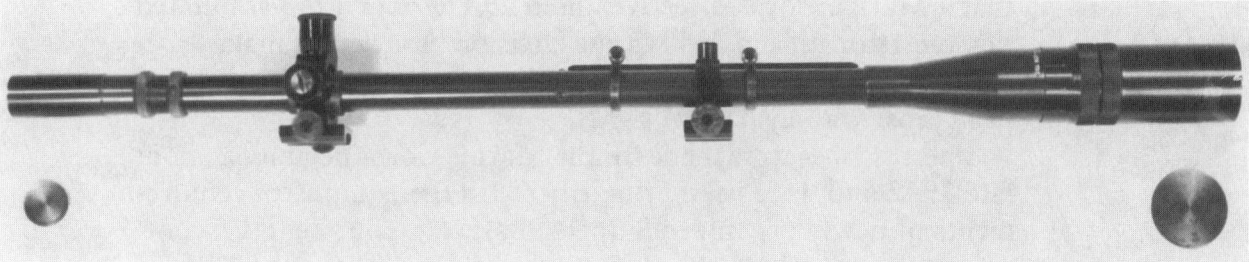

A typical World War II-era USMC contract sight as furnished by the John Unertl Optical Company. The 8-power scope was 24 inches in length with a 3/4-inch main tube diameter. Threaded dust caps were provided for both ends of the scope. Though reasonably effective, the end caps were frequently lost. (Peter R. Senich.)

As then followed, the U.S. Rifle, Caliber .30, M1903A1 (Springfield), mounting the military version of the 1 1/4-inch objective Unertl target scope, was for all intent and purpose accepted by the Marine Corps as its sniper standard. Nevertheless, with overall conditions as hectic and fluid as they were at that time, so far as sniping equipment was concerned, the use of such terms as "accepted," "standard," or even "adopted" were at best loosely applied.

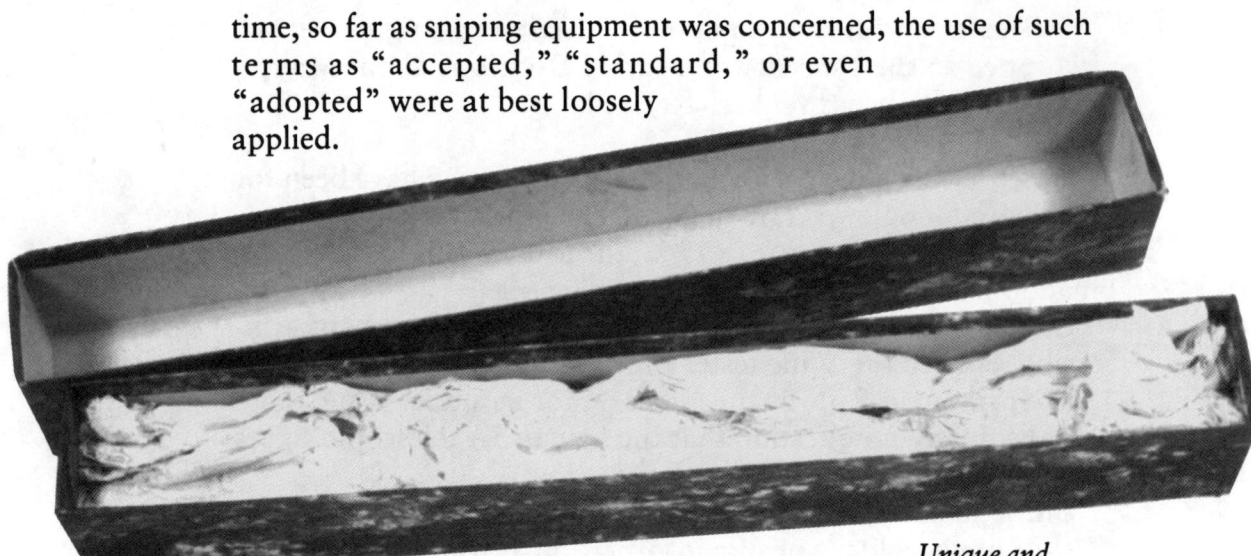

Unique and extremely rare, an original cardboard container used to ship the Unertl telescopic sights to the Marine Corps during World War II. A soft paper packing material widely used for shipping optical and laboratory instruments served to protect the sights in transit. (Peter R. Senich.)

In due course, "First Base Depot" (FMAC) was notified in early February 1943 that it could expect shipment of "150 Marine Corps rifle team rifles with selected barrels and fitted with Unertl sighting scopes." That number was subsequently increased to 250. This, then, was the initial, and as some Marine historians contend, perhaps the only, intended shipment of the M1903A1/Unertl system to USMC combat units in the Pacific.

Despite tacit acceptance of the Unertl, it is important to emphasize that an unspecified number of Lyman-equipped Springfields would continue to see combat as well. Receipt and field distribution of both types of equipment reached such a state of confusion that a Marine Corps directive dated 29 October 1943 stipulated that the 1st, 2nd, and 3rd Marine Division base depots make "special reference" to rifles with Unertl telescopes, as distinguished from those with Lyman 5A sights.

Unertl scopes were made for the Marine Corps beginning about late 1942 and were used primarily to fill the equipment requirements of newly organized Sniper-Observer-Scout Teams (scout-snipers) destined for action against the Japanese in the Pacific. While most of the Unertl scopes were installed on Springfields, a number were reportedly used with Model 54 and Model 70 Winchester rifles. These were not official issue, however.

While it is considered academic to some, inquiries made through the years to the Unertl firm by various interested parties addressing the number of Unertl contract sights produced for the Marine Corps often yielded conflicting figures. For example:

"The total quantity made was between 5,000 and 6,000."
and
"The total number manufactured was approximately 3500."

2420
10/62-tcg
01-41

HEADQUARTERS, FIRST MARINE AMPHIBIOUS CORPS,
IN THE FIELD.

29 October, 1943.

From: The Commanding General.
To : The Commanding General. 1MAC (ADM).

Subject: Snipers', Rifles.

Reference: (a) CMC CONF ltr to CG, FMAC, AO-347-hdl over
               (05A643), of 6Jan43.
           (b) CG, FMAC, CONF ltr (0091) to CG, 1stMarDiv,
               et al, of 16Feb43. (Copy to CO, 1st Base Depot).
           (c) CMC CONF ltr to CG, FMAC, AO-233-nsh over
               (03B3943), of 9Feb43.
           (d) CMC CONF ltr to CG, FMAC, 05B25343 over AO-347-ec,
               of 10Sep43.

1. Reference (a) informed this Headquarters that one hundred (100) Marine Corps team rifles with selected barrels and fitted with Unertl sighting scopes, together with one hundred (100) spotting scopes (40 B&L spotting scopes and 60 draw-tube scopes), were to be shipped to the First Base Depot. Reference (b) directed the distribution of this equipment upon receipt at the Base Depot. Reference (c) informed this Headquarters that one hundred fifty (150) telescope equipped rifles would be shipped about 15 February, 1943, pursuant to reference (a), and that this number would later be increased to two hundred fifty (250). It would be assumed, then, that two hundred fifty (250) rifles, two hundred fifty (250) Unertl sighting scopes, and two hundred fifty (250) spotting scopes, either prismatic or draw-tube type, were to have been provided. Reference (d) states that the two hundred fifty (250) rifles were shipped. It also requests recommendations that cannot be made upon present information.

2. Tables Of Organization provide for an authorized allowance of snipers' rifles in certain organizations. The standard equipment furnished in accordance therewith is a rifle fitted with Lyman 5-A sighting scope. The two hundred fifty (250) above mentioned rifles were specially selected rifles fitted with a more efficient sighting scope (Unertl), accompanied by special spotting scopes, all furnished in response to a special request from this Headquarters.

3. There is a possibility that the two types of equipment have been confused, under the general heading of "sniper's rifle". No return has been made on reference (b), and no direct

-1-

Marine Corps directive (29 October 1943) stipulating that the 1st, 2nd, and 3rd Marine Division base depots make "special reference" to rifles with Unertl telescopes, as distinguished from those with Lyman 5A sights. (U.S. Marine Corps.)

With proper regards to the Unertl firm, and recognizing the difficulty of maintaining records for over 50 years, so far as it is

Subject: Snipers' Rifles.   29 October, 1943.

report has been received from the Second or Third Base Depots as to the receipt of snipers' rifles nor have organizations reported their receipt. It is known that about 4 May, 1943, the Second Base Depot released fifty (50) snipers' rifles to the Second Marine Division, and that a small number of rifles and scopes were shipped by the First Base Depot to the First Marine Division.

4. It is requested that you secure and forward to this Headquarters, in order that requests from The Commandant for information and recommendations may be complied with, the following.

(a) A report from The Commanding General, Supply Service, showing receipts in all Base Depots of snipers' rifle equipment, and any distribution made.

(b) A report from units of this Corps of any snipers' rifle equipment received by them.

Make special reference in all reports as to the specially selected Rifle Team rifles, Unertl sighting scopes, and spotting scopes, referred to in references (a) and (c), as distinguished from the standard sniper's rifle with Lyman sighting scope.

/s/ G. C. Thomas

G. C. THOMAS,
By direction.

Copy to: CMC.

5/133-ab
Serial(0786)   1st Endorsement   6 November, 1943.
HEADQUARTERS, FIRST MARINE AMPHIBIOUS CORPS (ADM).

From: The Commanding General.
To :   All Units IMAC.

1. Forwarded for compliance, via this Headquarters, with paragraph 4(b).

F. N. REEVE,
By direction.

known, a total of 3,500 scopes appear to have been actually ordered by the Marine Corps, the initial order being for 1,000 and the second for 2,500. However, according to USMC records, 1,750 Unertl telescopic sights had been accepted by the Marine Corps by April 1945, and, as then stated, this figure represented the "total delivered." Though additional deliveries may have taken place before the war ended a few weeks later, considering the overall situation, the status of the war at that point, and the controversy surrounding the suitability of the Unertl scope, further deliveries are believed to have been highly unlikely.

Of further interest, judging from prewar Unertl target scope serial number marking practice, the Marine Corps contract sights were given their own serial number range. While proving very little at this juncture, the highest known "Unertl Sniper" serial number is in the 2700 range, the lowest just over 1000. All things carefully considered, Unertl contract sight numbering appears to have started at or near serial number 1000. Moreover, surviving sights serial-numbered just over 1000 are rarely encountered, these of course having seen the earliest USMC training and combat exposure during World War II.

When delivered to the Marine Corps, the Unertl sights, for most part, were shipped to the USMC Depot of Supplies (Philadelphia), where installation and basic targeting was effected by qualified armorers.

Regardless of their 8-power marking and reference, all sights were actually 7.8 power and were supplied without a recoil absorber, a spring that brings the tube back into firing position

Marine Corps Model 70 (47262) front mount and recoil spring assembly ("telescope recoil absorber"), which brought the scope back into position after firing. Offered as an accessory item, the Unertl recoil absorber was designed to fit any 3/4-inch tube and was often used with Lyman and Fecker scopes as well. The 1/8-inch "Pope-rib" top is clearly visible. The front mount also provided a three-point suspension for the telescope tube. (Peter R. Senich.)

NAVMC   OMB F-(Telescope)-1

ORDNANCE MAINTENANCE   U. S. MARINE CORPS HDQRS.
BULLETIN No. F-(Telescope)-1   Washington, D. C., 15 Dec. 1943.

OPERATION AND MAINTENANCE
UNERTL 8X SNIPERS' TELESCOPE

	Paragraph
Introduction	1
Operation	2
Maintenance	3

1. **INTRODUCTION**—The Unertl telescope is an eight power telescope for use on the U. S. Rifle cal. .30, M1903A1. (Fig. 1.) It is constructed to withstand the recoil of the rifle without necessitating a change in adjustment.

General Data:

    Magnification-8X
    Objective size (effective) 1¼"
    Exit pupil-4.2mm
    Field of view at 100 yds.-11'
    Luminosity-17.6
    Eye relief-2¼" to 2¾"
    Length-24"
    Resolution-3/32"
    Reticle angle-¼ minute
    Medium size cross wire with center dot
    Weight-24 oz.
    Maximum O. D.-1½"
    Main tube diameter-¾"
    Eye piece adjustable for individual eye
    *Target type ¼ minute click anodized.
        Duraluminum mounts with hardened steel
        bases and screws.

2. **OPERATION**—a. Focus the eyepiece against the sky until crosswire or aiming mark appears black and distinct. Then leave the eyepiece undisturbed for all ranges.

b. Focusing for ranges under 200 yards is accomplished by moving the objective focusing sleeve as follows: Loosen sunshade about one turn, follow with the graduated focusing sleeve to the indicated range markings on the objective cell, tighten sunshade again.

c. The rear mount provides an adjustment of approximately 200 minutes, each division on the graduated thimble representing ½ minute, each

The front cover of "Ordnance Maintenance Bulletin No. F—(Telescope)—1," 15 December 1943. The operation and maintenance instructions for the USMC Unertl 8X Snipers' Telescope. Seven thousand copies of the four-page pamphlet were published on 27 December 1943. An 8 1/2 x 11-inch, three-page version (31 August 1949) was circulated within the Marine Corps some years later. (Peter R. Senich.)

after each shot. It was thought that sand from the beaches working between the spring would score the tube. A ring located in front of the forward mount clamped to a rib affixed on top and in line with the tube, the combination of which served to prevent the telescope from rotating in its mounts. A second ring behind the front mount was simply a "spare," rather than an effort to limit the recoil of the tube, as some experts contend.

When the rifle was fired, the scope slid forward in the mounts and was pulled back into firing position by hand. Some rather ingenious recoil systems were used by Marine snipers in place of a regular recoil absorber. The simplest was a slice of rubber taken from a truck inner tube, which, stretched between the front clamping ring and the rear mount, brought the scope back into battery automatically.

The rear mount provided an adjustment of approximately 200 minutes, with each division on the graduated thimble representing 1/2-minute and each click a 1/4-minute adjustment. Later scopes were modified for 1/2-minute adjustments for each click.

A part of the original issue, a Micarta carrying case, also manufactured by Unertl, was supplied with every sight assembly. Although "belt-hooks" were fitted to the cases, the telescope carrying cases were designed to be carried on the combat packs rather than suspended from a cartridge belt. An aluminum version, similar in appearance to the Micarta case, was part of the original equipment proposal, but while mentioned in early documents, it does not appear to have ever reached issue status.

The military version of the Unertl "patented 3-point suspension mount" introduced in 1940: the target-type, USMC contract, 1/4-minute click, black anodized duraluminum mount with hardened steel parts and base locking screw. Machined from a single piece of aluminum alloy, the mount provides an adjustment of approximately 200 minutes, each division on the graduated thimble representing 1/2 minute, each click 1/4-minute adjustment. The micrometer "thimbles" were black enamel with graduations in white. Later model scopes were modified with each click a 1/2-minute adjustment. (Peter R. Senich.)

Operation and maintenance instructions for the Unertl telescope were set forth by U.S. Marine Corps Headquarters, Washington, D.C., in "Ordnance Maintenance Bulletin No. F—(Telescope)—1," (15 December 1943), a document that provided the following information:

General Data

Magnification	8X
Objective size	(effective) 1 1/4 inches
Exit pupil	4.2 mm
Field of view at 100 yards	11 feet
Luminosity	17.6
Eye relief	2 1/4 to 2 3/4 inches
Length	24 inches
Resolution	3/32 inch
Reticle angle	1/4 minute

Medium-size Crosswire with Center Dot:

Weight	24 ounces
Maximum O.D.	1 1/2 inches
Main tube diameter	3/4 inch

Eyepiece adjustable for individual eye.
Target type, 1/4-minute click anodized, duraluminum mounts with hardened steel bases and screws.

Marine Corps sights, furnished by Unertl under World War II contracts, bore the following legend on the tube, directly in front of the eyepiece:

J. Unertl
USMC - Sniper
2774

By any measure, it was a superb sight, with the only genuine question being its durability for sustained use in a combat environment. Despite any deficiencies, either real or imagined, noted riflescope authority and outdoorsman Bob Bell said it best perhaps:

> It was, theoretically, too long, too fragile, too whatever. But infantrymen and Marines—and even Navy sharpshooters at times—went on aiming with it and squeezing them off, and enemy soldiers kept dropping. It's hard to argue with results like that.

Not much need be said for the shooting capability of a select Springfield rifle. In response to the question of whether the Unertl was satisfactory, Stan Deka, a scout-sniper veteran of the Pacific campaign who survived Tarawa and the action on Saipan and

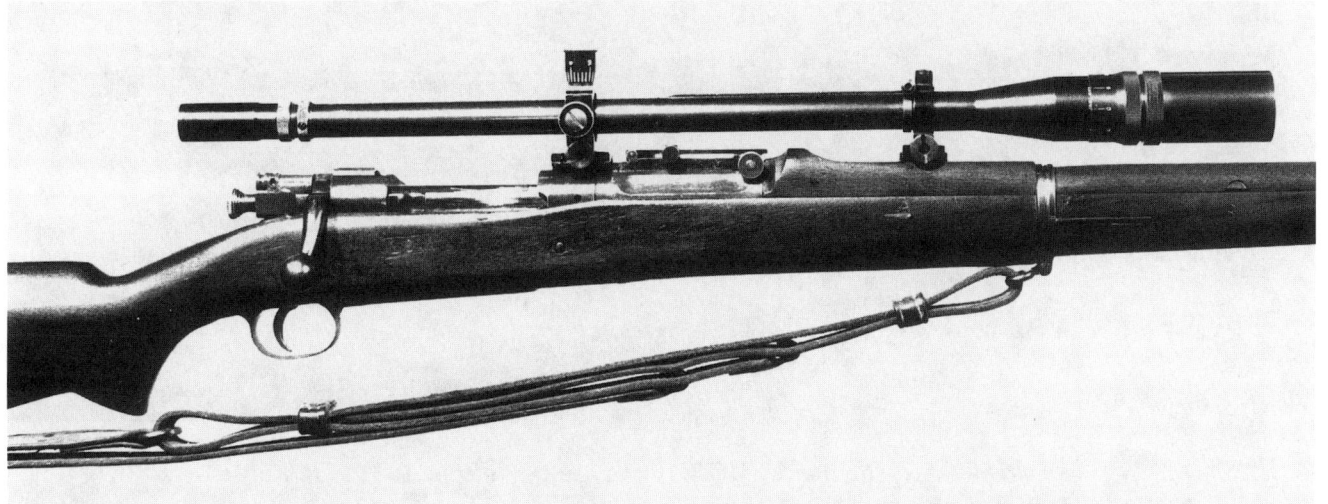

Marine Corps M1903A1 sniper rifle, serial no. 1531443, 6-39 barrel date, with Unertl 8-power contract sight no. 2299. An original USMC "conversion rifle" with a well marked stock (arsenal and inspection stamps), the rifle has various National Match (NM) characteristics and was also fitted with the USMC No. 10 front and rear sight components. (Kogan Collection.)

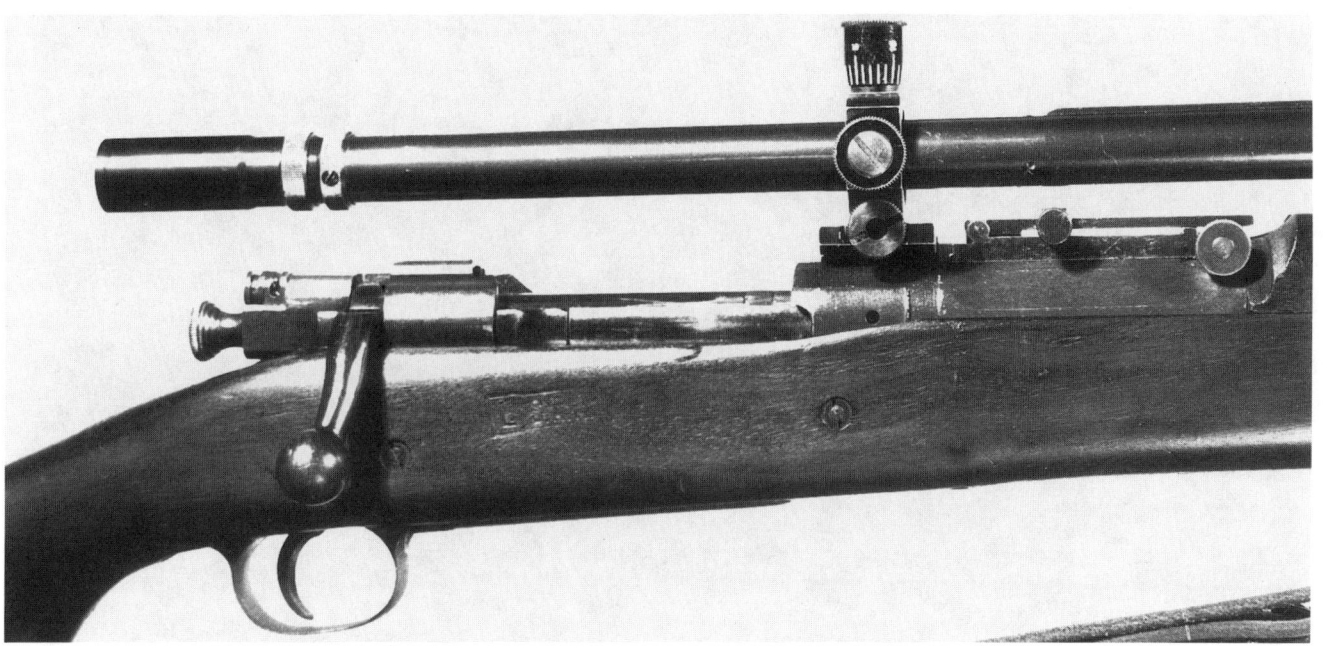

A close-up view of USMC M1903A1 sniper rifle no. 1531443, a prime example of a late-production Springfield Armory rifle modified for Marine Corps sniper use. (Kogan Collection.)

Tinian with the 2nd Marine Division, simply replied, "We found it quite adequate. We found no faults with the scope."

Regardless of the combat use of the Lyman 5A and other scopes, the M1903A1/Unertl combination remained as the principal, if limited, issue for Marine Corps sniping specialists throughout the war. Although the Springfield had outlived its usefulness as a basic infantry arm, it would continue to serve as a sniping weapon in Korea as well.

An alternate view (left) of USMC M1903A1 sniper rifle no. 1531443. (Kogan Collection.)

Sniper Issue: A Match Grade System

CHAPTER 4

A superb rifle in competition trim, the .30-caliber M1903 Springfield would serve as the principal military match rifle during the 1920s and 1930s.

Even though the Springfield became the "official National Match rifle" in 1908, it was not until 1910 that M1903 rifles were selected for match shooting on the basis of star-gauging barrels and test-firing (targeting) to determine their accuracy. For the most part, however, these were still standard service rifles.

In line with ongoing ordnance efforts to field the optimum match rifle, by 1921, a "special version" of the M1903 was assembled at Springfield Armory for the express purpose of National Match (NM) competition.

As then followed, M1903 match rifles were produced under controlled conditions using specially selected components, carefully assembled and fitted under a rigid inspection program.

Though it was improved and modified slightly during the 1920s, the greatest change to the Springfield match rifle came in 1929, when a new pistol-grip stock was adopted (Type-C) in place of the nonpistol-grip standard service stock (Type-S), otherwise known as the "straight stock."

In this form, the NM rifle was then referenced as Rifle, U.S., Caliber .30, Model 1903A1, National Match, and, as such, most represented the rifle adopted by the Marine Corps for sniper use in World War II.

The Springfield Armory description of the Model 1903A1 National Match rifle was as follows:

> The U.S. Rifle, Caliber .30, M1903A1, National Match has a pistol grip stock (D1836) especially selected for workmanship and grain. It is made of black walnut. The receiver, bolt, and ejector are made of nickel steel. The sear and cocking piece are made of chrome-vanadium steel. The barrel is specially selected for the finish of the bore, rifling, and chamber. The bolt is polished all over to a bright finish. The runways for the bolt in the receiver and the extractor cam surface are polished after Parkerizing. It has the service firing pin assembly and safety lock assembly. The sleeve, sear, trigger, follower, and ejector are oil blackened. The trigger is serrated, and the trigger pull is between 4 and 5 pounds with-

out creep. The bolt functions smoothly, and the bolt lift does not exceed 15 pounds. All components are specially manufactured. All working surfaces are polished after hardening. The barrel is National Match, star-gauged. The rifle is targeted, and the target and star-gauge record are furnished with each rifle. All components not mentioned above have the same finish as those of the service rifle. The rifle weighs about 8 pounds, 14 ounces.

When combined with an excellent sight such as the Unertl target scope and a competent marksman, the M1903A1/Unertl system provided the Marine Corps with a potent combination. By any measure, it was perhaps the finest military sniping equipment then in use.

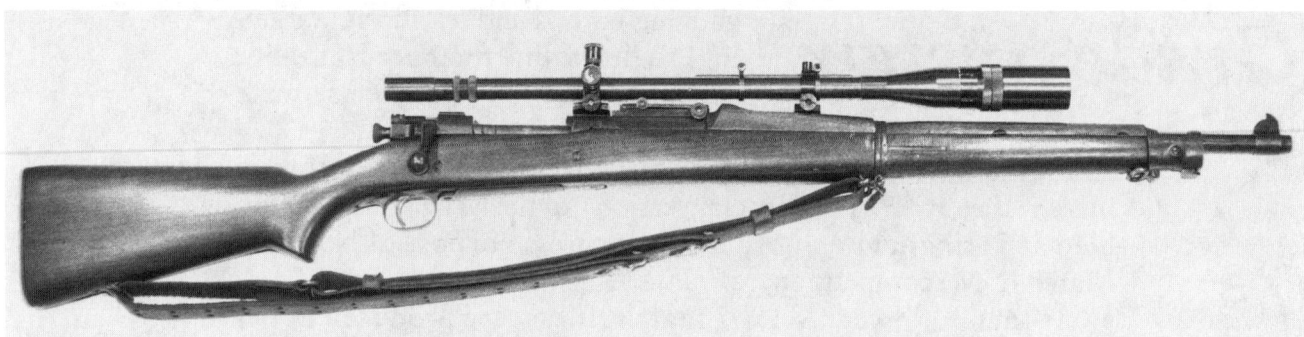

Marine Corps M1903A1 Sniper Rifle (1526591, 3-39 barrel date) with 8-power Unertl target telescope (USMC contract no. 2214), as issued for scout-sniper use in World War II and the Korean War. The rifle is part of the small-arms collection at the Marine Corps Museum. (Peter R. Senich.)

Documents indicate that both M1903 National Match and M1903 "special target" rifles (reconditioned National Match rifles) were to be "taken up" as sniper equipment (i.e., serve as a mounting platform for a telescopic sight). They also list the rifles as being "on hand" at the Depot of Supplies in Philadelphia:

> There are on hand at this depot the following rifles, U.S. cal. .30, M1903:
>
> 104 Rifles, U.S., cal. .30, M1903 national match, held for U.S. Marine Corps Reserve Rifle Team.
> 369 Rifles, U.S., cal. .30, M1903 national match, held for U.S. Marine Corps Rifle Team.
> 574 Rifles, U.S., cal. .30, M1903 special target rifles, held for Division, Marine Corps and Elliot Trophy Team matches.

The extent of such use in conjunction with the USMC sniping program, if any, remains obscure and subject to debate.

A close-up view of the USMC M1903A1 Unertl target-type (split frame) rear telescope mounting. A postwar commercial mount in this case, Unertl, and occasionally Lyman, rear target mounts were used with the Unertl USMC contract sight in the years following World War II. Even though the USMC "Unertl 8-power Sniper" sights were not procured after 1945, commercial target scopes were obtained from the major manufacturers for Marine Corps rifle team use. (Peter R. Senich.)

The rib located on top of the Unertl tube prevented the scope from rotating in its mounts. The front clamping ring was used to reposition the sight after the weapon was fired. A second ring behind the front mount was simply a spare, rather than an effort to limit the recoil of the tube. The three-point suspension front mount was issued with the sight. (Peter R. Senich.)

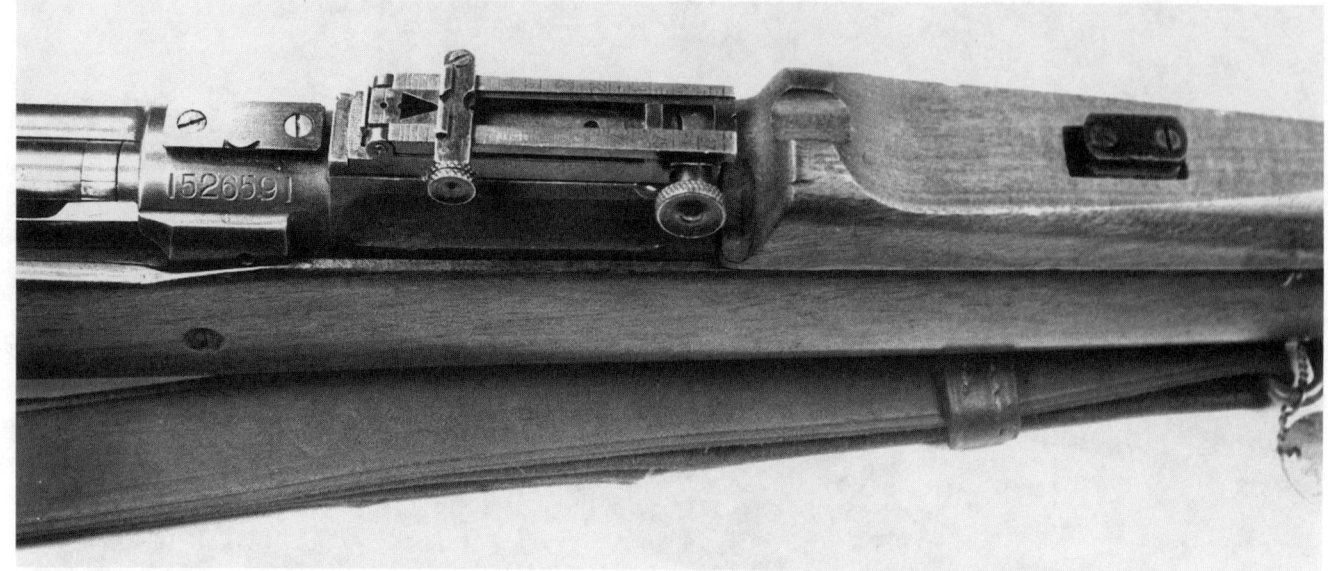

A close-up view of the USMC M1903A1 Springfield sniper rifle (1526591) depicting the manner in which the Unertl bases were attached to the barrel and receiver ring. Although base spacing (7.2-inch centers) remained constant, specimen rifles with the rear base positioned at the back edge of the receiver ring have been noted. The standard rear sight has the 2,850-yard notch at the top of the leaf. Some USMC sniper rifles were fitted with the No. 10 (USMC special) and National Match sights, however. (Peter R. Senich.)

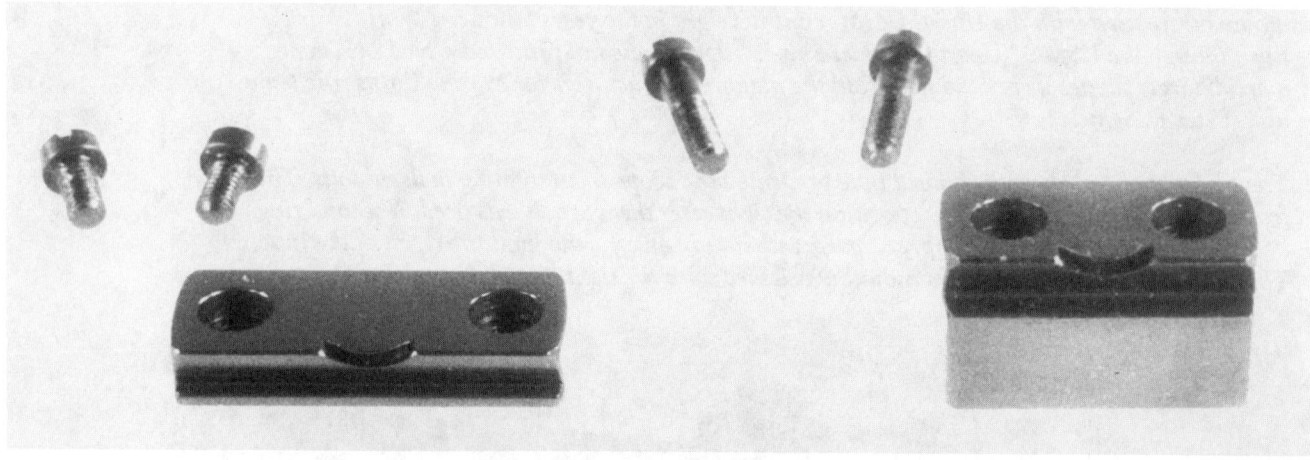

Unertl Optical Company "O" and "E" telescope bases (typical) used to mount the 8-power USMC Unertl sniper telescope on the M1903A1 rifle. The rear base (O) was attached to the receiver ring. The front base (E) was attached to the barrel. The distance on centers was 7.2 inches. The hardened steel bases were provided with a "circular beveled mill cut" to facilitate mount tightening. Though rarely encountered, both Lyman and Fecker telescope mounting bases were also used with this weapon system. (Peter R. Senich.)

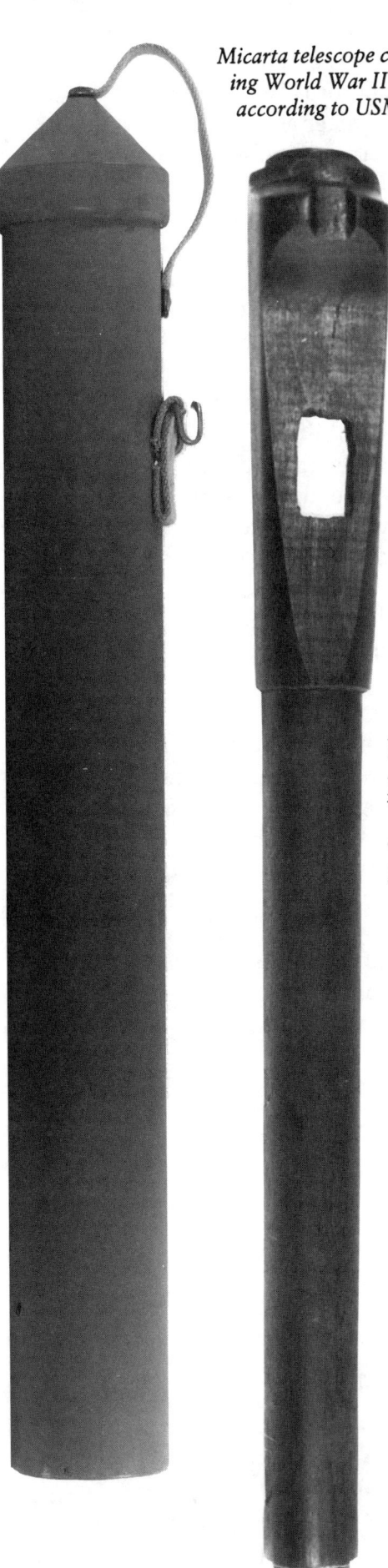

Micarta telescope carrying case (left), as furnished to the Marine Corps during World War II. Even though belt hooks were fitted to the cases, according to USMC documents, the telescope carrying cases were designed to be carried on the combat pack rather than suspended from a cartridge belt. An aluminum version similar in appearance to the Micarta case was part of the original equipment proposal made by the Unertl firm to the Marine Corps (1940–41). (Cors Collection.)

An original USMC sniper rifle (M1903A1) handguard, as modified by a Marine Corps armorer during World War II. The handguard "swell" was milled flat approximately .660-inch above the bore line, with the opening centered 2 1/4 inches behind the lower band. Though machine-made, the rectangular telescope base opening was roughly finished. (Peter R. Senich.)

It has long been presumed in some quarters that the National Match and special target rifles held at the USMC Depot of Supplies, with modifications to the handguards and the installation of telescope bases, were issued or set aside for sniping purposes. As a matter of interest, the late Lt. Col. William S. Brophy, USAR, Ret., commenting on this topic in his classic work, *The Springfield 1903 Rifles*, related:

> During many discussions with the late Brigadier General George Van Orden, USMC (Retired) in the early '50s when he operated Evaluator's Limited in Triangle, Virginia, the General proudly related his part in having the Unertl 8X telescope chosen for use by the U.S. Marines. His recollection of the rifle was not firm, but he believed that if they were not National Match rifles, they were rifles assembled to National Match specifications and would appear to be so, as the Marine Depot in Philadelphia had the skill, know-how, and equipment to equal Springfield Armory work and had for years done such work for the Marine shooting teams.

A veritable beehive of ordnance activity, the Ordnance Section of the Marine Corps Depot of Supplies at Philadelphia had been charged with "the maintenance of rifles, pistols, bayonets, machine guns, and other small ordnance material of the Marine Corps."

The Ordnance Section was created in 1919 after the demobilization and reduction of the Corps from war strength to a peacetime quota. More than 50,000 rifles and large quantities of other arms and equipment were shipped to the Depot for maintenance and storage.

According to an article entitled "Ordnance Section," by Major H.L. Smith, USMC, in the December 1925 issue of Marine Corps Gazette:

> The rifles and other arms were in widely varying conditions of serviceability. Due to the hasty demobilization of units newly arrived from overseas, it was apparent that all ordnance should be inspected, segregated into classes and prepared for storage. Accordingly the Ordnance Section was organized to handle this work. Men selected for their experience in this work were detailed and suitable space was allotted at the Depot. . . . In connection with the Ordnance Section, an ordnance school has been opened to train finished armorers for use through the service.

Though lacking the capability to produce major components such as rifle barrels and receivers, for example, the Ordnance Section, in addition to repairing and reclaiming small arms, also "manufactured" certain small parts for Marine Corps use, including "telescopic sight bases, the USMC No. 10 front sight, No. 10 drift slide and the front sight cover for the M1903 rifle."

(Note: The telescope sight bases were known as the "taper block Marine Corps type developed and made at the Depot." The bases were used to mount Winchester A5 and, later, Lyman 5A target scopes to the M1903 rifle. The No. 10 sight components adopted shortly after World War I consisted of a special front sight blade and rear sight drift slide for USMC M1903 rifles.)

As Major Smith further stated:

> The section makes sporting rifles for officers in the service, according to their own specifications as to stocks, barrels, sights, and triggers. The Marine Corps rifle team and the American international team have been consistent winners with rifles worked upon by the Ordnance Section.

So far as the USMC M1903A1/Unertl sniper system was concerned, however, regardless of whether the base weapons' point of origin was Springfield, Massachusetts, or Philadelphia, Pennsylvania, the actual work necessary to adapt existing NM rifles, select and convert standard service rifles, or assemble rifles in entirety to match specifications, was carried out by Marine Corps armorers based at the USMC Depot of Supplies.

A close-up view of two original USMC M1903A1 sniper rifle handguards provides an effective comparison of the 1 x 1/2-inch (+/-) telescope base opening. Although both openings were clearly machine-made, one was carefully finished while the other was left rough. The handguard (top) has an oil finish; the other is varnished. Even though handguards were modified according to the "specifications" for this weapon, this was never intended to be a precision operation. Handguard variations between weapons considered original are known to exist. USMC armorers' practice of using pencil or chalk to initial, date, or apply the rifle serial number to the underside of the handguard appears to have been conducted on a random basis. Most USMC M1903A1 sniping rifles believed to be authentic have no handguard markings whatsoever. (Peter R. Senich.)

Model 1903 Springfield rifle barrels selected by star-gauging were so stamped on the crowned portion of the muzzle at the six o'clock position. Developed in 1905, the star gauge was used as a quality control device in the manufacture of M1903 barrels. As Capt. E.C. Crossman summed it up in 1931, "The star gauge has nothing celestial about it. . . . a rifle that is star-gauged is not in any way altered or enhanced." Army and Marine Corps rifle team armorers employed star-gauging equipment as a matter of routine. Rifle barrels checked by this gauging procedure were not always "stamped," however. According to various accounts, in many cases ungauged-unmarked barrels shot as well or better than some that had been "glorified" with a star-gauge stamp. (Peter R. Senich.)

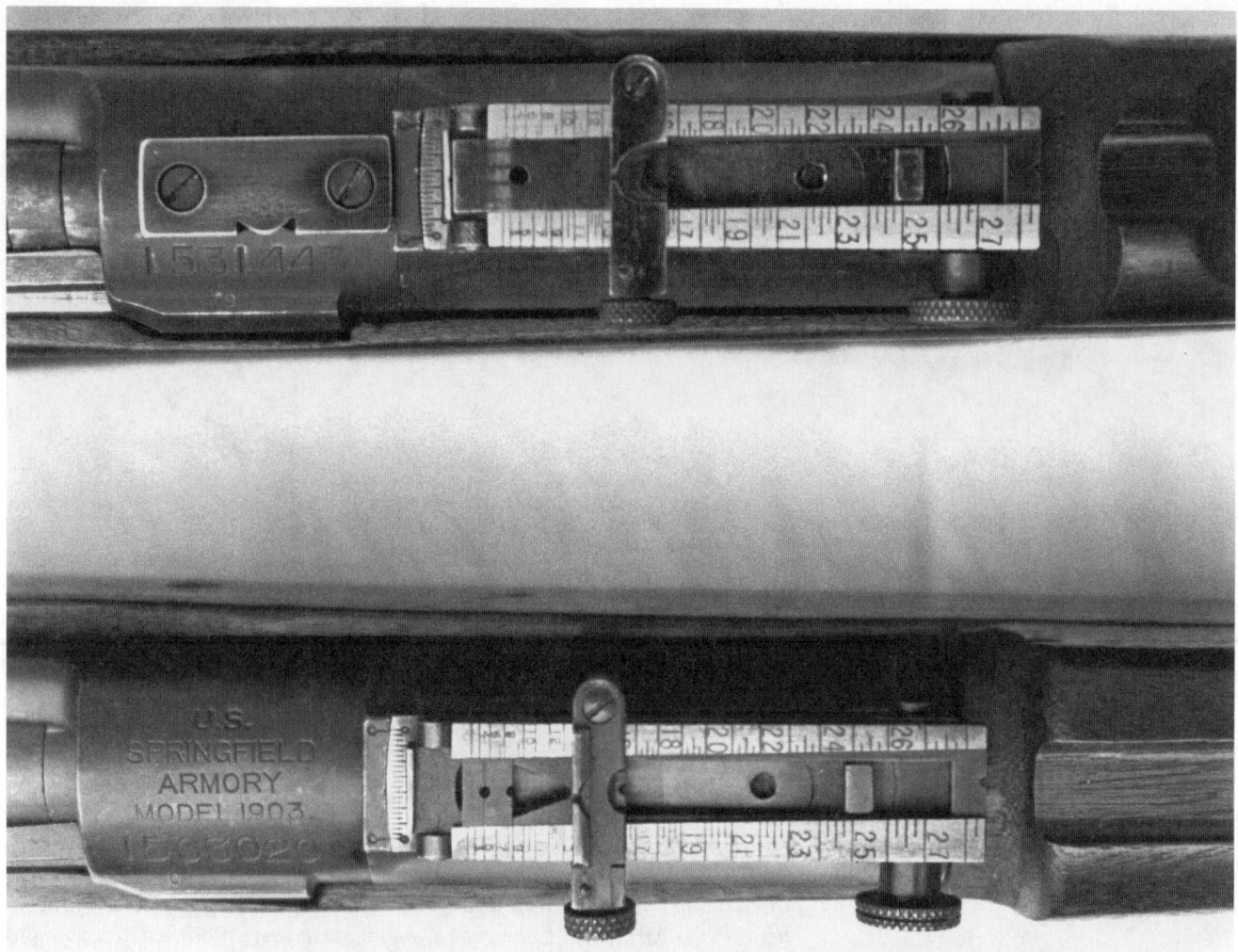

A comparison of the rear sight on a Marine Corps M1903A1 sniper rifle (serial no. 1531443, 6-39 barrel date) and a standard M1903 Springfield rifle. The sniper rifle has the USMC No. 10 drift slide (.100-inch aperture, no open U notches); the M1903 sight has the standard open U notches and .050-inch aperture. The special Marine Corps No. 10 sight components were adopted shortly after World War I. Though later deemed unsatisfactory in 1935, No. 10 sight assemblies continued in service and were fitted to some USMC M1903A1 sniper rifles. (Kogan Collection.)

Drawing from research involving the firsthand examination of original Marine Corps documents at the Suitland Federal Records Center, the National Archives, and the personal recollections of USMC ordnance personnel directly involved or in close proximity, military historian Kenneth Kogan provided the following insight on the USMC M1903A1 sniper rifle:

> The modifications involving the M1903 rifle were relatively simple. The upper handguard was milled down and cut out to accommodate the front scope block, the rear block being mounted on the receiver. National Match rifles were used for the initial lot of rifles and no further modifications were necessary. In due course, standard service models

of above average accuracy were utilized. The service models were altered to duplicate most of the special characteristics of the National Match rifle. This involved polishing magazine followers and bolt runways, adjusting trigger pulls, fitting deeply checkered National Match buttplates, and sometimes polishing the entire bolt body.

A comparison of the front sight on the USMC M1903A1 sniper rifle no. 1531443 (top) and the standard M1903 rifle. The USMC No. 10 front sight blade is .100-inch wide; "the sharp upper rear edge and undercut face resulted in a well-defined front sight even in poor light." The No. 10 blade was .075-inch higher than the standard M1903 sight and approximately twice the thickness. The Marine Corps front sight required a special sight cover. (Kogan Collection.)

Of parallel interest, former Master Gunnery Sgt. Harold E. Johnson, USMC, provided a brief description of ordnance activities involving the selection of M1903 sniper rifles:

Newly unpacked rifles were placed in a machine rest and fired for group size. The rifles that met certain requirements were set aside for conversion to sniper rifles. These usually, but not always, had star-gauged barrels. However, not all barrels marked as such shot all that well. Some ordinary barrels were found to shoot just as well, and sometimes better than those that were marked.

The selected rifles had Unertl scope blocks installed on the receiver and on the barrel ahead of the rear sight. The issue sights were retained.

Trigger pulls were adjusted, and all of the latest pattern components were installed. Bolts were carefully fitted and electro-pen engraved with the rifle serial number.

Model 1903A1 C-stocks were used and the handguard was modified by planning the top surface flat. A small rectangular hole was cut in the handguard for the front scope block.

The rifles were then re-tested for accuracy with the Unertl scope in place. If they didn't meet performance standards they were rejected and re-converted into service rifles.

By no means limited to conversion work, efforts to produce suitable sniper equipment would also involve the selection of various components necessary to assemble a complete rifle—a practice much the same as that used to supplement the annual requirements of the Marine Corps rifle teams.

As Kogan continued:

> When it became necessary, Marine armorers reworked and assembled parts received directly from Springfield Armory. Due to the use of bulk parts, there was no correlation of serial numbers and barrel dates.
>
> The armorers stated they had used re-heat-treated low number receivers as well as later NS actions and made no distinction between the two.
>
> Type-C stocks were chosen for density of grain (less likely to warp) and barrels selected that conformed to pre-star star-gauge specifications. Bolts were polished bright, numbered to the receiver and then blued.
>
> A total of five armorers were involved. Two would work with the star-gauge selecting barrels while the others did the machining and final fitting.

As a point of interest, Marine ordnance personnel who were active then insist that when modified or assembled for scout-sniper use, the weapon was referenced as the "Model 1941 Sniper Rifle."

Although variations between Marine Corps M1903A1/Unertl sniper rifles considered authentic have been duly noted, apart from the obvious difficulty of finding a 50-year-old military weapon in original "as issued" condition, there is nothing to indicate whether the rifles in original form were consistent in configuration or a subtle mix of minor variations, as authentic examples suggest.

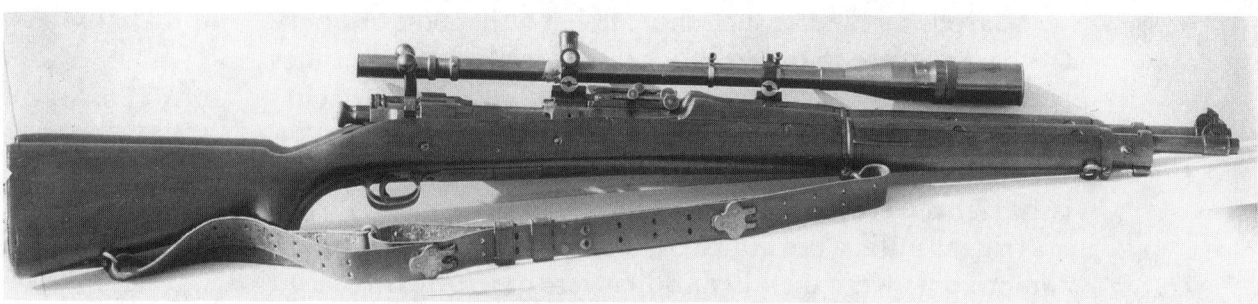

What appears to be a "double exposure" is actually two closely grouped USMC M1903A1 sniper rifles circa 1945. Authentic beyond question, the two rifles and three 8-power Unertl telescopic sights were recovered from a U.S. Navy minesweeper by a crew member when the ship was decommissioned following World War II. A part of a private collection for more than 40 years, the M1903A1 rifles are believed to have been among the late war USMC sniper issue allocated to the Navy in early 1945. The rifles and telescopic sights are in unused condition. (Collection West.)

Whereas prescribed "specifications" for modifying or assembling rifles slated for sniper use did in fact produce some constant characteristics, most of the weapons originating at the

Philadelphia depot did, to some extent, reflect the "signature" of a given armorer (gunsmith, in civilian parlance)—particularly where certain obvious techniques, such as inletting, for example, would indicate the level of workmanship or competence of the armorer doing the work.

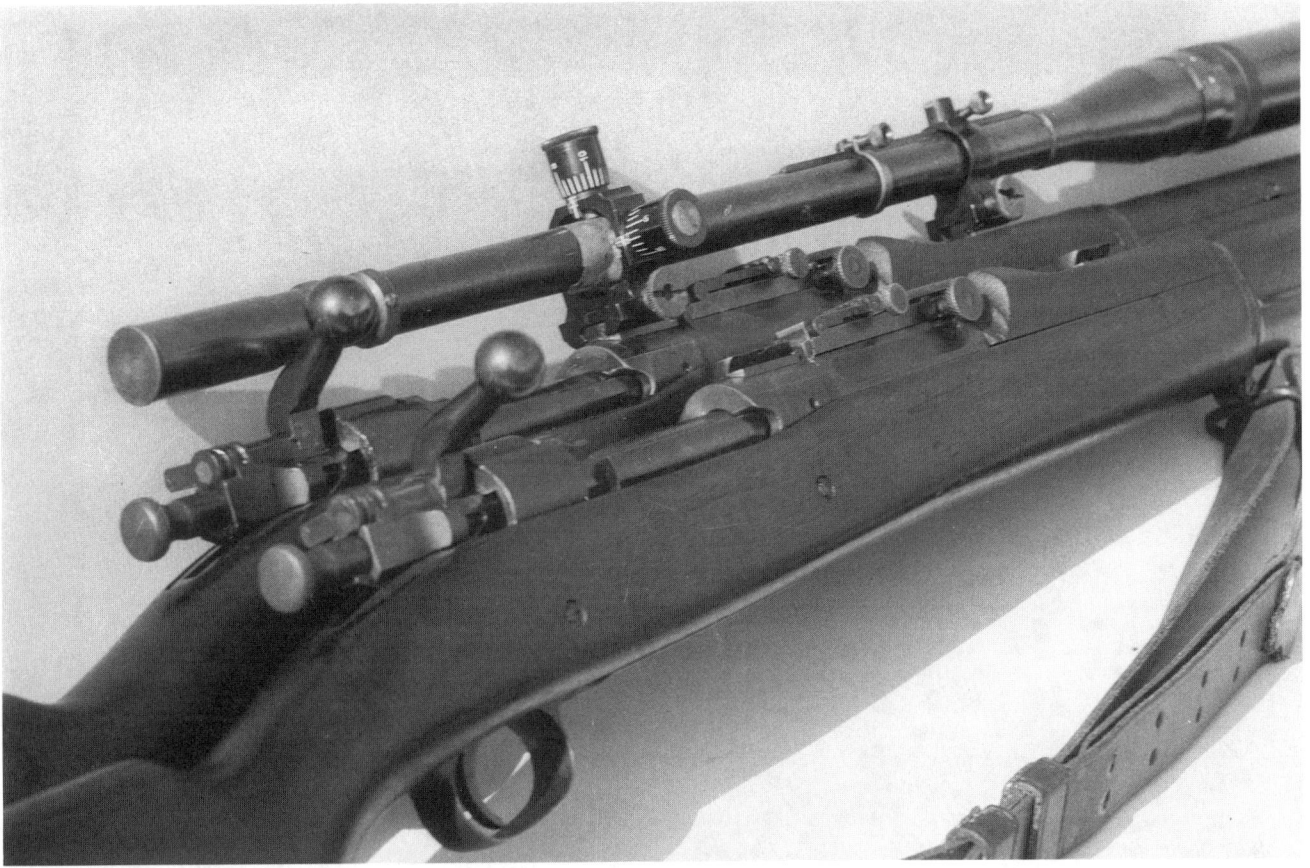

USMC/U.S. Navy M1903A1 sniper rifles, serial no. 1496576, 3-38 barrel date, and serial no. 1526537, 3-39 barrel date. Despite the presence of various National Match grade components, the unique weapons are essentially "late manufacture" Springfield Armory rifles converted to National Match specifications. Though rarely encountered, even in rifles alleged to be authentic, both rifle stocks have been inletted carefully to provide a "six o'clock bed." A part of the USMC rifle team equipment (RTE), match rifle specifications for the Springfield Rifle at the time, the barrel touches the stock only at the forepart at the six o' clock position. The correct relationship between wood and metal (bedding) was essential in a match grade rifle. Marine Corps rifle team and sniper rifles were "bedded in accordance with the Springfield Armory bedding system." (Collection West.)

The USMC sniper rifles were not officially marked in a manner consistent with their configuration or point of origin, and while it was "just a job" to some, Marine armorers were known to apply their personal trademarks to the weapons they worked on—a matter of individual pride in some cases. In addition to the practice of "chalking" or pencil-marking initials and rifle serial numbers inside the handguard, armorers also stamped their initials at inconspicuous places in the stock.

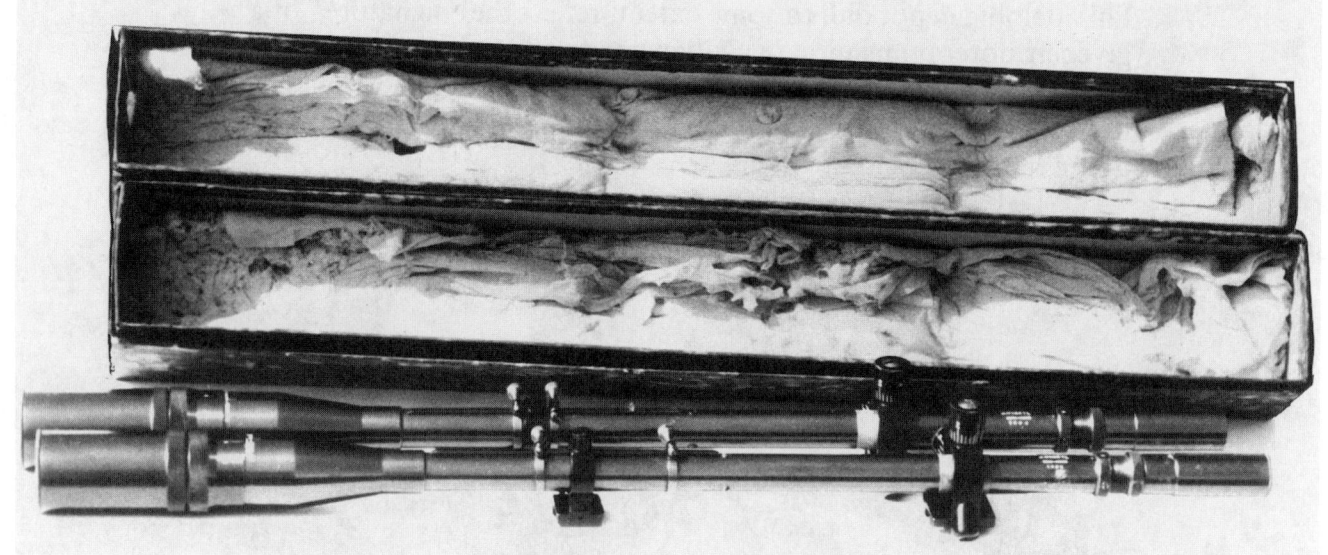

A prime example of the Unertl USMC contract sights, as shipped to the Marine Corps during World War II. Two consecutively numbered Unertl scopes (no. 1670 and no. 1671) are shown with their original shipping cartons. The third scope, also in new condition, is closely numbered to those illustrated. The naval equivalent of "ordnance disposal," the M1903A1 sniper rifles were to be used for clearing errant sea mines. Both conventional and telescopic sighted rifles have been used for minesweeping operations for many years. (Collection West.)

Close-up, USMC/U.S. sniper rifle with the bolt drawn back. In both cases, the bolts were polished, engraved with the rifle serial number by electric pencil, and blued afterward. Heavy paper wrapping was placed around the telescopic sight at the rear mount to protect both the tube and the bearing points of the elevation and windage adjustment "screws" during transit. This was done before the telescopes were shipped—a common practice. Most, if not all, of the target scope manufacturers protected their sights in the same manner. (Collection West.)

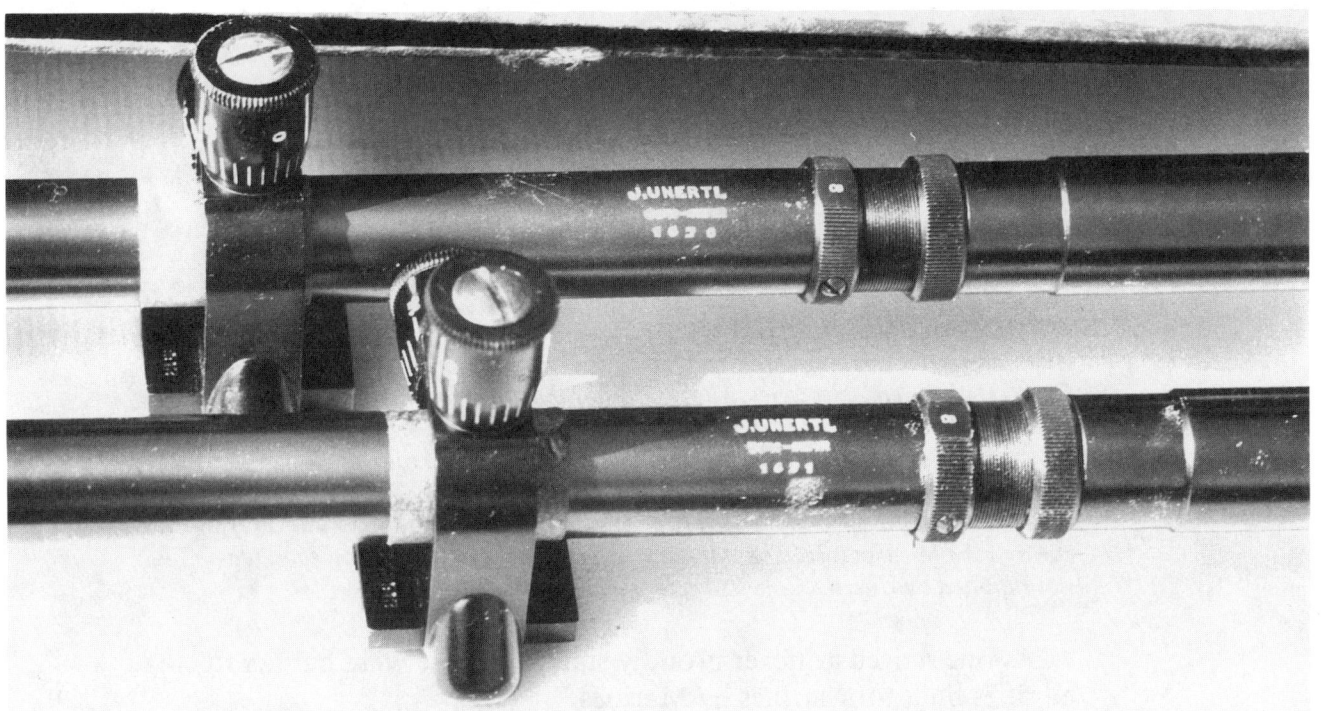

A close-up view of the 8-power Unertl USMC contract sights (1670-1671) provides a good look at the typical manufacturer's legend and the left side of the rear mount. The number "8" stamped on top of the eyepiece locking ring (right) indicates the power, or magnification, of the sight. Although 10-power (marked Unertl [USMC]) contract sights have been noted, the Unertl firm believes these were "altered after World War II" when their "interchangeable eyepieces" became readily available. According to Unertl, the USMC sniper scopes were only furnished in 8 power (7.8X). (Collection West.)

One of the USMC/U.S. NAVY 8-power Unertl telescopic sights with its original shipping container. The 3 1/8-inch square, 24 1/4-inch long cardboard boxes have no markings whatsoever. The box cover has a dark grey mottled-pattern paper glued to the cardboard. When recovered from the Navy minesweeper, "the telescopic sights were still packed in their containers." (Collection West.)

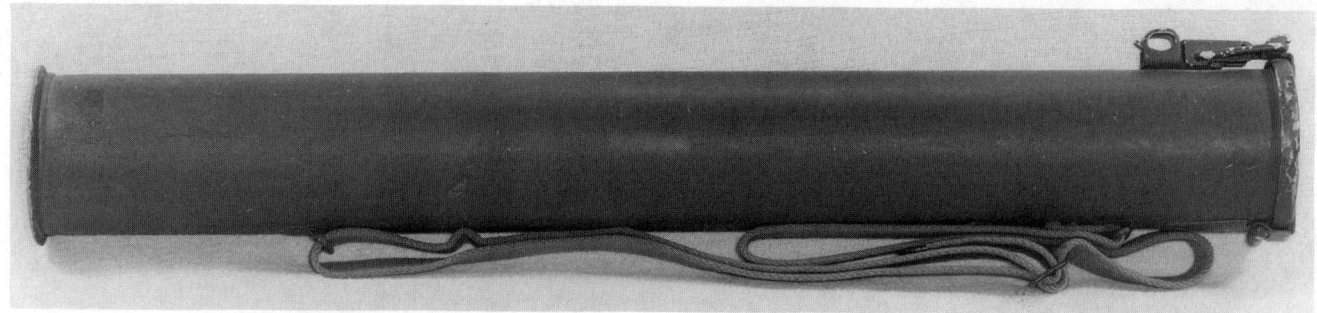

A tubular metal carrying can furnished by the Marine Corps in limited numbers for use with Unertl telescopes. The bottom of the tube was fitted with a wood disc having a recess in its center for the objective end of the sight, while the rear mount was held by a formed sheet-metal rail located inside the tube toward the opening. The shoulder strap provided an efficient means of carrying the accessory item. According to the Unertl firm, it supplied the early aluminum carrying can and the Micarta case. The tubular metal version illustrated, however, was not supplied by Unertl. (Cors Collection.)

As one retired armorer proudly stated, "These were handcrafted rifles built for Marines by Marines."

A facility acknowledged to have had the greatest concentration of USMC small-arms talent in the United States, the Ordnance Section of the Philadelphia Depot of Supplies was unquestionably the best place to produce the Marine Corps sniper rifle.

CHAPTER 5

The Riflescope in Combat: Problems in the Field

However suited for combat the M1903A1/Unertl system may have been, as events transpired, the newly adopted Marine Corps sniper rifle would fall from official favor.

Despite only limited combat exposure following its introduction, by late 1943 the value of the M1903A1/Unertl system had been placed in doubt as a direct result of unsatisfactory field reports.

It was a subject of some controversy at the time, according to an unpublished essay by Capt. Mark K. Edmondson, USMC (Ret.), an authority on World War II Marine Corps sniping efforts:

Although initial reports based on the Guadalcanal experience had helped to provide impetus to the beginning of a true sniper training and equipment program in 1942, favorable impressions were later lost at HQMC back in Washington, where other reports were received from the Raider Battalion which participated in operations with Army units on New Georgia Island in mid-1943. This unit filed a very unfavorable report on the effectiveness and value in combat of scope-fitted '03s, apparently based on experience with the Lyman 5A fitted '03 since there is no evidence that Unertl-equipped '03A1s were yet in the field. Apparently, the Raiders were impressed with the Army's newly-fielded '03A4 with Weaver 330/M73B1 scope combination. Select units comprised of specially trained combat personnel, the Raiders' opinion carried a lot of weight in wartime Washington in the early part of the war.

Apparently, in mid-1943 scope-fitted sniper rifles were in short supply in Marine line units in combat and those that were available—such as the Lyman 5A-equipped '03s that the Raiders would have had in New Georgia—were unsatisfactory. Unfortunately, the initial field evaluation of the Unertl, based on the 2nd Division on Tarawa later that year, was also negative. Meanwhile, the Army had a program fielding large quantities of new M1903A4s and scopes, which seemed to some influential Marines in the field better than the Lyman or Unertl.

In the long run, of course, the '03A1/Unertl turned out to be the superior sniper weapon, but in those hectic days of the

IN REPLYING ADDRESS
THE QUARTERMASTER
AND REFER TO NO.

HEADQUARTERS U. S. MARINE CORPS
WASHINGTON   10 February 1944.

MEMORANDUM FOR LT. COL. W. A. KENGLA, DIVISION OF PLANS AND POLICIES:

Subject: Sniper Rifles.

    1.   Present stock of scopes, Unertl, 8X, in Philadelphia is 355.

    2.   Undelivered portion of contract with Unertl is 1300.

    3.   Data on Sniper equipment standard with U. S. Army is as follows:

    1. Army Ordnance has procured to date 20,000 Rifles, U. S., Caliber .30, M1903A4 (Snipers) which are equipped with Sight, Telescopic, Assembly (Weaver 330C). Also believe an additional quantity of rifles are on order (probably about 10,000). This rifle is basically the M1903 Springfield action. However, it has a pistol grip stock and the receiver has been changed somewhat to properly accommodate mounting of scope. No other rear sights are provided other than the scope.
    2. Army experience to date indicates that any repairs or adjustment of scope must be done at a depot or arsenal (5th Echelon) and rifles in hands of organizations are returned to such establishments and new rifles issued as replacement.
    3. No other scopes have even been procured or stocked by Army Ordnance which could be obtained by the Marine Corps for mounting on M1903 Springfield rifles on hand.
    4. Unofficial information from Army Ordnance this date indicates approximately 2,000 M1903A4 rifles on hand, not obligated, and it is believed up to 1,000 of these could be obtained by the Marine Corps through proper channels.

    4.   In view of these facts, it is recommended that the unfilled portion of contract for telescopes with Unertl, 8X, be cancelled.

R. B. Warye,
Major, U.S.M.C.

As a result of unfavorable combat reports concerning the Unertl telescopic sight, at one point, the Marine Corps had begun moving toward formal adoption of the M1903A4 sniper rifle as a replacement for the M1903A1/Unertl system (10 February 1944). (U.S. Marine Corps.)

war, when performance counted for everything, HQMC was responding to the negative reports.

In USMC correspondence of February 1944, the Commandant of the Marine Corps (CMC) had ordered the acquisition of Unertl scopes terminated at the earliest possible time since "The Unertl 8X Sniper Telescope has not proved effective in combat." When depot stocks were exhausted [355 at the time] the Quartermaster was "to take steps to substitute the rifle U.S. Cal. .30, M1903A4 (Snipers) equipped with Sight, Telescopic Assy (Weaver 330C)." The '03A1s and Unertl scopes in inventory were recommended for disposal as excess property. The contract with Unertl was to be terminated and, apparently, no more rifles assembled from available stores of USMC rifle team equipment. Evidence indicates that from this point no more '03A1/Unertl sniper rifles were assembled and/or shipped from Philadelphia until very late in the war, if at all.

An example of the dense jungle conditions encountered during the island campaign against the Japanese. As stated best perhaps: "Seeing, much less identifying, moving shapes only a few feet away was often impossible." The limitations of sniping equipment in a jungle environment are readily apparent (Cape Gloucester, 1943). (Mark K. Edmondson, U.S. Marine Corps.)

There was no comparing the shooting capability of an Army M1903A4 in issue condition with that of a handcrafted M1903A1 match grade rifle; yet, though never adequately explained, the M1903A4/Weaver combination was employed by Marine marksmen in the South Pacific beginning in mid-1943.

Though deemed "unsatisfactory in service," it is believed the Unertl sight was found to be unsuitable due to its unwieldy nature rather than for any inherent problem with the scope itself. In view of the difficulty associated with conducting combat operations in dense tropical vegetation, there was no denying that the diminutive Weaver scope was better suited for jungle warfare—if for no other reason than size.

Nevertheless, apart from personal preferences and any possible size factor, both telescopic sights were plagued with moisture problems as well as reticle damage. Although problems with the reticles (cross-hair damage) were duly attributed to the rigors of combat, and in some cases to careless handling, insofar as optical manufacturers had not perfected the art of optimum lense sealing, the temperature, humidity, and rainfall extremes found in the South Pacific combined to create severe "moisture-retention problems" with telescopic sights and binoculars as well.

In what amounted to more than a simple matter of physical size, optical characteristics, and internal adjustments versus external adjustments, both the Unertl and Weaver telescopic sights were clearly out of their elements, even though both were entirely capable of producing satisfactory results within the limits of their designs and original intended use for match shooting and hunting purposes.

As a result of initial U.S. combat involvement in the Pacific (Solomon Island campaign) early in World War II, the Infantry Board and the Ordnance Department, in efforts to meet urgent requirements for telescopic sighted rifles, conducted tests and evaluations for the purpose of adapting a commercial telescope to the Springfield rifle.

In late 1942, Headquarters, Army Ground Forces, recommended that the readily available Weaver 2.5-power 330C hunting telescopes be adopted for use with M1903 or M1903A1 rifles. The rifles were to be especially selected for accuracy and smoothness of operation; type "C" stocks were to be used and the bolt handles remodeled to eliminate interference with the sights.

According to Ordnance records:

> The rifle adopted in December 1942 met established requisites through the use of a modified Redfield "Junior" type of mount fastened to the receiver of the M1903A1 Rifle, less iron sights, utilizing the 2 1/2X Weaver Telescope.

While acceptance of the new sniping arm had been predicated on tests conducted with the Model 1903A1 Springfield Rifle, in lieu of its status at that point, the War Department directed Remington Arms of Ilion, New York, to divert 20,000 of the new, simplified M1903A3 variants from regular production for conversion to sniping weapons.

As a result, Remington commenced manufacture of a sniping variant officially designated as the U.S. Rifle, Caliber .30, M1903A4 (Sniper's) in February 1943. Although the 03A3 and the A4 were essentially the same, the primary difference rested with the A4 having a concavely forged bolt handle with a considerable amount of metal machined from the outside to allow for a low telescope mounting. As such, the Weaver 330 or the Lyman Alaskan, with its larger tube diameter, could be fitted to this rifle.

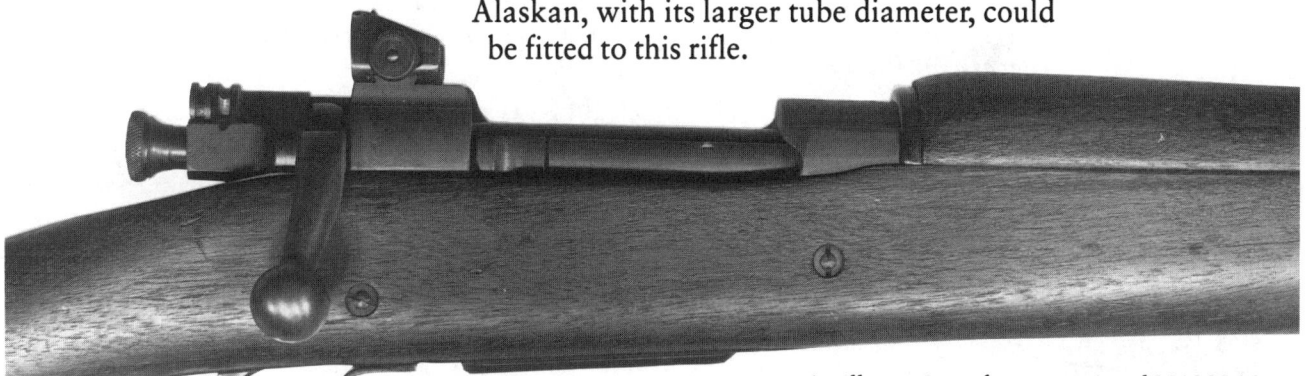

An illustration of a conventional M1903A3 rifle (serial no. 4114560, 8-43 barrel date) provides a comparison between a standard and sniper version of the World War II-era Remington rifles. In addition to the conversion of A3 rifles for sniping purposes in Korea, though viewed with some reservation, reports of "unofficial" USMC field expedient M1903A3 rifles fitted with "salvaged target scopes" during the later stages of the Pacific campaigns have surfaced as well. (West Point Collection.)

Contrary to the intent of the memorandum dated 16 February 1944, though employed by Marine marksmen in the Pacific, the "Army Sniper Rifle" was neither formally adopted nor procured directly from the Remington Arms Co. The M1903A4 rifles used by the Marine Corps were obtained through regular supply channels directly from the Army. Securing rifles, submachine guns, machine guns, and other materiel by direct transfer from the Army was common practice during World War II. The M1903A4 did not replace the M1903A1 Unertl system. (U.S. Marine Corps.)

```
2000-40-50
AO-644-lms
                                    16 February 1944.

From:       Commandant of the Marine Corps.
To:         The Quartermaster.

Subject:    Sniper rifles and telescopes.

    1.      The Unertle, 8X, sniper telescope has not proved
effective in combat. Accordingly you are requested to cancel
existing contracts for this item. Upon exhaustion of depot
stocks of Unertl telescopes, please take steps to substitute
the rifle U. S. cal. .30, M1903A4 (Snipers) equipped with
Sight, Telescopic Assembly (Weaver 330C).




                                    D. Peck
                                    Acting
```

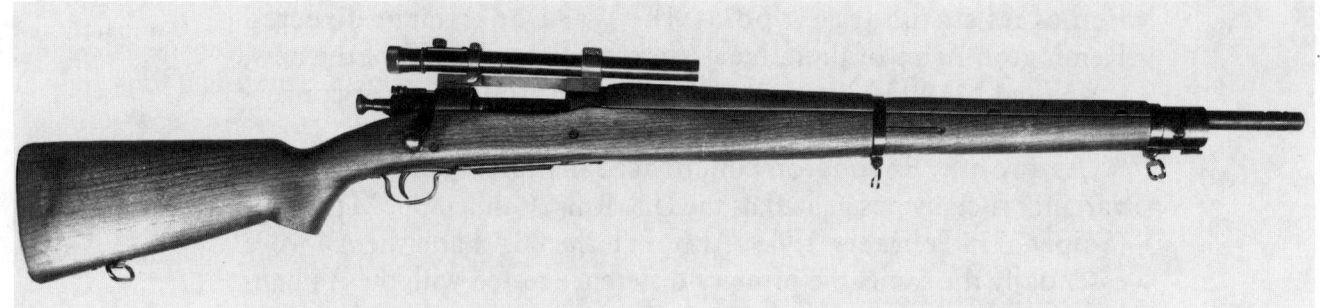

U.S. Rifle, Caliber .30, M1903A4 (Sniper's) with Telescope M73B1 (Weaver 330C) and Type-C pistol grip stock. Featuring one of the very first production rifles, the photograph was made at the Remington plant in early 1943. The early A4 rifles were issued with the "C" stock; the scant grip variation emerged later as a production expedient. (Donald Urtz.)

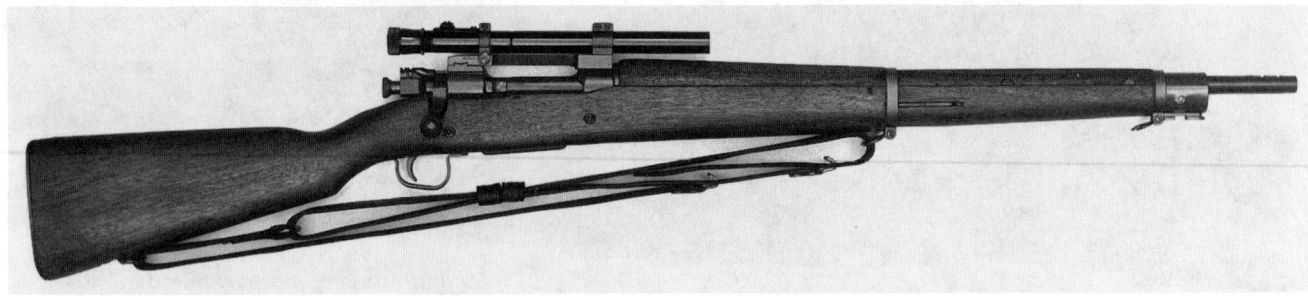

U.S. Rifle, Caliber .30, M1903A4 (Sniper's) with telescope M73B1 and "scant-grip" stock fitted with the enlarged trigger guard introduced in mid-1943 to provide clearance for a gloved trigger finger. Both types of trigger guard were apparently used through the course of production, however. (Peter R. Senich.)

Initially, pistol-grip Type-C stocks were furnished with the M1903A4 sniper rifles. A production expedient referenced as the "scant-grip" stock was later issued with the A4.

The receiver mount secured the scope over the bore by means of a recess which engaged a corresponding lug located below the front ring. The lug was inserted into the mount, eyepiece to the right, and rotated 90 degrees clockwise to bring it into battery. Two slotted screws threaded into the mount clamped the rear scope ring from both sides. After basic lateral zero had been established by adjusting the left screw, the right screw was tightened, locking the telescope in place.

While comparatively simple, once in the field, the "windage-screws" were easily broken and virtually impossible to obtain through supply channels. Basic vertical zero was established by placing shims between the base and the receiver. This was necessary even though the base was made for this rifle.

In an effort to facilitate rapid production, the Ordnance Department deemed it inadvisable to redesign the receiver bridge or introduce additional machining operations necessary for mounting conventional sights. As it was then stated, "Since the telescope sight is a self-contained unit, there is no necessity for a normal rear or front sight." Critics were quick to point out that, should the scope be knocked out of adjustment or damaged, the rifle would be virtually useless. Nevertheless, "iron" sights were not furnished with M1903A4 rifles.

Additional objections stemmed from the proximity of the mount to the receiver, which prevented loading with a standard five-round clip. Instead, the A4 had to be operated as a single-loader, with one cartridge being placed into the chamber, or with cartridges loaded into the magazine one by one. Prior to final shipment, all rifles were individually targeted by Remington personnel, at a range of 100 yards with a minimum of five shots, using both muzzle and elbow rest.

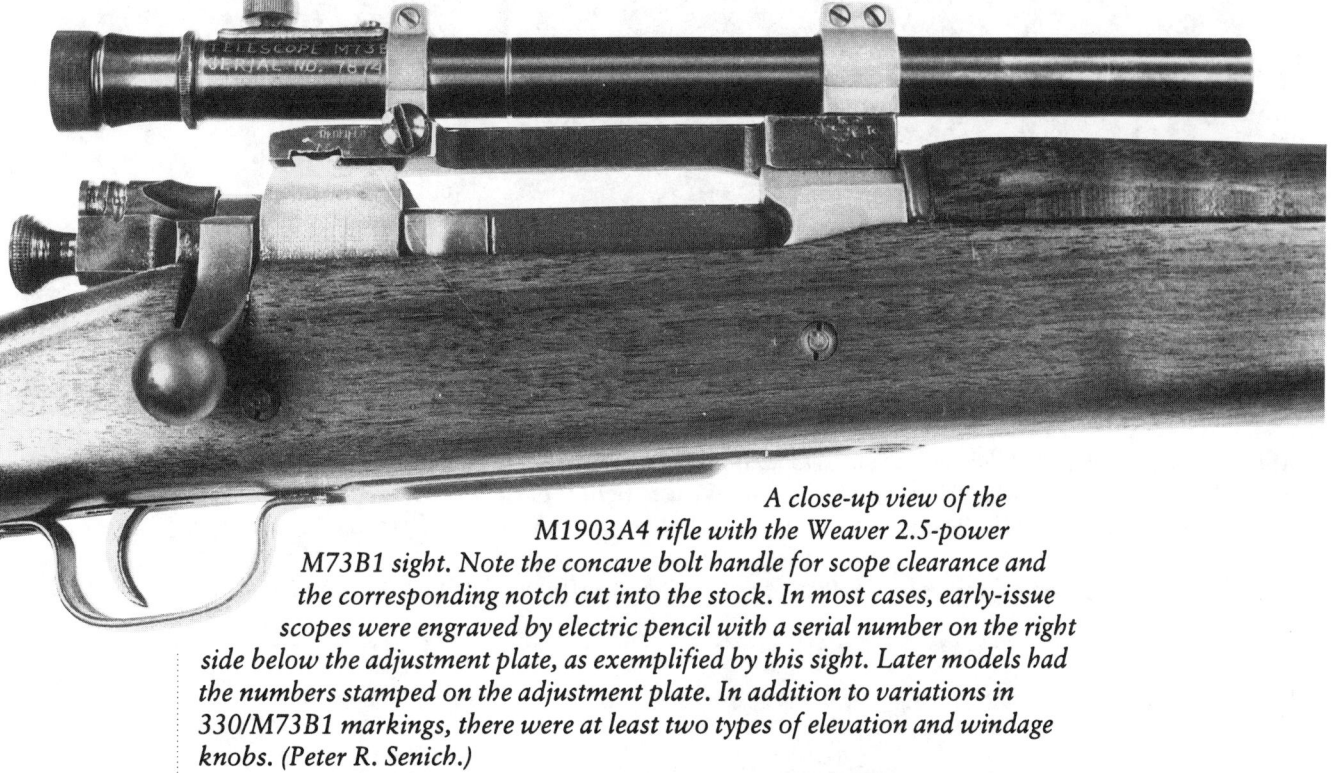

A close-up view of the M1903A4 rifle with the Weaver 2.5-power M73B1 sight. Note the concave bolt handle for scope clearance and the corresponding notch cut into the stock. In most cases, early-issue scopes were engraved by electric pencil with a serial number on the right side below the adjustment plate, as exemplified by this sight. Later models had the numbers stamped on the adjustment plate. In addition to variations in 330/M73B1 markings, there were at least two types of elevation and windage knobs. (Peter R. Senich.)

The first rifle/scope combinations finding their way to the combat zones utilized regular commercial Weaver sights; that is, sights originally manufactured for the civilian market. Alluding to this fact, W.R. Weaver, president of the Weaver firm, stated shortly after the war:

> When the need arose for a sturdy, dependable sniper's scope, we were ready to go into instant production. It was not necessary to design a new scope nor to retool our plant to make scopes from a Government design. Our regular Weaver Scope Model 330 was just what the Army wanted. We merely stepped up production and diverted our shipments from sporting goods dealers to the Army.

Marine combat personnel during close-quarter action at Cape Gloucester, December 1943. The rifleman in the foreground is armed with an M1903A4 sniper rifle; the Weaver sight is partially obscured. Note the bayonets "fixed" in anticipation of contact with the Japanese. (Mark K. Edmondson, U.S. Marine Corps.)

A Marine Corps rifleman displays his M1903A4 rifle at Pavuvu (Russell Islands), 13 May 1944. According to the original caption, "A Cape Gloucester veteran is shown with the sniper rifle he had used during the New Britain campaign." From all indications, the M1903A4 was available for USMC combat use by mid-1943. (U.S. Marine Corps.)

The front cover of War Department Technical Manual TM 9-270, 28 September 1943. The World War II ordnance pamphlet detailed the operation and maintenance of the M1903A4 and Weaver 330C telescopic sight. (Peter R. Senich.)

Although the Weaver sight was officially designated M73B1, the initial pamphlet covering the characteristics and operation of the M1903A4 (Sniper's) rifle (War Department Technical Manual TM9-270, dated 28 September 1943) referenced this scope only as the "Weaver Telescopic Sight No. 330-C."

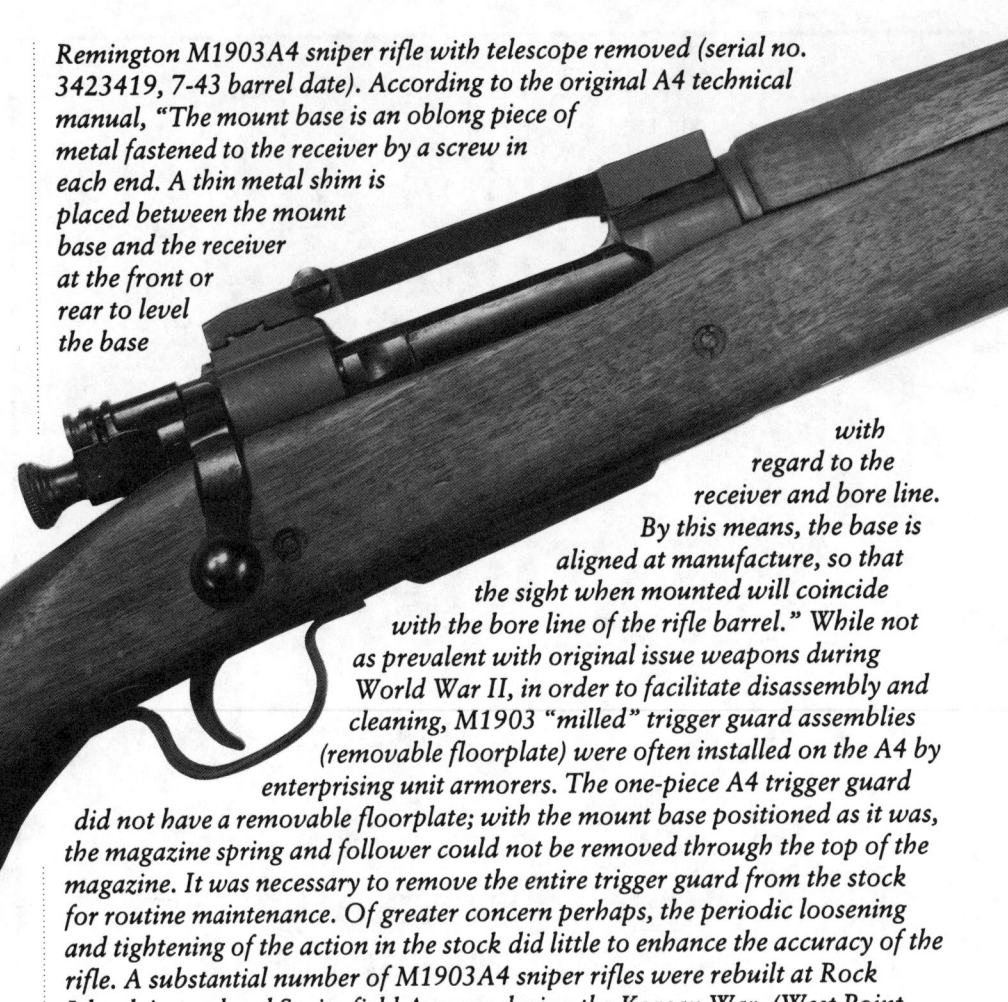

Remington M1903A4 sniper rifle with telescope removed (serial no. 3423419, 7-43 barrel date). According to the original A4 technical manual, "The mount base is an oblong piece of metal fastened to the receiver by a screw in each end. A thin metal shim is placed between the mount base and the receiver at the front or rear to level the base with regard to the receiver and bore line. By this means, the base is aligned at manufacture, so that the sight when mounted will coincide with the bore line of the rifle barrel." While not as prevalent with original issue weapons during World War II, in order to facilitate disassembly and cleaning, M1903 "milled" trigger guard assemblies (removable floorplate) were often installed on the A4 by enterprising unit armorers. The one-piece A4 trigger guard did not have a removable floorplate; with the mount base positioned as it was, the magazine spring and follower could not be removed through the top of the magazine. It was necessary to remove the entire trigger guard from the stock for routine maintenance. Of greater concern perhaps, the periodic loosening and tightening of the action in the stock did little to enhance the accuracy of the rifle. A substantial number of M1903A4 sniper rifles were rebuilt at Rock Island Arsenal and Springfield Armory during the Korean War. (West Point Collection.)

The commercial Lyman "Alaskan" telescope was also authorized for use with the M1903A4 rifle and was to phase out the Weaver on a "one-to-one" replacement basis beginning late in 1943. However, this sight could not be furnished in quantity since the Lyman firm was operating at capacity on small-parts contracts for the government. In addition, Bausch & Lomb, supplier of matched lenses for the Alaskan, was involved in war production, which prevented manufacture of the optics used in this sight. While approximately 2,000 receiver mounts (rings, etc.) were procured from Redfield to accommodate the Alaskan, according to Remington records, delivery of the Lyman sight never materialized and, excepting the few scopes used for evaluative purposes, only the Weaver sight was furnished with the A4 during World War II.

The 330 scope in original form was introduced to the American market in the early 1930s by W.R. Weaver and quickly earned recognition as a durable, low-priced hunting telescope—the result being its placement high on the list of commercial scopes considered for military application when the war began.

The 9 1/2-ounce, 10 1/2-inch sight possessed a double-cemented, compound achromatic lense system, a field of view at 100 yards of 35 feet, and universal focus from about 25 feet to infinity.

Changes in elevation and windage were affected internally by means of 1/4-minute click adjustment dials located at the top and side of the drawn steel tube.

Although Ordnance had considered the Weaver Model 330S (Silent) variant having adjustment dials (elevation and windage) equipped with lock nuts, it adopted the Model 330C scope with click adjustments instead (the "C" referencing "click" adjustment). Eventual modifications included the addition of Ordnance-designed adjustment dials having a graduated scale. Telescopes supplied to the military were furnished in commercial blue-black, and lens covers consisting of two leather caps joined by a strap were issued with each rifle. From all indications, the lens caps were the only protective measure for the Weaver sights. According to Frankford Arsenal records, the M65 web telescope carrying case, though variously referenced as "issued with" the A4, was to be furnished "when the Telescope M82 was mounted on the U.S. Rifles M1903A4 and M1C."

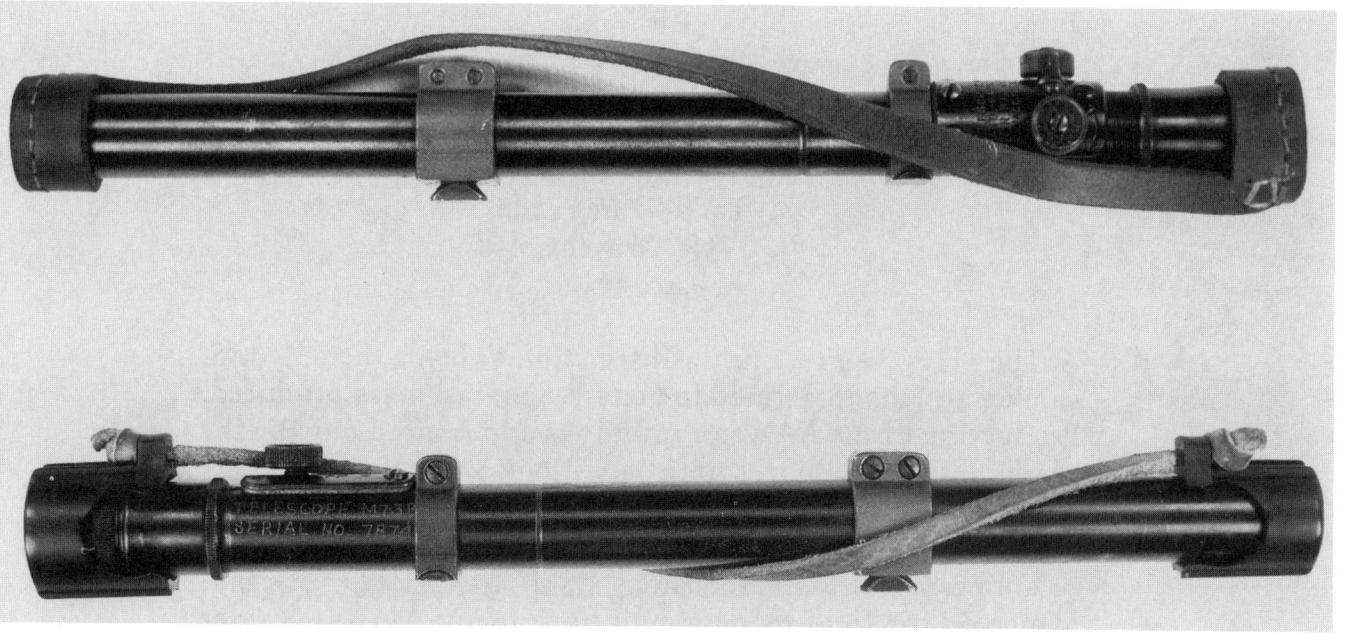

Weaver M73B1 telescopic sight with original issue leather dust caps (top) and the plastic cap assembly introduced following World War II. A unique design, the plastic caps snapped onto the scope tube when not protecting the lenses. Although dust caps and even telescope carrying cases served to protect the telescopes in the field, they were usually lost or simply discarded. Referenced as the "rotary dovetail system" in prewar sales literature, the front scope ring simply rotated into the receiver base from a 90-degree angle. The Redfield "Junior" mounting positioned the scope altogether too far to the rear, to the extent that many A-4 riflemen recall "bouncing" the Weaver eyepiece off of their helmet or eyebrow every now and then. Although tapered-post or cross-hair reticle patterns appear to have been the most common, variant reticle patterns have been noted as well. (Peter R. Senich.)

Attempts to rectify early cross-hair difficulties resulted in the adoption of a tapered-post reticle. Nevertheless, the vast majority of sights furnished for the A4 utilized the standard .001-inch cross hairs. In prewar commercial form, the Weaver had offered the shooter an option of either the tapered-post or cross-hair reticle. However, the military decided in favor of the latter when it adopted the Weaver. The first sights to see combat with the M1903A4 rifle were fitted with cross-hair reticle patterns.

Despite a functional eye-relief of 3 to 5 inches, additional field complaints centered on the sight recoiling against the sniper's helmet, thereby damaging the telescope and/or lens. As a result, moving the sight forward on the receiver and developing a rubber guard to protect the tube were under consideration when the M1903A4 was reclassified to "Limited Standard" (out of production, with use temporary until replacement) in June 1944. At this juncture, further development of the M73B1 telescope became low priority.

Although variations in markings have been noted, including sights bearing an "M8" designation, the following legends are representative of those appearing on the adjustment plate:

> Model 330
> Pat. Pend.
> W.R. Weaver Co.
> El Paso, Tex. USA
>
> Telescope M73B1
> Pat'd—Pats.Pend.
> W.R. Weaver Co.
> El Paso, Tex. USA

The M1903A4 retains the distinction of being the only U.S. sniping arm manufactured in quantity, that is, mass-produced. Production of the A4 was continuous and limited only by the availability of telescopes until June 1944, when the last orders were canceled in favor of Army procurement of its successor, the U.S. Rifle, Caliber .30, M1C (Garand).

Curiously, whereas Headquarters, USMC had placed great significance on the field recommendations of the Marine Raider Battalions, in regard to the question of why the M1903A4/Weaver system was preferred over the Marine Corps M1903A1/Unertl combination in the first place, the abbreviated USMC "Chronological History of the Sniper Rifle" offered the following rationale:

> As so often happens, it appears that the experiences of one unit in one operation: that is, Raider Battalion at New Georgia, have been sufficient to effectively damn a piece of equipment.
> The Unertl 8X scope was evidently procured early in the war because it appeared, at that time, to answer the requirements.
> Because the Unertl scope was not satisfactory does not mean that all scope-fitted rifles are useless for Marine Corps operations. The 1st Division at Cape Gloucester was unable

to effectively use scope-fitted rifles because of climate and terrain. The 2nd Division at Saipan used scope-fitted rifles very effectively.

And as Captain Edmondson summarized it:

> Success with the '03A1/Unertl on Saipan and Peleliu during 1944 helped change official opinion. The more open terrain had favored employment of snipers with a long-range capability and the feedback to HQMC by early 1945 was considerably better than it had been. Another factor was the Army's successful development of a telescope mounting system for the M1, the M1C, which gave snipers a semiautomatic capability. This eliminated the tell-tale movement required for operating the bolt on the '03 to chamber a second round should another shot be necessary. The USMC was testing the M1C against the 03A4 as the war ended. Meanwhile, snipers using the '03A1/Unertl, and even regular '03s mounting Unertls, were being employed with great success on Okinawa. These developments apparently led to the official reinstatement of snipers and their equipment in Marine Corps organizations late in the war.
>
> Finally, on 10 August 1945, 108 scoped sniper rifles per division were allocated by the CMC primarily to make space for the M1C which by that time had been recommended for adoption by the Marine Corps Equipment Board in early 1945. Nevertheless, there is no evidence that such allocations were made from the Philadelphia depot before the war

Taken immediately after a Marine sniper had fired his rifle, this photograph shows the Unertl scope in the forward, or recoil, position (Saipan, July 1944). The olive drab fabric bandolier held .30-caliber ammunition in cartridge clips—a convenient means of carrying rifle ammunition. Cartridges were simply stripped from clips as needed. (U.S. Marine Corps.)

ended a few days later. The end of hostilities undoubtedly caused the cancellation of any shipments.

So far as the overall efforts to provide Marine combat personnel with the best equipment available were concerned, selecting an effective sniping rifle and telescopic sight played a relatively small role. While the system may not have always worked as intended, these were extremely difficult times and, in total fairness to the Marine Corps, the efforts were both genuine and sincere.

A Marine sniper team armed with the ever-effective M1903A1/Unertl combination in action on Okinawa in May 1945. Note the rifle (left) with a Type-S straight stock (grasping grooves). Sniper use on Okinawa is considered to have been the high point of the USMC sniping program during the war in the Pacific. (U.S. Marine Corps.)

While it seems that training and equipping the scout-snipers may have been viewed as controversial, when compared to the almost insurmountable problems of organizing, training, and equipping entire combat divisions, as was then taking place, the efforts associated with fielding snipers was undoubtedly more of a nuisance than a controversy.

As for the Army sniper rifle and the Marine Corps, however, the M1903A4/Weaver system, while not adopted formally, would serve the Marine Corps as supplemental sniping equipment during World War II and again in Korea.

IN REPLYING ADDRESS
THE QUARTERMASTER
AND REFER TO No.
215-12-62

HEADQUARTERS U. S. MARINE CORPS
WASHINGTON   20 April 1945

From: The Quartermaster General of the Marine Corps.
To: Commandant of the Marine Corps.

Subject: Rifle, U.S., Cal..30, M1903A1, Snipers Equipment, with Telescopes, Sighting, Unertl, 8X, disposition of as excess property.

References: (a) CMC ltr 2000-40-50/AO-644-lms to QMG of 16Feb44.
            (b) Telcon Lt. E. A. May, Jr. (Navy BuOrd-Mn5e) and Lt. Purrington (MarCorps) of 14Apr45.

    1.   Reference (a) directed the cancellation of existing contracts for the Telescope, Sighting, Unertl, 8X as same had not proven effective in combat. However, materiel already delivered, and that on which production had reached a point where cancellation would have been impractical, netted a total delivery as follows:

```
1750 - Telescopes, Sighting, Unertl,  @68.00   $119,000.00
       8X complete with Mounting
       blocks and screws
2565 - Cases, carrying                @14.60     37,449.00
 750 - Blocks, mounting, with         @ 1.50      1,125.00
       screws (sets)
                              Total             $157,574.00
```

    2.   In view of reference (a) and the fact that current tables of allowances do not include any reference to a sniper rifle, it is recommended that authority be given this office to dispose of as excess property without reimbursement all sniper rifles, scopes, carrying cases, and sets of mounting blocks remaining on hand.

    3.   At present approximately the following quantities remain on hand in depot stocks:

```
 975 - Telescopes, Sighting, Unertl, 8X
       complete w/mounting blocks and screws
1790 - Cases, carrying
 750 - Blocks, mounting, w/screws (sets)
```

Late war correspondence from the Quartermaster General, USMC, concerning the "disposition" of Unertl scopes and related hardware (20 April 1945). Although some Unertl sights were disposed of as surplus following the war, an unspecified number remained in Marine Corps service as late as United States involvement in Southeast Asia some twenty years later. Unertl contract sights procured during World War II were used with Model 70 Winchester rifles against Communist forces in Vietnam. Of further interest, in response to the

4.   There are also approximately 800 Rifles, U.S., Cal..30, M1903A1 in depot stocks which either have mounting blocks assembled thereto or have been set aside for use as sniper rifles. In order to dispose of the above telescopes it will undoubtedly be necessary to provide the rifle fitted with the mounting blocks and authority to do so is also requested.

5.   At the present time informal information received by telephone from Lt.Col. R. C. McGlashan (MarCorps) and Lt. E. A. May, Jr. (Navy BuOrd-Mn5e) indicates an initial requirement for the Navy of 400 Rifles fitted with telescopes for use in minesweeping operations.

6.   Shipping instructions for the first 100 such rifles have been received in accordance with reference (b). No shipment will be made, however, pending receipt of authority or other instructions from your office regarding disposition of this materiel.

L. E. Rea,
By direction.

AUG 18 1945

FILE

Navy request for "400 rifles fitted with telescopes for use in mine-sweeping operations," though barely visible, a handwritten notation (page 2) reads: "give Navy 100 until further notice." (U.S. Marine Corps.)

The Bolt-Action Sniper Rifle: The End of an Era

CHAPTER 6

The period between World War II and Korea saw little advancement in Marine Corps sniper equipment and training. Despite having proved their worth during the later stages of the war, few scout-snipers were fielded after 1945.

With the war in the Pacific all but over, the Army M1C had been tested and deemed suitable for Marine Corps use. In connection with tacit acceptance of the semiautomatic sniping rifle, the M1903A1/Unertl system was authorized for issue on the basis of 108 rifles per Marine division. Though few in actual number at that point, the '03 Springfield would serve as the interim USMC sniping rifle following World War II.

As a result, when the North Korean army attacked South Korea in June 1950, the M1903A1/Unertl system was the only Marine Corps sniper equipment readily available for combat use. At this juncture, however, the M1 sniping rifle (M1C) was not available in any quantity. Therefore, according to individuals then active, in addition to the few remaining original World War II M1903A1 sniper rifles held in stores at various locations, "complete rifles" were assembled at the Philadelphia Depot of Supplies for the express purpose of scout-sniper use in Korea.

From all indications, however, many of the Korean War "Springfield sniper rifles" were reworked or assembled at other Marine Corps facilities as well.

An integral part of the Ordnance Division at the USMC Depot of Supplies, the Rifle Team Equipment (RTE) subsection of the small-arms repair section located in the Depot "annex" (Schuylkill Avenue Annex) still carried out special work such as assembling or converting rifles for sniper use.

As then stated:

> This section continually maintains equipment for Marine Corps rifle and pistol teams, match conditions rifles, pistols, and "bull-guns" (used by the Marine Corps for Olympic Match Firing), and performs modifications on weapons as directed by the Target Practice Section of Headquarters Marine Corps.

Though limited in scope as compared to similar activities during World War II, production of the M1903A1/Unertl system was,

An early Korean War combat photograph (September 1950) showing Marine Corps Lt. Fred Tees firing an M1903A1 sniper rifle at Communist troops at the Seoul Railroad Bridge (Han River, Korea). Note the sidearm, field glasses, and spent cartridge cases. Tees was a Marine air officer tasked with maintaining a link with USMC ground forces during the operations at Inchon and Seoul. His rifle was "retrieved" from an enemy soldier rendered hors de combat during earlier action in what was an unusual situation—the USMC sniper rifle was being used by a Communist marksman. (U.S. Marine Corps.)

at best, intermittent, with rifles produced only on an "as-needed basis." At this juncture, however, in addition to the few remaining Unertl "Marine Corps contract sights" and mounting hardware, by all accounts, "some" of the Lyman and Fecker rifle team target scopes were mounted as well—in some cases, with either Lyman or Fecker scope mounting blocks (bases).

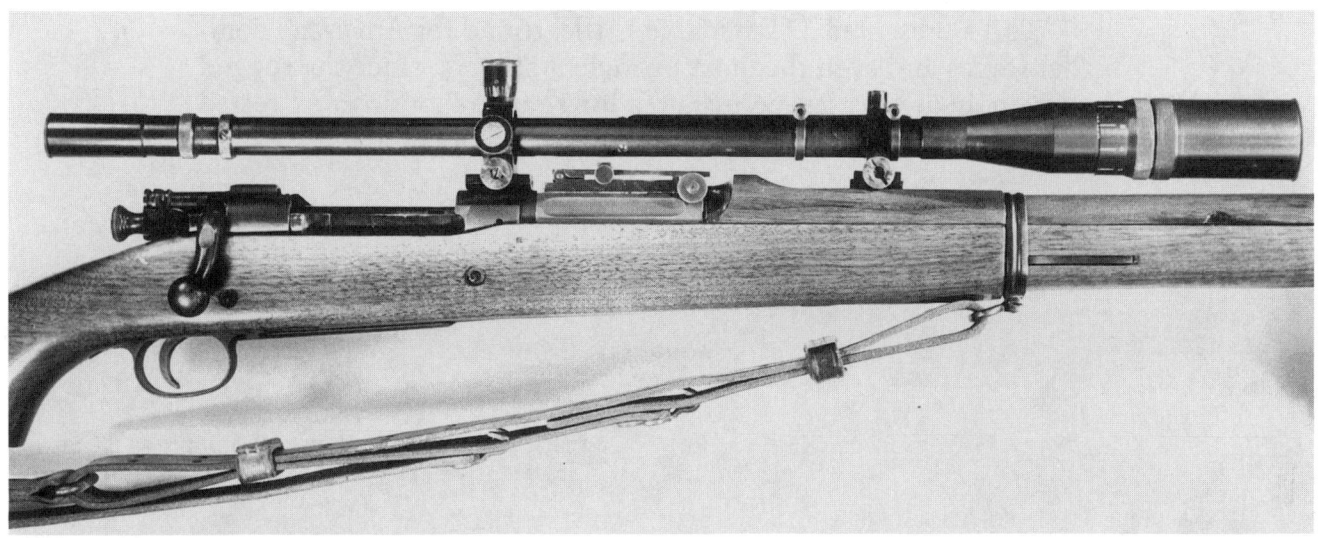

Marine Corps Model 1903A1/Unertl sniper rifle. The bolt handle has a telescope clearance notch. From all indications, Springfield sniper rifles were assembled at various Marine divisional depots on an "as-needed basis" following World War II. The conversion of an M1903 rifle to USMC sniper configuration was readily accomplished by any competent Marine Corps armorer. (Conway Collection.)

A comparison between two USMC M1903A1 sniper rifle bolt assemblies. The bolt (top) was polished, engraved with the rifle serial number, and then given a blue finish. The other is parkerized, does not have a serial number, and the bolt handle was notched to provide additional clearance between the handle and the telescope. Although similar notched bolts have been noted on USMC Springfield sniper rifles owing their origins to the Marine Corps, such modifications do not appear to have been part of the original World War II specifications for this weapon system. A replacement item or postwar modification at best, the origin of the bolt handle clearance notch has not been clearly defined. (Peter R. Senich.)

Though virtually identical in appearance to the Unertl bases, authentic USMC M1903A1 Korean War-era sniper rifles have been noted with telescope mounting bases made by Lyman and Fecker.

Standard target scopes could be readily affixed to

bases made by any of the principal manufacturers, an industry practice dating from "before the war." For that matter, any of the "standard" target scopes (3/4-inch main tube diameter) could be used with mounts from another manufacturer and bases from yet another. It was not uncommon to encounter a match shooter with a Unertl telescope in Lyman target mounts affixed to Fecker bases, for example. This was common practice.

Korea presented a formidable battleground for American combat forces and even the most proficient snipers, since the rugged terrain, in most cases, necessitated long-range shooting that rested beyond the resolving power of the issue telescopes.

Even though target scopes provide a limited field of view at extreme ranges, Marine snipers registered a number of 1,000-yard kills with the Unertl sight. Many considered the M1903A1/Unertl combination to be the most effective sniping arm employed in Korea (May 1951). (U.S. Marine Corps.)

With most of the Korean peninsula covered by an intricate mass of hills and ridges, much of the action took place on or between the ridges, especially after the war had settled into a static defense of fortified positions. The typical Korean ridge, rising from rice paddies and a stream at its base and slanted upward on an angle of 45 degrees or more, required an hour or more of steady climbing to reach the top. Once an infantryman reached the path-wide crest, he saw another ridge ahead, and others beyond it.

First Marine Division snipers (2nd Battalion, 5th Marines) during a practice firing session in Korea. The M1903A1/Unertl system and the semiautomatic M1C served as the principal Marine Corps sniper equipment during the Korean War. By all accounts, most snipers preferred the M1 Garand over the bolt-action Springfield. (U.S. Marine Corps.)

Under the circumstances, many considered the Marine Corps M1903A1 mounting the Unertl or an occasional Lyman or Fecker target scope to be the most effective sniping arm in Korea, inasmuch as Marine Corps scout-snipers had accounted for some rather impressive long-range kills with this weapon. Despite this fact, however, the M1903A1/ Unertl combination would be relegated to "Limited Standard" as a direct result of a Marine Corps study to update the requirements for a telescopic sighted weapon.

In late 1951, based upon the results of these studies, the Marine Corps Equipment Board recommended that:

(1) The U.S. Rifle, Caliber .30, M1903A1 now in use and in stock as snipers' rifles be declared limited standard.

(2) The Unertl 8X Telescope be declared obsolete.

(3) The Unertl mounts for the Unertl Telescopes be declared obsolete.

(4) The U.S. Rifle, Caliber .30, M1C, with telescope, cheek-pad and flash-hider, be standardized for the Marine Corps.

In use until the cease-fire ended combat in Korea, the venerable "Springfield Snipers" gradually disappeared from Marine Corps service.

From a collector's standpoint, there are, in effect, three categories of M1903A1 Marine Corps sniper rifles: those originating within the Marine Corps during World War II; those owing their origins to the Marine Corps following the war, particularly those intended for use in Korea; and finally, those surreptitiously "put-together" for sale on the collector's market.

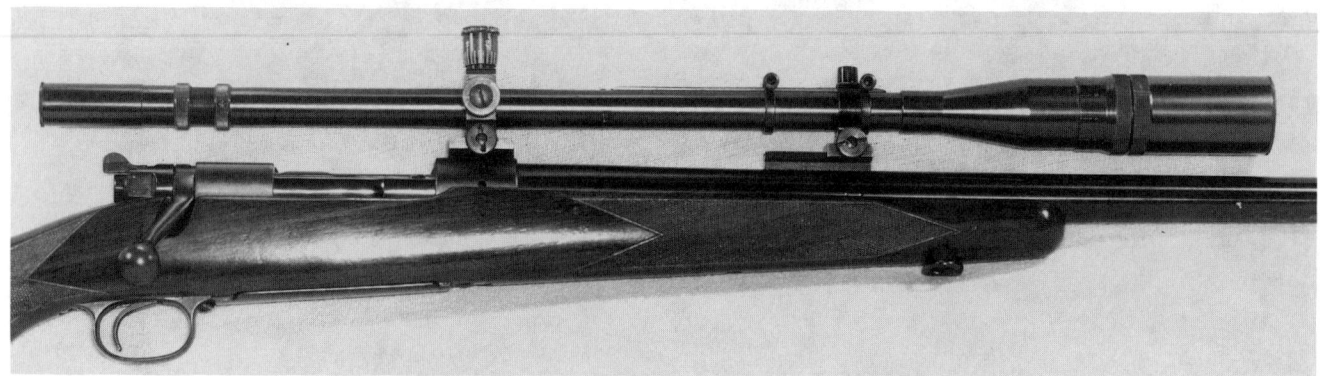

Close-up view, USMC Model 70 (48218) with Unertl contract scope. Although medium-heavy target barrels supplied by Winchester (24-inch length) and Douglas (26-inch length) were reportedly used to rebarrel some of the World War II Marine Corps Model 70s during the 1950s, in this case, the target barrel was made by Winchester and bears a 1952 date of manufacture. Of further interest, many of the same rifles were shipped out as supplemental sniping equipment during early Marine Corps involvement in Southeast Asia. A Model 70 of similar configuration was employed by Carlos Hathcock, who had 93 confirmed kills in Vietnam. (Cors Collection.)

Unfortunately, in most cases it is all but impossible to tell these weapons apart.

Interestingly, in a segment of the extensive "Study of Sniper's Rifles, Telescopes and Mounts" conducted by the Marine Corps Equipment Board at Quantico, Virginia, in 1951, the Winchester Model 70 was reconsidered for USMC sniper use, but rejected for basically the same reasons cited during World War II:

There is no Marine Corps requirement for a special rifle for use by snipers in the Marine Corps. It is undesirable to inject another rifle into the supply system, and if another rifle is injected into the supply system, it is necessary to inject non-standard ammunition for this rifle into the supply system in order to exploit fully any gain in accuracy. The U.S. Rifle, Caliber .30, M1C is sufficiently accurate for use by snipers in the Marine Corps.

Despite its rejection of the Winchester, the review board held the rifle in high regard:

> Investigation of the better grades of commercial rifles indicate that the Model 70 Winchester is the most accurate American made rifle, Caliber .30, on the market.

Originally, Winchester had offered the match shooter three exceptional target rifles based on the Model 70. In the years following World War II, Winchester continued development of its Model 70 with extremely heavy barrels to meet the requirements of long-range target shooting.

Nothing more need be said about the quality and desirability of these rifles, which were just about the only over-the-counter factory arms made for target shooting following the war. There just wasn't enough enthusiasm for "big-bore" shooting to induce other manufacturers to get into the picture. As a result, Model 70 target rifles gained considerable favor among Army and Marine Corps rifle teams for match-shooting purposes.

Winchester Model 70 (serial no. 48218) with a USMC contract, 8-power Unertl telescopic sight. A Winchester "Standard Rifle" in original form, the "sporter barrel" was replaced with a 24-inch medium-heavy target barrel during the course of Marine Corps service. The barrel channel (stock) was enlarged to accommodate the thicker barrel. According to Winchester records, rifle no. 48218 was manufactured in 1941. (Cors Collection.)

So far as the events preceding this and Marine Corps involvement in Korea, were concerned, however, despite the often alluded to "rifle team influence" and "unrelenting pressure" to have the Model 70 procured for sniper use, the Model 70 Winchester would not see combat as "duly authorized" sniper equipment until United States intervention in Southeast Asia (Vietnam), when it wound up as the quasi-official sniper arm of the Marine Corps in 1965.

Apart from the infrequent "unauthorized use" of the Model 70 Winchester in one form or another (target scope or hunting scope), the only other "bolt gun" to see Marine Corps sniper use in Korea besides the M1903A1 was the Remington M1903A4. Despite official relegation to Limited Standard, the Weaver/A4 combination was brought forth and employed in large numbers during the Korean War by Army and, to a lesser extent, Marine Corps marksmen. At this juncture, the "bolt-guns" would share this application of harassing North Korean and "Chi-Com" forces with the M1C and M1D.

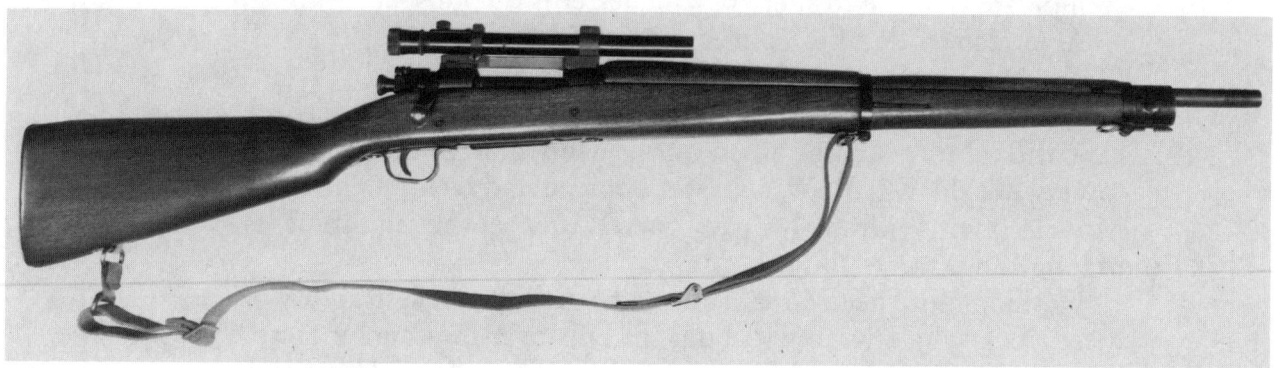

Remington Model 1903A4 sniper rifle with Telescope M73B1. While hardly a match rifle, the A4 was utilized by both Army and Marine Corps marksmen in virtually every combat theater during World War II and was issued again for use in Korea. (West Point Collection.)

Even though the Lyman sights (Telescopes M81 and M82) were still not considered "issue" items, a limited number of these scopes were mounted on the A4 at the field level in Korea. An unspecified quantity of base mounts and 7/8-inch rings were procured from the Lyman Gun Sight Corporation during this period.

While capable of producing satisfactory results when carefully prepared by qualified unit armorers, the M1903A4 was not favored by U.S. marksmen, particularly among those possessing the knowledge to recognize its deficiencies. A "Report of Sniping Activities" (dated 25 March 1952) dealing with the tactical employment of snipers in Korea, presented the following consensus among snipers familiar with the M1903A4 rifle:

> A discussion of issue sniper rifles and telescopes indicated the following:
>
> A. Present telescopes do not have sufficient magnification (2-1/2X).
>
> B. Adjustments for elevation and windage cannot be readily made.
>
> C. The Weaver 330 telescope is easily thrown out of adjustment.

Korean War-era Marine Corps marksman with the M1903A4/M73B1 combination. USMC snipers were known to employ—though sparingly—the A4 rifle with military and civilian versions of the Weaver 330C (M73B1) and Lyman Alaskan (M82) in Korea. As combat veterans insist, "When prepared and handled properly," the A4 was capable of acceptable accuracy, especially at a range of 200-300 yards. (Max Crace illustration)

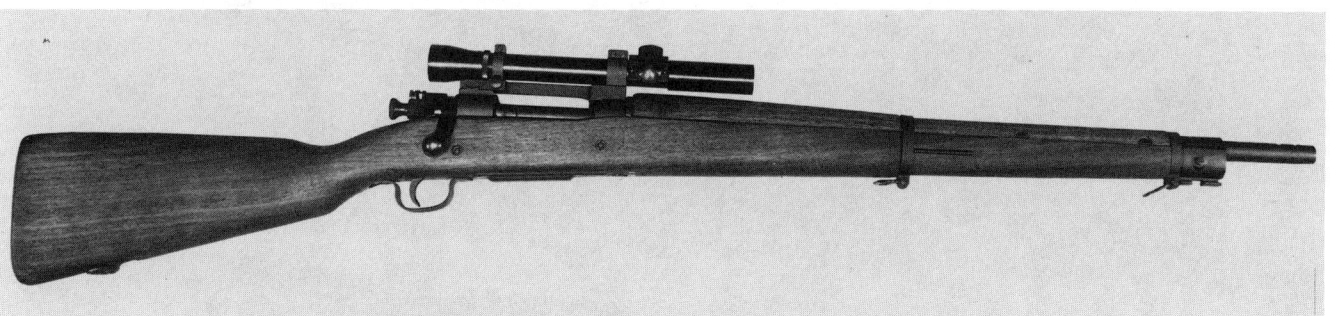

Model 1903A4 sniper rifle with a 2.5-power M82 telescopic sight. Even though Lyman sights (Telescopes M81 and M82) were not considered "official issue," a number of these scopes were mounted on the A4 for combat use in Korea. In one case in early 1951, Marine armorer reports from the 1st Battalion, 5th Marines indicated "the receipt of reworked '03A4s" fitted with straight stocks, Redfield Junior mounts, and commercial Lyman Alaskan scopes (so marked.) An expedient perhaps, the A4s were fielded before the M1Cs were available in quantity. (West Point Collection.)

  D. Telescope cross hairs are too coarse and obscure the target.

  E. Stocks should be better designed to facilitate taking good firing position.

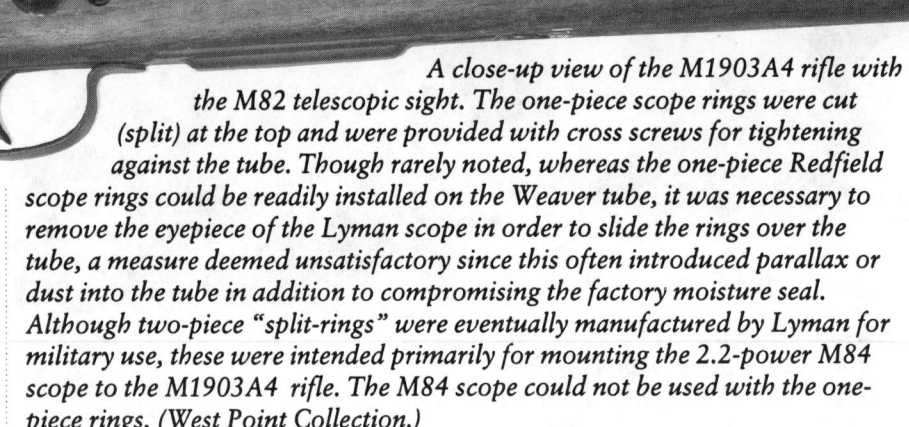

A close-up view of the M1903A4 rifle with the M82 telescopic sight. The one-piece scope rings were cut (split) at the top and were provided with cross screws for tightening against the tube. Though rarely noted, whereas the one-piece Redfield scope rings could be readily installed on the Weaver tube, it was necessary to remove the eyepiece of the Lyman scope in order to slide the rings over the tube, a measure deemed unsatisfactory since this often introduced parallax or dust into the tube in addition to compromising the factory moisture seal. Although two-piece "split-rings" were eventually manufactured by Lyman for military use, these were intended primarily for mounting the 2.2-power M84 scope to the M1903A4 rifle. The M84 scope could not be used with the one-piece rings. (West Point Collection.)

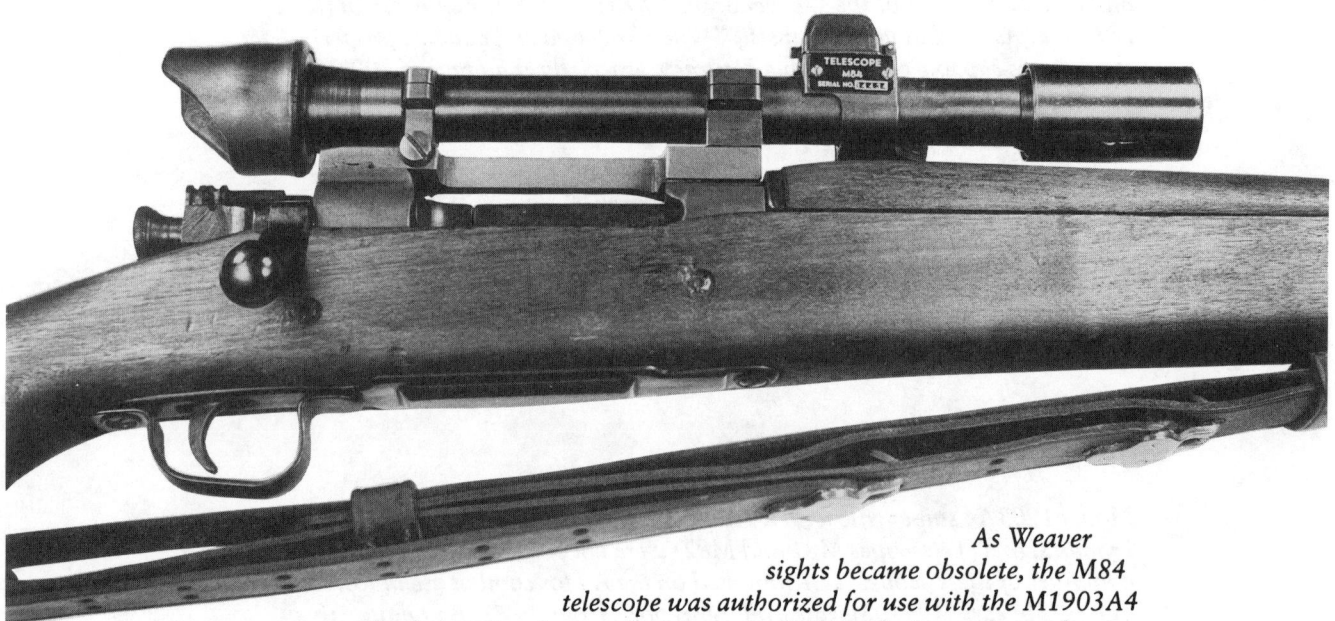

As Weaver sights became obsolete, the M84 telescope was authorized for use with the M1903A4 rifle. Despite its vintage, the A4 saw limited use during early combat in Vietnam when sniping arms were in short supply. A USMC museum rifle, a M1903A4 (serial no. 3419836, 8-43 barrel date) is shown with an M84 telescopic sight (no. 34434) and late-issue Lyman two-piece scope rings. (Peter R. Senich.)

Model 1903A4 sniper rifle with a commercial Lyman "Alaskan" 2.5-power telescopic sight (serial no. Z4002185, 9-43 barrel date), a part of the small-arms collection at the Marine Corps Museum. In this case, the elevation and windage adjustment housing is positioned directly behind the front scope mount (ring). Even though Lyman sights had been earmarked for use with the A4 during World War II, the specific manner in which Ordnance had intended their mounting has not been revealed. Despite an effective eye relief of 3 to 5 inches, the use of Lyman Alaskan-type sights (military/commercial) with the Redfield "Junior" mount assembly positioned the scope too far one way or the other by some standards. (Peter R. Senich.)

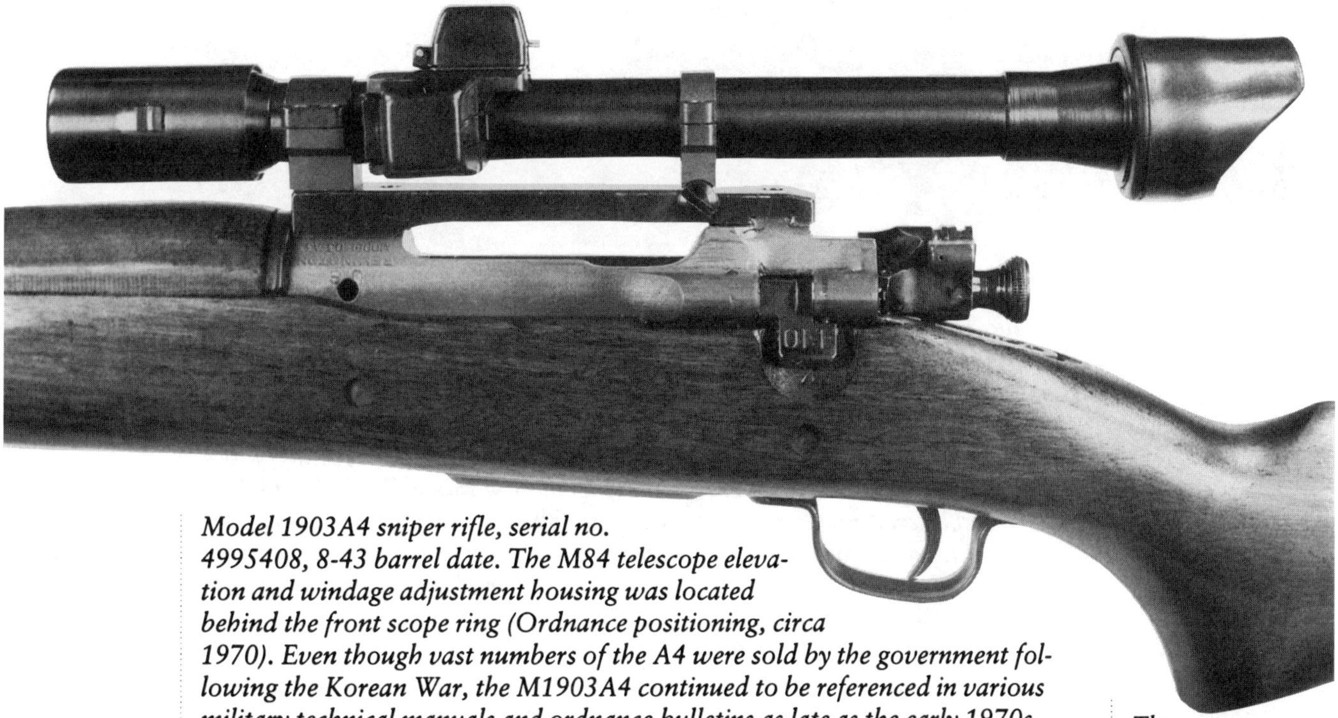

Model 1903A4 sniper rifle, serial no. 4995408, 8-43 barrel date. The M84 telescope elevation and windage adjustment housing was located behind the front scope ring (Ordnance positioning, circa 1970). Even though vast numbers of the A4 were sold by the government following the Korean War, the M1903A4 continued to be referenced in various military technical manuals and ordnance bulletins as late as the early 1970s during the height of U.S. involvement in Vietnam. (Peter R. Senich.)

F. Trigger pulls are neither adjustable nor crisp enough to permit a good squeeze.

G. Accuracy of the M1903A4 is questionable due to the bedding of the barrel and the fact that wartime production runs of M1903A3 rifles are believed to have been converted to the M1903A4 rifle, without screening out those rifles not suitable for such a purpose.

H. Present sniper rifles do not maintain their "zero" from day to day, thus requiring frequent targeting.

Despite the fact that vast numbers of the A4 were declared surplus and sold by the government to commercial arms dealers in the years following the Korean War, the M1903A4 continued to be referenced by the Department of the Army in various Technical Manuals and Ordnance Bulletins throughout U.S. involvement in Southeast Asia. While such reappearance of the A4 might suggest its use by U.S. snipers in Vietnam, except for infrequent use by Army and Marine marksmen during early combat activity when sniping equipment was in short supply, the M1903A4 was not employed to any great degree.

Winchester, Caliber .30, Model 70 Sniper, serial no. 254544 (1953) with special "sporter stock" (uncheckered) and a 12-power Lyman Super Targetspot telescopic sight. The rifle illustrated was purchased from Evaluators Ltd. by the U.S. Army in August 1953 for tests involving various telescopic sighted .30-caliber rifles, special long-range .50-caliber antitank rifles, and Browning (M2) machine guns, under the direction of Capt. William S. Brophy. The rifles marketed by Evaluators Ltd. were based on "special order Model 70s" obtained from Winchester. A highly respected organization catering to the weapon and equipment needs of law enforcement agencies and the military, Evaluators Ltd. was owned and operated by George O. Van Orden and his wife, Flora Mitchell Van Orden. (U.S. Army [APG].)

SPECIFICATIONS FOR THE VAN ORDEN SNIPER

RIFLE, 30-06 SNIPER: 24 inch medium heavy barrel, precision grade, mounted in the Winchester M70 special clip-slotted receiver: barrel mounted with bases for Lyman 77A Front Sight and Lyman SuperTargetSpot Sighting Telescope (telescope not furnished); barrel and action hand bedded in dense walnut 4-Position Sniper Stock with length of pull, drop and pitch approximating that of the U.S. Rifle cal 30 M1903A1; stock smooth finished and drenched to saturation with linseed oil, without checkering or lacquer; 1 1/4" selected sling swivels with 1 1/4" first quality leather military sling; rifle equipped with Lyman 48WH 1/4' Micrometer Receiver Sight with Target Disc and Lyman 77A Front Sight with 9 interchangeable discs; triggers and actions finished to target standards with allowances for wear in training to result in durable smooth final performance without further adjustment; overall weight approximately 10 pounds; tested with Western 30-06 Super-Match 180gr Boattail Handload to assure zero and grouping within requirements of national competition; final assembly, inspection and test under supervision of experienced ordnance and target practice technicians; delivered complete with operating instructions, ammunition handbook, metallic and telescopic sight manuals, and warranted ready as received for competition without further modification or adjustment other than the determination of the user's zero.

George O. Van Orden
Brig.Gen., U.S.M.C., Ret'd
President

An original copy of the Evaluators Ltd. "Specifications for the Van Orden Sniper." Even though Evaluators Ltd. marketed its M70 rifles to various branches of the Armed Forces, the extent of Marine Corps involvement with Van Orden and his Winchester rifles remains a topic of some debate. With exceptions possible, so far as it is known, Van Orden Sniper rifles did not serve the Marine Corps for combat purposes during the Korean War. (Blair M. Gluba.)

EVALUATORS LTD.
QUANTICO, VIRGINIA

LAW ENFORCEMENT AND MILITARY ARMS · EQUIPMENT AND SERVICES
TECHNOLOGISTS · CONSULTANTS · FACTORS

NOTES ON THE WINCHESTER M70 30-06 SNIPER (SPECIAL TARGET)

The Winchester M70 Sniper is a specially constructed precision target rifle built on special order of Evaluators by the Winchester Repeating Arms Company to specifications determined by field tests by Brig.Gen. George O. Van Orden, USMC Ret'd, and the late Major Calvin Lloyd, USMC, to provide the greatest stability and accuracy obtainable commensurate with the portability and flexibility essential in an efficient Sniper's rifle.

The barrel of the Sniper is classified as of medium-heavy weight and is assembled to the standard Winchester M70 clip-slotted receiver, mounted in a low-comb oil-finished stock of selected walnut and of special dimensions providing suitable and comfortable drop in all four standard firing positions. The action is hand-bedded and the barrel is as free-floating as the basic design permits.

The Sniper is mounted with the Lyman 48WH Receiver Sight, $\frac{1}{4}$' adjustments, the Lyman 77AK Hooded Front Sight with nine interchangeable inserts, and scope blocks positioned and zeroed to accept the Lyman SuperTargetSpot Sighting Telescope in standard target mounts.

The trigger pull is of the single-pull type and adjusted to approximate the minimum allowable competition weight plus a sufficient number of ounces to allow for wear as the rifle is broken in. Likewise, special attention has been paid to the cocking cams to assure a quality of smoothness reasonably expected in a new rifle of target quality.

The rifle is mounted with standard $1\frac{1}{4}$" sling swivels and is fitted with a $1\frac{1}{4}$" military type oil-finished leather sling.

The overall weight of the Sniper, without sling, is ten pounds or less and has been certified by the National Rifle Association as qualifying for the National Match Rifle Class in registered competition.

Each Sniper assembled for Evaluators has been targeted with Western 30-06 SuperMatch Handloads 180gr Boattail and, from the prone position with metallic sights, has delivered a group of $1\frac{1}{2}$' of angle or less.

The most striking characteristic of the Sniper is its ability to hold a zero over long periods under a wide range of conditions. This characteristic was sharply demonstrated during tests by the delivery of V-5 hits on the first shot at 1000 yards on 27 consecutive days, with sights at zero for that range modified by computed adjustments for temperature and wind. An ability to so closely hold a zero is of vital importance to the scout-sniper and of extreme value in competition.

A detailed description of the Winchester Model 70, .30-06 Sniper (Special Target) rifle offered by Evaluators Ltd. in 1953.

The first use of the Sniper in competition was during the 1941 Virginia State Championship Matches in which a fourteen year old girl, Miss Audrey Richard, then classified as a Smallbore Marksman, won the State Big Bore Championship. In the 1952 National Rifle Matches, for which the Sniper was for the first time commercially distributed by Evaluators, twenty five Snipers were used by men with a wide range of skill to completely dominate the NRA Match Rifle Class events, with the National Championship being won by Lt.Col. Walter Walsh, USMC, followed in second place by a civilian competitor attaining a numerically equal but outranked aggregate, both firing Snipers as delivered. Reports of scores attained in local matches and in practice with Snipers assembled in 1953 indicate that the extraordinary competition record of this rifle will be maintained in this year's Nationals.

No special instruction or care is required for the use and maintenance of the Sniper. It is recommended that no alteration of the setting of the guard screws be made so long as the rifle remains in zero and is delivering satisfactory groups with commercial standard ammunition of the type of Western SuperMatch Handloads or Western SuperX 180gr Boattail. The stock should be frequently dressed with linseed oil to assure exclusion of moisture from the wood. The bore should be cleaned from the breech daily after firing and the bore and action lightly oiled. Warm, soapy water is recommended for initial cleaning after firing corrosive primers: Hoppes Solvent #9 affords adequate protection in cleaning after firing noncorrosive primers. Following cleaning and lubrication it is well to stand or hang the rifle muzzle down to drain excess oil away from the tang and firing pin sleeve. Marking the initial position of the slots of the guard screws to enable detection of any displacement of these screws during firing is good practice. Should the guard screws slack off they should be firmly tightened, beginning with the after screw first: as a result of this it should be assumed that the rifle will acquire a new zero.

Given reasonable care as described above, with the rifle cleaned and lubricated following each day's firing, and when used with Western SuperMatch or SuperX cartridges, Winchester M70 Snipers distributed by Evaluators are guaranteed to perform as represented, limited only by the skill of the user. Should the rifle fail to perform properly Evaluators expects that the rifle will be returned to them or to the Winchester Repeating Arms Company for readjustment. Deviations from the above described practices or alterations by other than armorers of Evaluators, the Marine Corps Rifle and Pistol Team Detachment or the Winchester Repeating Arms Company voids all warranties regarding this rifle.

GOVO - 1953

CHAPTER 7

The Target Telescope

The acquisition of the Stevens and Winchester telescope business by the Lyman Gun Sight Corporation had left only two other companies (Belding & Mull and F.W. Fecker) to cater to the American target shooter during the early 1930s.

Though deemed "satisfactory" by all accounts, the Belding & Mull sights never achieved the popularity of the Lyman and Fecker scopes for competitive shooting and were not used to any great extent.

A succession of improved Lyman, Fecker, and eventually Unertl target scopes would serve the needs of the Marine rifle teams in the years prior to World War II.

An early summation of the target telescopic sight, a precision optical instrument developed primarily for match shooting purposes, was set forth by Edward C. Crossman in the original *The Book of the Springfield* (1931):

> The target shooting glass has as its chief requisite the matter of high accuracy, both in glass and in adjustments for varying ranges and varying wind conditions. To this end simplicity of mounts and strength of glass and shortness of tube and size of field and quickness of placing on the rifle are all sacrificed. The tube is long both for optical reasons and for long intermount spacing without having any of the adjustments on the tube interfere with its sliding freely in its mounts when the rifle recoils or when the rifleman desires to clear the bolt handle of his rifle of that type. The tube has to be pulled "into battery" for each shot after it slides under recoil from the previous shot. It must be pushed forward to clear the bolt handle of most rifles of this type, to permit the rifle to be operated at all. It has fine and more or less delicate micrometer screw mounts. It is slow and clumsy to put on the rifle and equally so to remove and its general construction is fragile.

In what was perhaps as relevant a statement in 1931 as it remains today, Crossman continued:

> As a rule, the use of the hunting glass for target shooting is about as unsatisfactory as the use of the target glass for hunting.

Ironically, the combat use of target scopes under conditions many believed better suited for hunting sights would pose a vexing problem for the Marine Corps through most of World War II.

In retrospect, however, of the firms then active, the F.W. Fecker Co. was considered to be the foremost target scope manufacturer through most of the 1920s and early 1930s.

Based in Pittsburgh, Pennsylvania, the Fecker company offered the competitive rifleman a choice of three target scopes: a 20-inch model in 4.5, 6, 8, and 10 power with 3/4-inch objective; the 22-inch version in 6, 8, 10, and 12.5 power with a 1 1/8-inch objective; and the 25-inch scope in 8, 10, 12.5, and 16 power with a 1 1/2-inch objective. Tube diameters were 3/4-inch, and all sights were available with 1/2- or 1/4-minute target mounts.

Focusing for range was effected by rotating a collar located near the center of the tube, a characteristic considered unique among target scopes of that era. According to Fecker sales literature, each scope was designated by its magnifying power and object lens, as "Fecker 1 1/8" 8-power Scope," for example. While Fecker target scopes were an integral part of the USMC rifle team equipment inventory during the 1930s and were among the telescopic sights considered for Marine Corps sniper use in 1941, the extent of any subsequent combat use by Marine riflemen in the Pacific has not been clearly defined.

A classic example of USMC rifle team members on the firing line during the early 1930s. The photo provides a good view of the rifle team equipment then in use. The M1903 Springfield Match Rifle (foreground) has the P.J. O'Hare front and rear sight protectors. The canvas seat, folding "shooting stool" also served as a rest for the telescope used for sighting targets. The leather covered "shooting boxes" were used to hold cleaning equipment as well as the miscellany every shooter deemed essential. (U.S. Marine Corps.)

When the Lyman firm entered the rifle scope business in 1929, it dropped the Winchester "Style B" models and concentrated on the No. 5A Telescopic Sight, the only scope listed in its original catalog. In addition to improving on the "basic defects" of the Winchester sight,

Lyman added a "Pope-type rib" to the tube to provide a more positive means of keeping the sight in vertical alignment, while using compound achromatic lenses manufactured by Bausch & Lomb to eliminate the "color fringes" common to the earlier scopes.

As with the Winchester device, the Lyman 5A made use of target-type mounts, the design of which were described in the 1929 Lyman catalog:

> The front mount is designed to give the tube a bearing on a convex surface instead of on rivets or screws. A spring plunger engages with a rib on the underside of the tube and keeps it from rotating, but permits the required sliding movement.
>
> The rear mount is designed to allow for elevation and windage adjustment for different ranges. Two springs, one exerting pressure vertically, the other horizontally, hold the tube in contact with the elevation and windage screws. These are micrometer screws reading to .001 of an inch, with division markings in white. The sight can be removed from the barrel without changing the adjustments.
>
> The bases for both front and rear mounts are of steel, having a dovetail cross section. If the bases are 7 3/16 inches apart "on centers," a change of one graduation in either elevation or windage adjustment will move the center of impact on the target one-half inch per 100 yards of range. If the bases are 6 inches on centers, the corresponding change per graduation is one-tenth of an inch for 50 feet of range.

Interestingly, even though the Marine Corps is known to have procured telescopic sights directly from Lyman, details surrounding the acquisition of the early Lyman scopes have not been fully revealed thus far. From all indications however, the 5-power Lyman target scopes were procured in quantity by the Marine Corps prior to World War II.

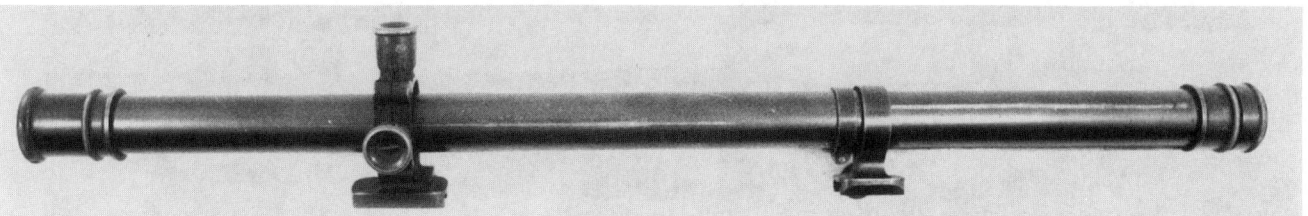

A 5-power Lyman 5A telescopic sight typical of those fielded by the Marine Corps during the 1930s. Even though USMC records mention "887" Lyman 5A sights at the Philadelphia Depot in October 1940, a significant number of Winchester A5 sights with the "special mounting" are believed to have been a part of that total. Despite the fact that the exact number or actual mix may never be known, from all indications both Lyman 5A and Winchester A5 sights saw early combat use with the M1903 rifle in the Solomon Islands. A matter of some confusion even before the war, the early target scopes were often referenced as "Lyman-Winchester sights" by the Marine Corps. (Gil Parsons.)

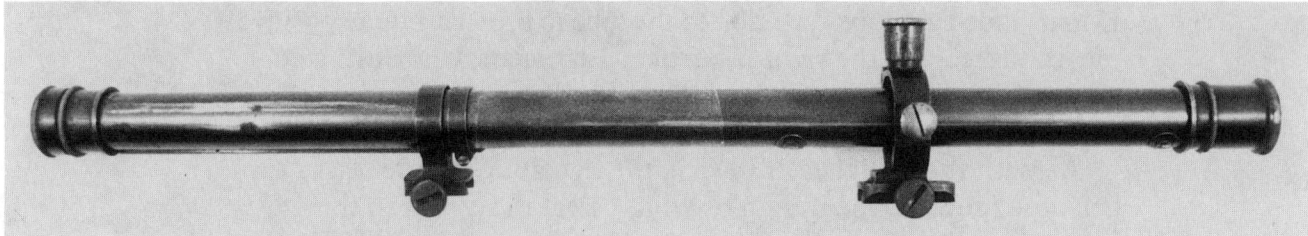

A left-side view of the Lyman 5A target scope. Apart from the Pope-rib beneath the front of the tube, the Lyman sight was virtually identical in appearance to the Winchester scope. (Gil Parsons.)

As a matter of interest, according to official correspondence dated 28 October 1940, there were 887 Lyman 5A sights held in stores at the Philadelphia Depot of Supplies. The question of whether these were originally procured to service the needs of the rifle teams or, in part, to train the "snipers" or "telescopic sight riflemen" mentioned in prewar Marine Corps marksmanship training manuals remains unanswered.

Even though the Lyman 5A sights had demonstrated their comparative worth on the firing line, the early Lyman target scope represented the state of the art as it existed in 1920. Recognizing this fact, Lyman developed and introduced a far more efficient telescope in 1934—the Lyman Targetspot.

The first in a series of what proved to be a highly successful line, the original "Targetspot" was 22 inches long with a 1 1/8-inch objective, 3/4-inch tube diameter, and it was available in either 8 or 10 power. The objective lens was adjustable for range from 50 feet to infinity, and the ocular unit could be adjusted for focus as well. A target-type rear mount provided 1/4-minute micrometer adjustments.

Rifle, U.S., Caliber .22, Model 1922 (M2) Gallery Practice Rifle with a USMC contract 8-power Lyman Junior Targetspot telescopic sight. Commonly known as the "Springfield .22-caliber rifle," the military training and practice rifles were fitted with the Lyman NRA No. 48B receiver sights. Note the added "telescope recoil absorber" and bolt handle relief (notch) for scope clearance. The scope is marked "USMC." (Conway Collection.)

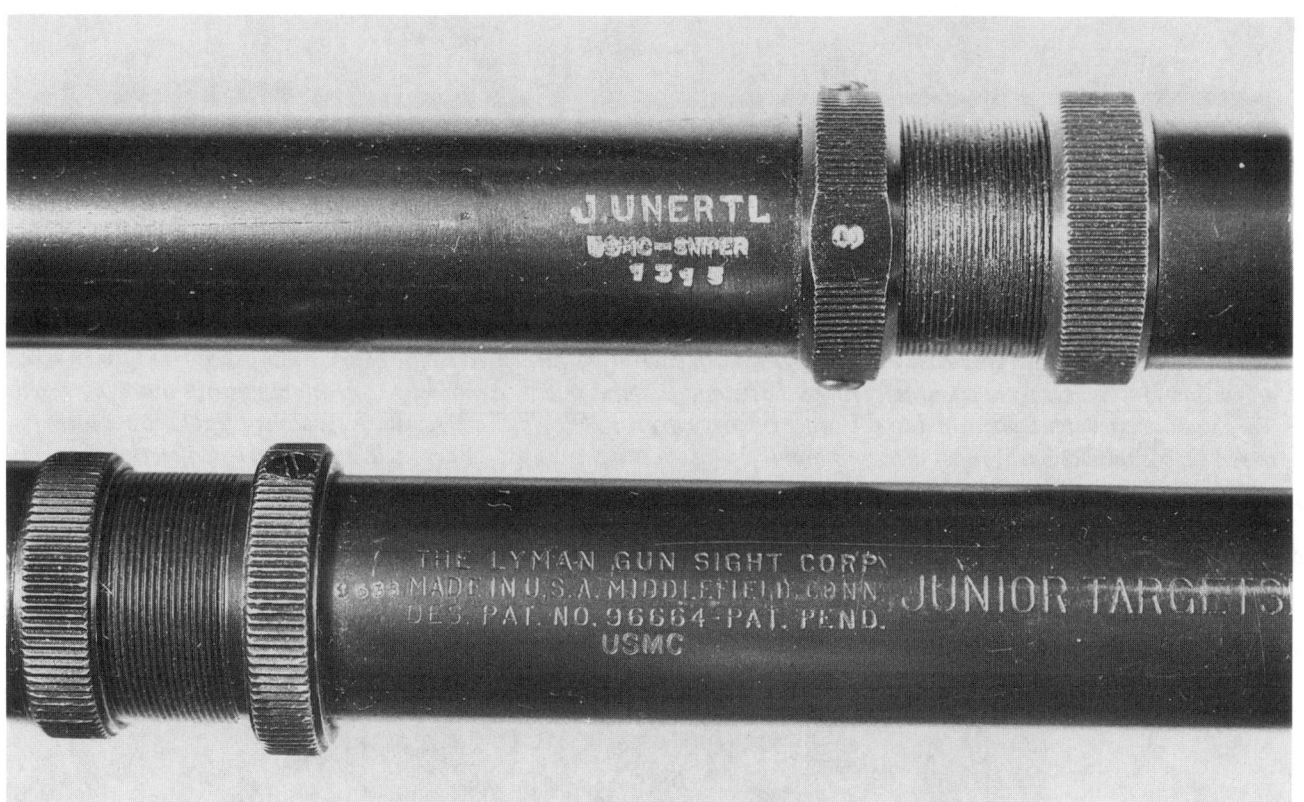

A close-up view provides an effective comparison between the roll-engraved "USMC" markings on an 8-power Unertl scope and the 8-power Lyman Junior Targetspot. According to company records, Lyman furnished "USMC marked" target scopes to the Marine Corps prior to World War II. (Conway Collection.)

By 1937, two new Lyman models, The Junior Targetspot and the Super Targetspot, were added to the line. The Junior Targetspot was 21 1/2 inches long with a 3/4-inch objective, 3/4-inch tube. When originally marketed, it was available in 6 and 8 power, with a 10-power model introduced in 1942. The Super Targetspot was made in 10, 12, and 15 power, with a 20-power option added in 1942 as well. A scaled-up version of the original Targetspot, the Super Targetspot was 24 inches in length with a 1.340-inch objective and 3/4-inch tube diameter. The flagship of the Lyman Targetspot series, the Super Targetspot was in production from 1937 until 1978.

Focus adjustment for the Junior and Super Targetspot models was essentially the same as that of the Targetspot. A three-point suspension rear mount introduced in 1937 was used with the three sights. When bases were installed on 7.2-inch centers, one click changed the group center 1/4-inch (1/4 minute) at 100 yards. The front mount used with the Targetspot series had a top spring and plunger to hold the scope and a rib to keep the scope from turning.

The Target Telescope

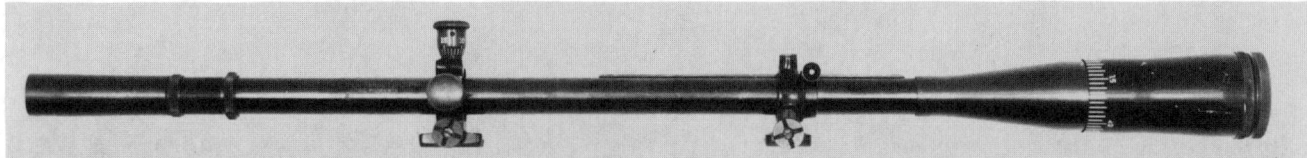

A 20-power Super Targetspot telescopic sight furnished to the Marine Corps by the Lyman Gunsight Corp. in 1949. A contract sight in this case, the tube is marked "USMC PROPERTY." The Super Targetspot came with a "3-point suspension," 1/2-minute click rear mount. The scope weighed 25 ounces and measured 24 3/8 inches long. The standard reticle was an extra fine cross hair; normal eye relief was 2 inches. A rubber eye cup, hardened steel bases, dust caps, and a wooden carrying case were included with each sight furnished to the Marine Corps. Storm Queen molded rubber lens covers were eventually offered as standard equipment. According to Lyman, various models from the Targetspot series were furnished to the Marine Corps prior to World War II. Although some target scopes were procured on a contract basis, most were apparently random purchases. (Gil Parsons/De La Fortrie Collection.)

A close-up view of a typical "USMC PROPERTY" marking on the Lyman Super Targetspot contract sight. Apart from the factory applied markings, Marine Corps target scopes were often marked "USMC PROPERTY" and eventually "U.S. PROPERTY" after 1962 with an electric pencil. From a collector's standpoint, however, the presence of one or the other electric-pencil markings does not guarantee the Marine Corps origins of a given sight. (Gil Parsons/De Le Fortrie Collection.)

NOMENCLATURE OF TARGET SCOPE

1. Rubber eye cup.
2. Eyepiece containing ocular lenses.
3. Eyepiece clamp ring.
4. Reticule levelling ring.
5. Rear, double micrometer, mount.
6. Front mount.
7. Eye relief stop ring.
8. Distance focus scale.
9. Object lens in tube.
10. Distance focus clamp ring.

Of all the Targetspot scopes in the Lyman line, the Super Targetspot was the most successful. Introduced in 1937, the "Super" model was manufactured until 1978. In original form, the sight was available in 10-, 12-, and 15-power models. A 20-power sight was added in 1942, a 25-power version in 1949, and a 30-power model in 1953. (Gil Parsons.)

Lyman three-point suspension, 1/4-minute click rear target mount with postwar-manufacture "straight-edge bearings." When bases were installed on 7.2-inch centers, one click changed the group center 1/4 inch (1/4 minute) at 100 yards. The original Lyman three-point, micro-click mount was introduced in 1937. The mounts were designed to fit all "standard dimension" bases. (Gil Parsons.)

The Lyman Targetspot series was also considered for Marine Corps sniper use in 1941 and, while never formally adopted, Lyman target scopes, in one form or another, were employed by Marine Corps rifle teams and to some degree, by USMC combat personnel during World War II and in Korea as well.

Perhaps the best-known target scopes fielded by the Marine Corps were those furnished by the John Unertl Optical Co. of Pittsburgh, Pennsylvania, a viable part of the riflescope industry beginning in the mid-1930s. Even though the Unertl firm was producing "hunting and big game" scopes prior to World War II, its target scopes were to draw the most attention.

Marine Corps marksmen during the National Rifle and Pistol Matches at Camp Perry, Ohio, in 1930. The heavy barrel match rifles are fitted with J.W. Fecker 1 1/8-inch objective target scopes. The center of the universe so far as match shooters were concerned, the National Matches were also known as the "Camp Perry Nationals" and the "Camp Perry Matches." (U.S. Marine Corps.)

In some respects, the early Unertl target scopes were similar to those made by J.W. Fecker, the firm John Unertl had worked for prior to starting his own optical company in 1934. For a time, Unertl made only scopes, using either Fecker or Lyman mounts, but eventually introduced an aluminum alloy (Dural) target mount based on the same principle as the others. As such, the three-point suspension, double-micrometer target mounts made by Fecker, Lyman, and Unertl during this period were all similar in design and function. Despite subtle differences, the principal Fecker, Lyman, and Unertl target scopes (3/4-inch tube diameter) could be interchanged from one set of mounts to another and the mounts, in turn, could be fitted to any of the "standard target bases" then available.

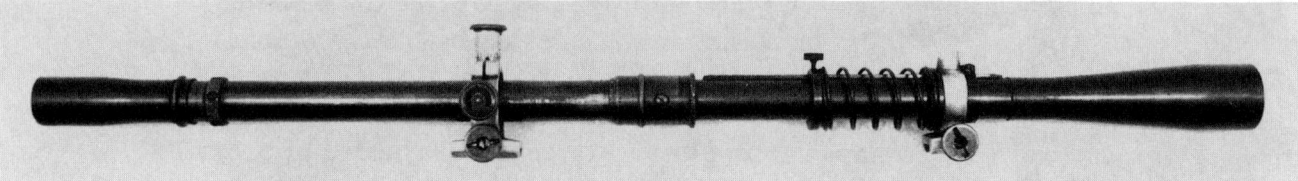

A Fecker 1 1/8-inch objective, 10-power target scope (22 inches long, 3/4-inch tube diameter) typical of those employed by the Marine Corps for match shooting purposes during the 1930s and 1940s. Fecker target sights were available with three-point suspension, duraluminum front and rear mounts with or without click adjustments. The target mounts made by Fecker, Lyman, and Unertl were all similar in design. Fecker scopes were focused for range by rotating the collar located near the center of the tube. The eyepiece was adjustable for definition of reticle. Cross-hair reticles were available from superfine to coarse. Sights were furnished with dust caps and a leather carrying case. A viable part of the USMC rifle team equipment inventory for many years, Fecker target scopes were among the telescopic sights considered for Marine Corps sniper use before World War II. The J.W. Fecker Co. was absorbed by a major optical firm some years after the Korean War. An excellent rifle scope, the Fecker target sights are highly prized by target shooters and collectors alike. (Gil Parsons.)

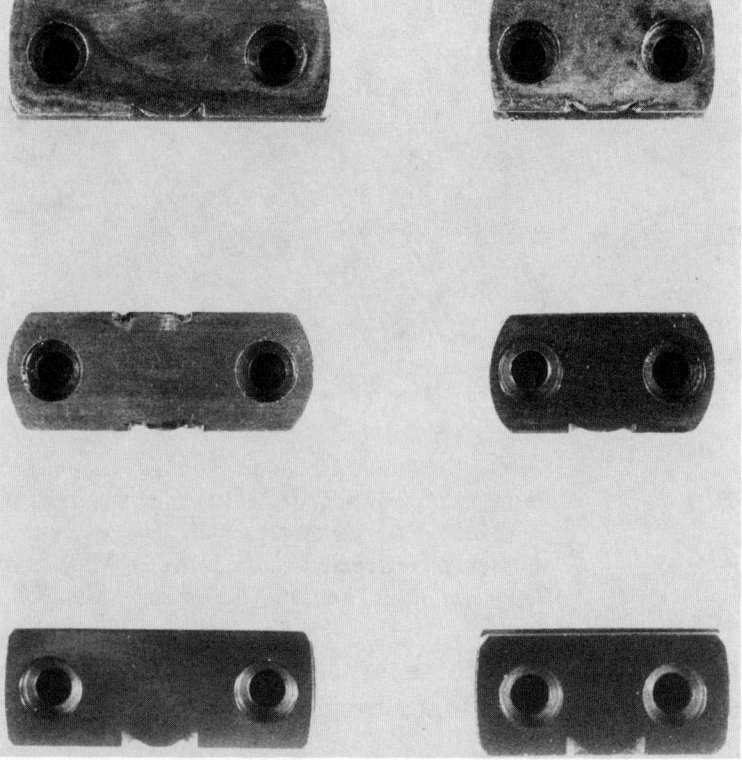

A comparison of Unertl, Fecker, and Lyman target scope mounting bases intended for use with the M1903 Springfield Rifle. Although base dimensions varied slightly, the hole size, counterbore, and spacing were identical. The base underside was radiused to fit the barrel and receiver ring; the dovetail form is the same on each base. The steel bases were machined and hardened accordingly. Even though Unertl hardware saw the most frequent use with the USMC M1903A1 sniper system, Lyman and Fecker bases were also used in the years following World War II. (Peter R. Senich.)

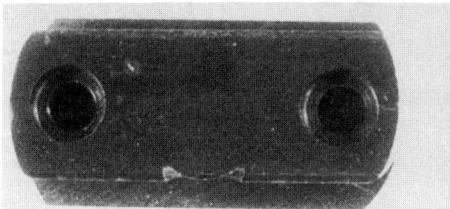

Typical Model 70 target telescope mounting blocks. The base (left) was attached to the receiver ring, the other to the barrel. When positioned on the rifle, the beveled mill cuts (mount-locking notches) provided both 6-inch and 7.2-inch spacing for the target mounts. Although target telescopes could be fitted to the Model 70 Standard Rifle (standard barrel), it was necessary to use a different front base. The front base shown was sized for use on a target barrel. (Peter R. Senich.)

Although Unertl would eventually offer a line of target scopes that would include 1-, 1 1/4-, 1 1/2- and 2-inch objective models of varying magnifying powers. The 1-1/4-inch objective, 24-inch long "Combination Target Scope" would serve as the basis for the Unertl 8-power "Sniper" sight eventually adopted by the Marine Corps for combat use.

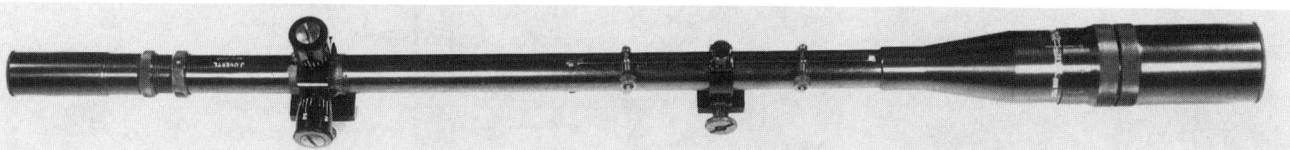

The military version of the prewar 1 1/4-inch objective Unertl target sight known as the "Combination Target Scope," an 8-power Unertl USMC "Sniper" sight as furnished to the Marine Corps during the war in the Pacific. In addition to combat use in Korea, the Unertl scopes served the Marine Corps during the early stages of its involvement in Vietnam. (Peter R. Senich.)

Popular target sights prior to World War II, the Unertl scopes were noted among competitive marksmen for their outstanding optical qualities.

According to product information then available:

> The Combination Target Scope is designed with a 1 1/4" clear aperture objective, which enables the shooter to spot his group, thus eliminating a spotting scope. It will spot bullet holes at 100 yards and under reasonable light conditions spotting at 200 yards is not a difficult task.

Referenced as the "Unertl Sniper" scope in military trim, the Combination Target Scope's attributes were duly noted in the 1941 Marine Corps study, "Equipment for the American Sniper," by Van Orden and Lloyd. The Unertl Sniper scope was one of 29 models of telescopic sights tested in evaluations conducted at Quantico, Virginia, beginning in late 1940.

July 23, 1940. J. UNERTL 2,208,913
MOUNTING FOR TELESCOPE GUN SIGHT
Filed March 30, 1940

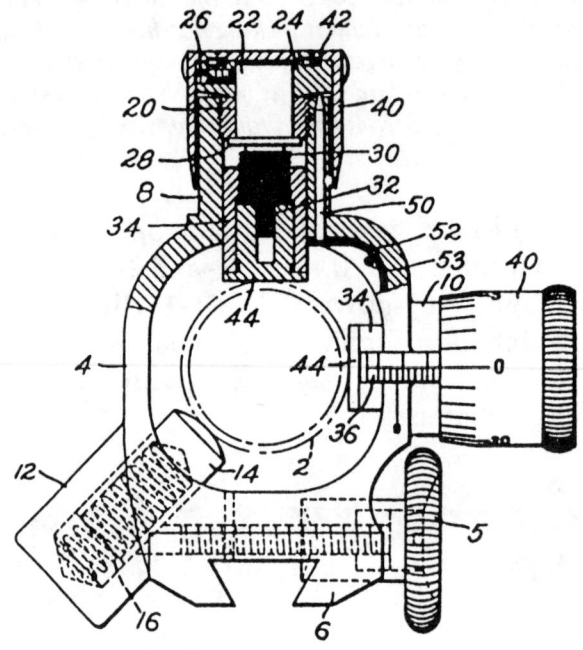

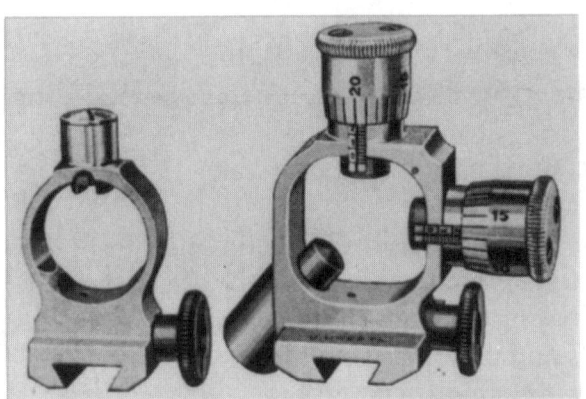

INVENTOR
John Unertl.
ATTORNEY

U.S. Marine Corps Scout-Sniper: World War II and Korea

Original patent drawing for the John Unertl "Mounting for Telescope Gun Sight" filed 30 March 1940. Prior to developing its own mounts, Unertl supplied its target rifle telescopes with Lyman 1/4-minute click micrometer mounts. An example of the original Unertl "Dural" aluminum alloy target mounting is also shown. In slightly modified form, the Unertl Dural mounting served as the mount system for the 8-power USMC contract sight. Patent No. 2,208,913 was granted to John Unertl on 23 July 1940. The patent number also appears on the Unertl target telescope mounts. (Donald G. Thomas.)

An accomplished rifleman and bench rest shooter, the late John Unertl is shown in competition with his 2-inch target scope in the late 1940s. According to his son, John Unertl, Jr., the force behind the company and designer of the Unertl line, John Unertl had worked in the optical division at Spandau Arsenal during World War I, but he had not been a sniper in the German Army as frequently reported. John Unertl was engaged in the optical instrument field from 1909 until his passing in 1960. His experience encompassed many phases of precision instrument manufacture from commercial to military. In one form or another the Unertl firm has furnished telescopic rifle sights to the Marine Corps for more than 50 years. (John Unertl Optical Co.)

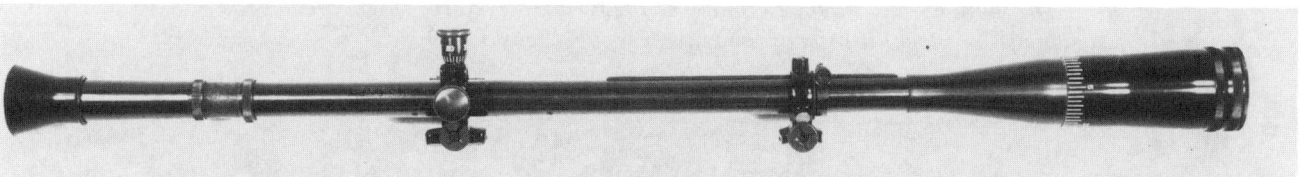

Another USMC marked Lyman 20-power Super Targetspot telescopic sight (no. 17515, circa 1949) shown with the rubber eye cup, an accessory item furnished with each sight. (Peter R. Senich.)

A full view of the factory-applied "USMC PROPERTY" markings on the 20-power Lyman Super Targetspot no. 17515. (Peter R. Senich.)

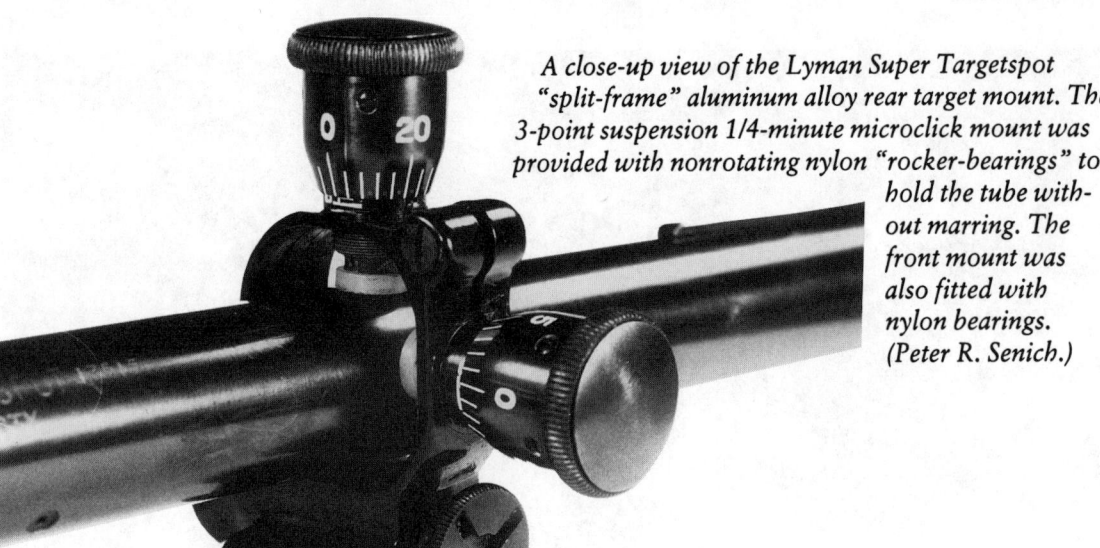

A close-up view of the Lyman Super Targetspot "split-frame" aluminum alloy rear target mount. The 3-point suspension 1/4-minute microclick mount was provided with nonrotating nylon "rocker-bearings" to hold the tube without marring. The front mount was also fitted with nylon bearings. (Peter R. Senich.)

The number "20" stamped on top of the forward eyepiece ring indicates the power or magnification of the Lyman scope. (Peter R. Senich.)

An example of the typical wood "scope box" furnished with the Marine Corps 20-power contract sights. This is a standard commercial box with "USMC PROPERTY" markings applied (stamped) at the Lyman factory. (Peter R. Senich.)

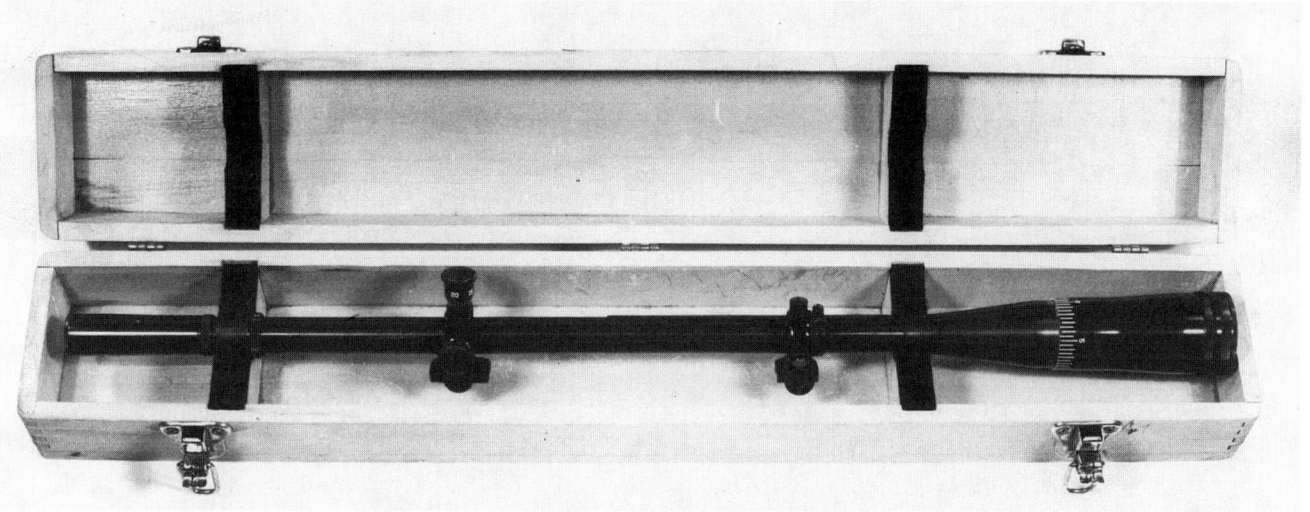

Lyman scope box with Marine Corps 20-power Super Targetspot in place. According to Lyman, "The special wooden carrying case was regularly furnished with new Targetspot and Super Targetspot scopes." The 4-inch square wooden box was 26 inches in length with electroplated metal hardware. (Peter R. Senich.)

Included among the equipment deemed satisfactory for Marine sniper use, the Unertl scope was considered "efficient to the extent that a sniper can hit any target he can see at any range up to at least one thousand yards." As a result, "The 8-power Unertl 'Sniper' telescopic sight, or equal, mounted in the Unertl 'Snipers Mounts,' or equal" was ultimately recommended for adoption by the Marine Corps Equipment Board on 27 March 1941.

However unsuited for actual combat target scopes may have been, in fact, the hunting or big game riflescopes then available shared the same major problems: they were just as susceptible to the effects of moisture and to reticle damage.

Inasmuch as the target scope had been an integral part of rifle team competition as well as the principal instrument used to train the few snipers or telescopic sight riflemen the Marine Corps fielded after World War I, and with much of the Marine Corps rifle team equipment and personnel involved in an emerging scout-sniper program as the war began (1940–41), it is understandable that a target scope would serve as the prime candidate for Marine Corps combat use at that juncture.

In any event, whether the military at large could have fielded a completely satisfactory telescopic rifle sight of any configuration during World War II remains open to speculation. By any measure, the demands experienced in the various theaters of combat operations, particularly those in the South Pacific, exceeded the technology then available.

Telescopic Sights: The M1 Rifles

CHAPTER 8

In the years following the adoption of John Garand's semiautomatic rifle design, continuing refinement of the new service weapon precluded any consideration of its suitability for sniping.

However, when combat requirements brought about a reassessment of priorities during the initial stages of World War II, the demand for telescopic sighted rifles resulted in the hasty adoption of the bolt-action 03A4 variant, and authorization to develop a sniping arm based on the M1 rifle as well:

> At the time Headquarters, Army Ground Forces recommended the standardization of the M1903A4 Sniper's Rifle, it was also recommended that the M1 be equipped with a telescope in such a manner as to permit clip loading and normal functioning of the weapon.

Nevertheless, by 1944, attempts to adapt a satisfactory telescope mount to the M1 according to guidelines established by Headquarters, Army Ground Forces, proved fruitless. In the face of mounting pressure, a concerted effort saw the emergence of two designs: the M1E7 Rifle and the M1E8 variation, both of which were reportedly developed at Springfield Armory.

The M1E7 incorporated a dovetail cam-operated pressure-plate type of scope mount requiring the drilling and tapping of three holes and the drilling of two tapered holes in the left side of the receiver to adapt the base. The M1E8 design, on the other hand, called for use of a machined block-type mount pinned to the chamber end of the barrel, which required a shortened rear hand guard to provide necessary clearance.

Even though both systems proved satisfactory and conformed to Ground Forces requirements, the M1E7 design fitted with the Griffin & Howe telescope mounting was chosen, as ordnance records recount, "because of its rugged characteristics." The workings of the telescope mount group of what became the M1C were described as follows:

> The telescope mount group consists of a mount base fixed to the receiver and a removable mount. The mount base is semi-permanently attached to the left side of the receiver by two taper pins and three allen-head screws. The top of the

mount base, which is male dovetail in shape, runs parallel to the bore of the rifle. The removable mount consists of two two-piece rings, secured to a slide, to hold the telescope. The rings are made in two halves that are held together by screws. The slide is an oblong block. Two locking levers (screws) hold a pressure plate (clamp) in a recess in the slide. When the levers are turned forward, the slide can be removed or replaced on the mount base. The levers are turned backward to lock the slide in place on the base. Turning the locking levers backward pulls them, by their threads, tightly against the pressure plate whose inner side forms part of the female dovetail. This locks the telescope and removable mount in position on the rifle. To aid in unlocking the removable mount there are two small springs under the pressure plate. These springs force the pressure plate outward when the unlocking levers are turned to the unlocked position. Two small screws on the left side of the slide and in the pressure plate make certain that the locking levers are in the correct position when unlocked.

As a matter of interest, the Griffin & Howe telescope mount group was not designed specifically for the M1E7, but rather was an adaptation of a mounting popular with sportsmen on bolt-action rifles prior to the war.

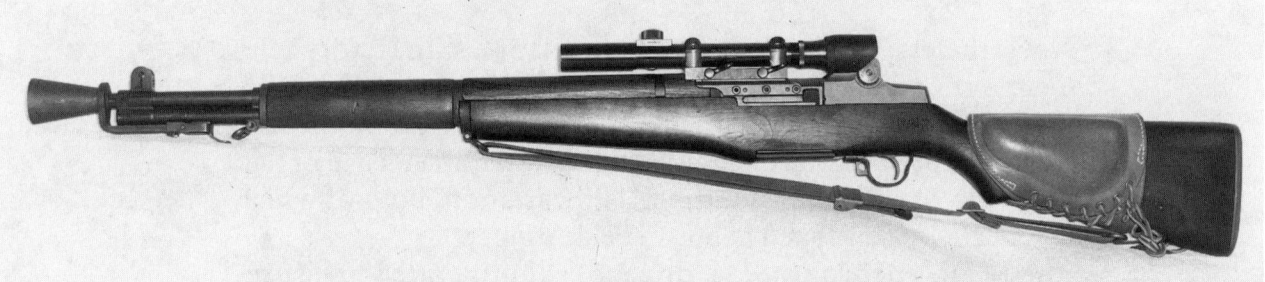

An original Springfield Armory-manufactured M1C sniper rifle (serial no. 3451813, 5-45 barrel date) with M82 telescope, M2 flash hider, and T4 leather cheek pad. A hefty package in combat trim, the M1C was approximately 46 inches in length with a weight of nearly 12 pounds. According to some combat veterans, the flash hider and cheek pad were often thrown away in combat. The elimination of both items made the weapon "less cumbersome." (Cors Collection.)

According to official record:

> On the basis of Infantry Board tests of the M1E7 and M1E8 Rifles, the M1E7 Rifle equipped with a two and one-half power telescope was standardized in June of 1944 as U.S. Rifle, Caliber .30, M1C (Sniper's), thus making the M1903A4 Sniper's Rifle Limited Standard. In order to assure production meeting requirements, the M1E8 Rifle was adopted in September 1944 as U.S. Rifle, Caliber .30, M1D (Sniper's).

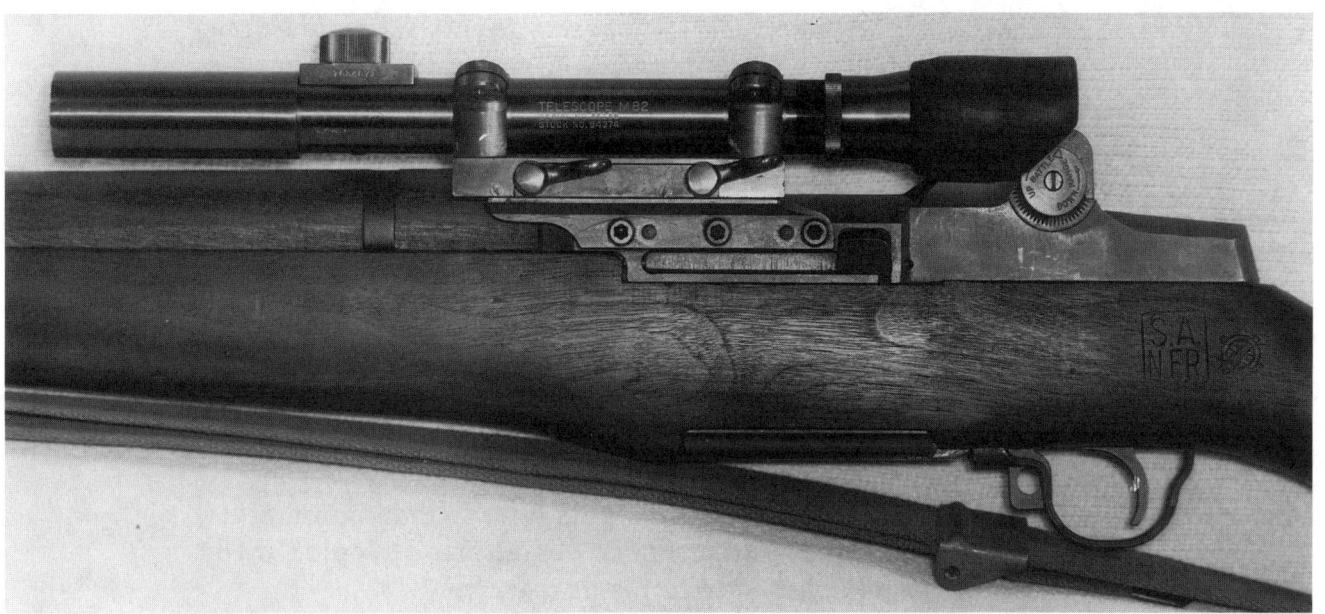

A close-up view of a typical M1C (3451813) with M82 sight and Griffin & Howe mount assembly. Though effective in principle, early M1C assembly and targeting problems at Springfield Armory had prompted the acceleration of the M1D development program in early 1945. In view of the situation then confronting the Ordnance Department, an M84-equipped M1D would have undoubtedly replaced the M1C had the war continued. (Cors Collection.)

The initial government contract placed with Griffin & Howe in mid-1944 called for a total of 8,300 telescope mounts for use with the M1C rifle. Fourteen thousand were completed by VE Day (8 May 1945), and on VJ Day (12 August 1945) only 2,000 remained in work. Upon completion of its final contract, Griffin & Howe had furnished a total of 37,000 mount assemblies (rings, mount, and receiver base).

When development of an M1 sniping variant finally went into high gear in late 1943, procurement of a suitable telescopic sight proved to be a difficult task. By this time, the Weaver 330 had clearly demonstrated its unsuitability for the rigors of combat, as evidenced by reports from the Pacific.

Even though the 330 had been tested and designated as an alternate sight when the M1C was adopted, its application never progressed beyond the testing stage. The Lyman firm had curtailed scope production due to pressing government contracts, and excepting the few Lyman Alaskan commercial telescopes used for evaluative purposes, they were not available in quantity.

When Lyman was able to resume telescope production, representatives from Frankford Arsenal visited the company on 29–30 September 1944, to finalize manufacture of Alaskan sights with a combination rain-sun shield for the objective end of the telescope and a protective rubber eyepiece for the ocular end. During this visit, pilot parts were carefully examined and re-toleranced where necessary in order to facilitate rapid production.

On 2 October 1944, Headquarters, Army Ground Forces approved the military version of the Alaskan and authorized manufacture of 2,000 sights with "cross-wire reticles." Efforts to supplement initial Lyman production included Springfield Armory's furnishing cross-fire reticle assemblies for the new telescopes.

In military configuration, the Lyman Alaskan was designated Telescope M81. However, in view of Frankford Arsenal studies which had indicated a definite preference for a tapered-post reticle with this type of telescope, manufacturing drawings were revised shortly after the M81 was approved to incorporate a tapered-post reticle (Lyman Catalog No. 6). This variant then became Telescope M82. Except for reticle patterns, both telescopes were identical.

Although early-production sights bore Lyman commercial markings as well as the military designation, typical M81 Telescopes furnished to the Army were marked:

Telescope M81
Serial No. 34097
Stock No. 84373

Following a brief period of production when components (scope tubes) originally made for commercial use were expended, all reference to their Lyman origin was deleted, leaving only the model identification, serial number, and Federal stock number. Telescopic sights having the tapered-post reticle were designated:

Telescope M82
Serial No. 35692
Stock No. 84374

Variations in Federal stock numbers will be encountered with this sight, however.

In commercial form, two types of this telescope had been produced by Lyman. The early type, with an aluminum alloy tube and exposed elevation and windage dials, was discontinued when alloy could no longer be obtained. The newer steel tube model, dubbed the Lyman Alaskan "All Weather" scope, was modified to include protection for the elevation and windage dials by means of screw-on dust and moisture covers.

The Alaskan, on which the M81 and M82 were based, had a magnifying power of 2 1/2 diameters, a field of view of 35 feet at 100 yards, and universal (fixed) focus. Although eye-relief was cited as 5 inches, the full field of view could be seen whether the eye was 2 1/2 or 6 1/2 inches from the eyepiece. The tube diameter was .866 inch, and the overall length of the scope was 12.875 inches with the rubber eyepiece and objective shield extended.

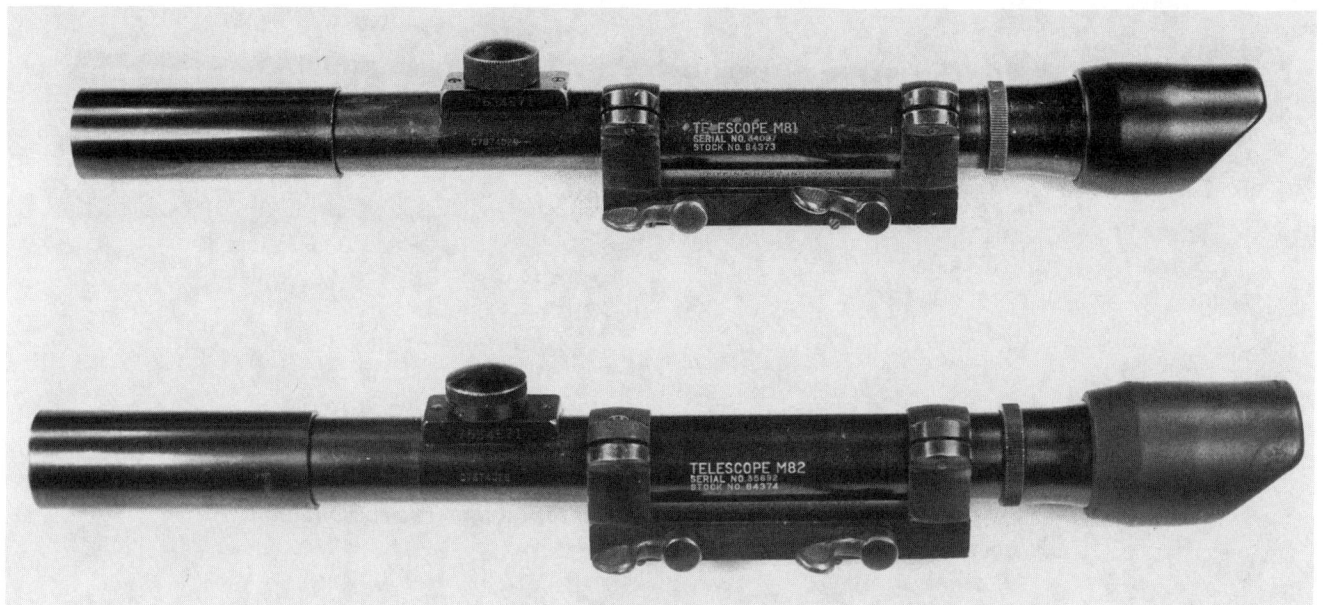

Comparative view of M81 and M82 telescopes with Griffin & Howe mounting as issued with the M1C sniper rifle late in World War II and again in Korea. An adaptation of the Lyman Alaskan "All Weather" commercial hunting scope, the sights were fitted with a retractable rain and sun shield and rubber eye guards for military use. A cross-wire reticle pattern was used in the M81 sight; a tapered post with the M82. Even though the primary function of the rubber eye guard was to protect the rifleman, the guard also served "to position the observer's eye at the proper distance" and to protect the scope if it recoiled against the steel helmet. The semicircular shape on the underside was designed to provide clearance for the elevation adjustment knob on the left side of the standard M1 rear sight. The same eye guard shape was later used with the M84 rifle scope. (Peter R. Senich.)

An early Korean War USMC combat photo depicts an M1C-equipped Marine rifleman "firing on North Korean troops from a ruined building." Semiautomatic M1 sniping rifles were in short supply during early action in Korea. (U.S. Marine Corps.)

A right-side view of an M82 telescope with the elevation and windage dial dust covers removed. The Griffin & Howe mounting positioned the telescope approximately 1 inch to the left of the center of the bore. In this case the M1C rifle number was stamped on the right side of the mount. The combination rain/sun shield is extended. (Peter R. Senich.)

A Marine marksman (2nd Battalion, 5th Marines) with an M1C mounting a 2.5-power Lyman Alaskan (All Weather) commercial sight during action near Chajang-ni, Korea, in February 1953. Lyman rifle sights "went to war" in both commercial and military configuration. By all accounts, it was not unusual to see Lyman commercial sights in use on the M1C in Korea. (U.S. Marine Corps.)

The reticle had internal adjustment for both elevation and windage. The top dial adjusted for elevation, and that on the right side of the tube adjusted for windage. The dials had an adjustment plate over them, which was engraved with a scale having 20 graduations around its diameter, each graduation having an adjustment value of two minutes. The dials clicked for each half graduation, giving the clicks a value of one minute. The graduations were numbered, the fifth graduation being numbered "10" meaning 10 minutes, and so on up to 30.

The plates were also engraved with an arrow and the word "UP" and letter "R" showing which way to turn the dials to increase or decrease the elevation or adjust the windage to the right or left. The plate could also be loosened by means of the center screw so that the dial could be turned until the rifle shot to the mark at the range desired. Then the plate was loosened and turned so that its zero came up even with the index line. The graduations would then read "zero" for that range and "zero" for windage.

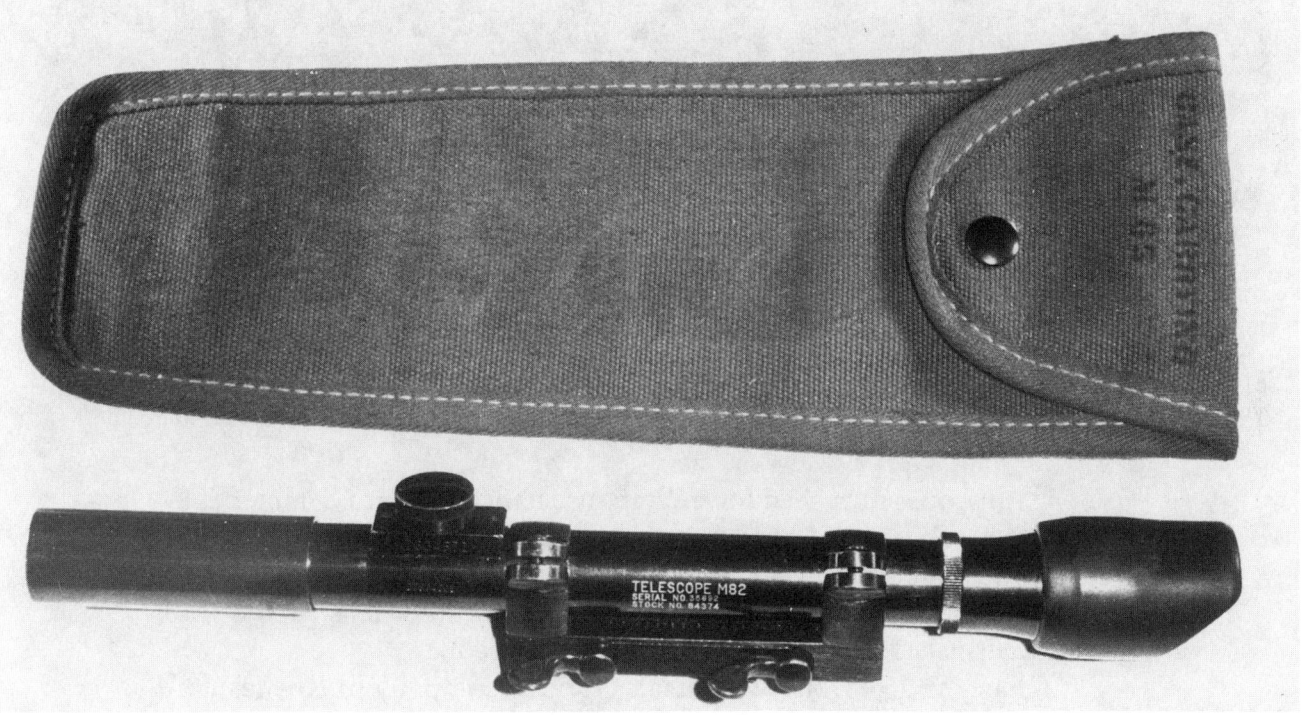

An original-issue "case, carrying, M65 (Telescope)" circa 1945 (D7692065), intended for holding the M1C telescope assembly when removed from the rifle. According to an early Ordnance description, "The telescope carrying case is made of olive drab cotton duck that has been treated to be fire-, water-, and weather-resistant. A snap fastener (lift-the-dot) keeps the case closed. A metal hook and web strap provide a means of attaching the carrying case to a cartridge belt or other equipment." Though manufactured in quantity, telescope carrying cases saw little use in a combat environment. The sights were rarely removed from the rifles. (Peter R. Senich.)

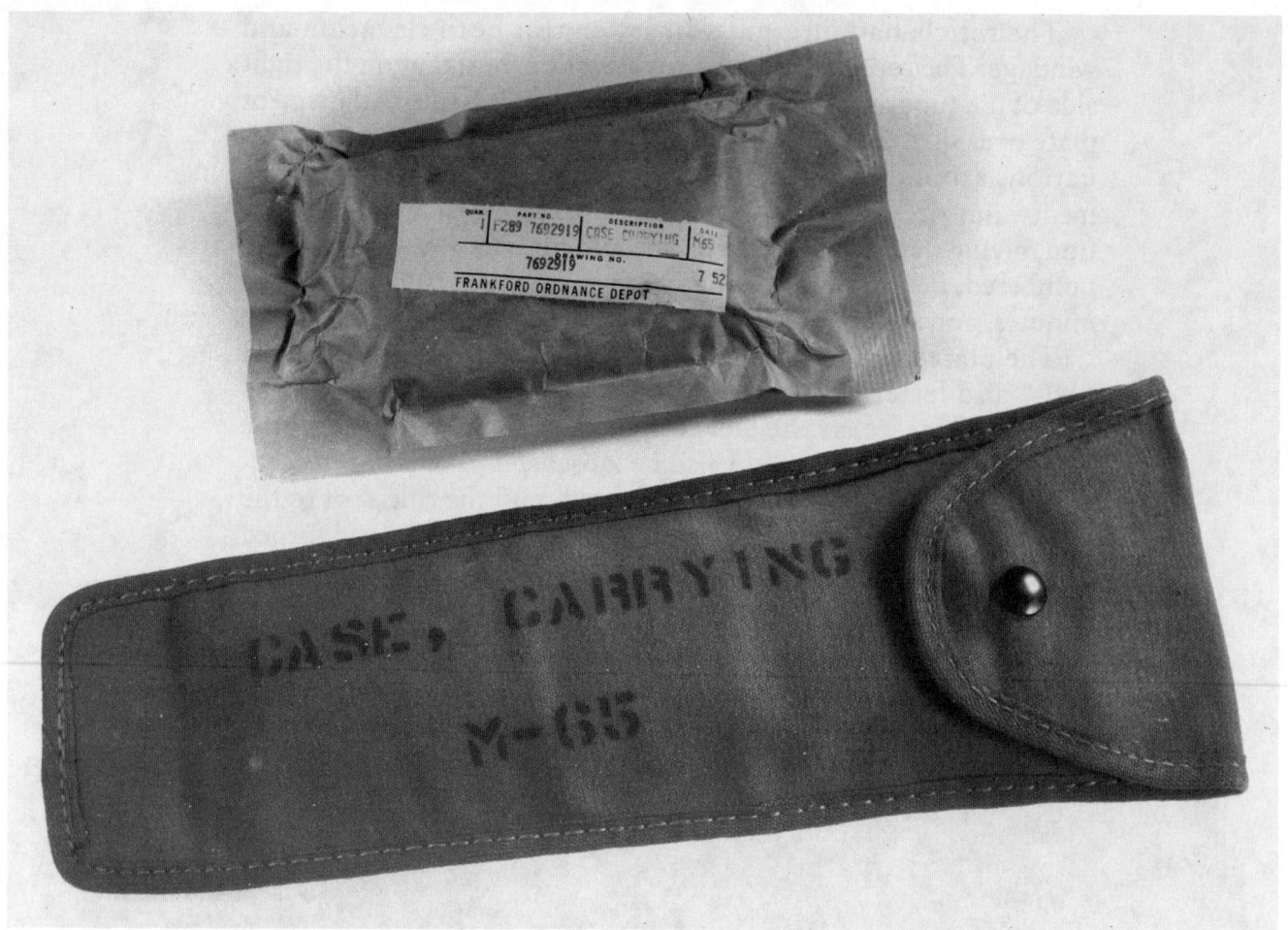

Korean War-era M65 telescope carrying case (D7692919) in a sealed Frankford Ordnance Depot package (the case is an example of the contents). The back of the case is marked "MRT 3-10-52" (mildew-resistant treatment). The package is dated July 1952. (Peter R. Senich.)

All scopes furnished for military use had a standard commercial blue-black finish. A web carrying case (M65) with "lift-the-dot" flap fastener and belt-hooks was designed to hold the telescope and mount when removed from the rifle. Leather lens caps were not furnished with either M81 or M82 telescopes.

Early in 1945, the Wollensak Optical Company of Rochester, New York, commenced production of M82 scopes for use with the M1C. Initial production tested at Springfield Armory indicated that "the optics became loose and out of adjustment after sustained test-firing (3,000 rounds)." However, this problem was rectified following a series of meetings between representatives of the Ordnance Department and Wollensak engineers. While the exact quantity of M82 scopes produced by Wollensak remains obscure, according to their records, "thousands of these instruments were supplied to the Army for sniper use."

Despite the government acquisition of a second source in this case, Lyman remained the principal supplier of M82 Telescopes through the end of the war in August 1945.

Frankford Arsenal, long a principal source of optical fire-control systems for the Army's artillery, embarked on research and development in quest of "an optimum telescope for sniper use" shortly after the beginning of the war, due to the pressing need for telescopic sights for small arms.

Although early sniper experience had indicated that a telescope must be fungus-proof, waterproof, and practically shockproof, it had become obvious that no commercial sight possessed the attributes necessary for sustained military use, and Ordnance development of a telescope to replace the commercial types commenced in earnest.

The Weaver 330 sight was to be replaced by the Lyman scope. As noted by Frankford Arsenal records, "The Telescope M73 (Alaskan) is to be used until a superior telescope is developed and standardized." Nevertheless, consideration was given to the Lyman Alaskan in a somewhat modified form, that is, with "new reticle patterns." However, the M73E1 and M73E2 telescopes, as they were designated for development purposes, did not progress beyond the testing stage.

By early 1945 a conventional 2.2-power sight, designated T134, had emerged as the most practical among those considered for adoption. Although development of 3-power and 4.5-power variants with characteristics similar to the T134 device had been initiated and were to be available for field-testing in June 1945, they were ultimately rejected for reasons that remain obscure. Telescope T134 was chosen, designated M84, and standardized on 12 April 1945.

The M84 was a straight tube telescope with universal focus, 2.2-power magnification, and a field of view of 27 feet at 100 yards. The reticle pattern consisted of a vertical post with horizontal cross-hair. Although eye-relief was listed as 5 inches, like the M82 in this case, the eye could be positioned somewhat nearer or further from the ocular end, as the shooter deemed necessary. The optical system was sealed with synthetic rubber gaskets in an effort to make the scope impervious to moisture.

The elevation dial, mounted on top of the tube, had a hinged protective metal cover that was held closed by a friction catch. The elevation screw had 32 threads to the inch. A complete turn gave 40 minutes of angular movement to the sight post. Each minute-of-angle change was held by a detent within the dial. While the click was not normally audible, it could be felt. One click was equal to 1 minute or 1 inch per 100 yards of range. The elevation scale started at zero yards and went up to 900 yards with marks every 50 yards and numbers at 100-yard indexes. When calibrated at any given range, the elevation dial was approximately correct from 1 to 900 yards.

The windage dial, also having a protective cover, was located on the left side of the tube. The windage scale was adjustable in minutes of angle and was graduated from twenty minutes left, through zero, to 20 minutes right. One click was equal to 1 inch per 100 yards range. A total movement of 100 minutes (two and a half turns of the dial) was available to permit the sight to be calibrated to correct for any mount misalignment.

Use of the M84 scope necessitated accurate estimation of target range and required the sniper to either hold over the target or adjust the elevating mechanism on the sight to the estimated range. Although the M84 was intended primarily for the M1C and M1D, it was authorized for use with M1903A4 sniping rifles as well.

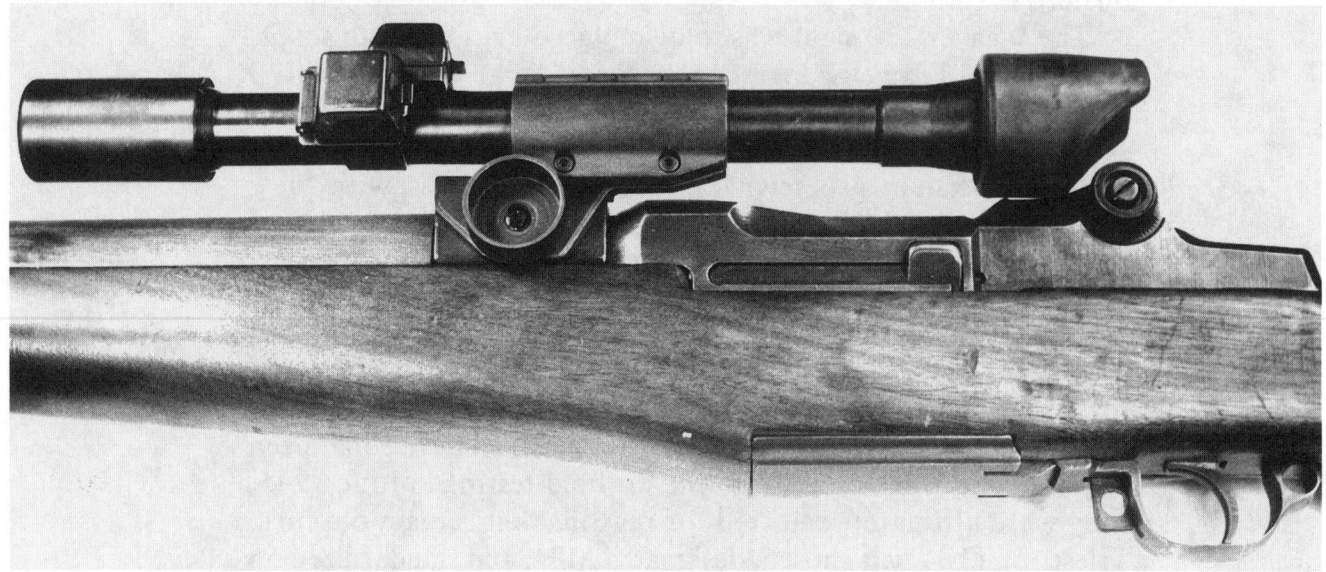

An original M1D sniper rifle with the 2.2-power M84 telescopic sight. As Ordnance records indicate, M1Ds were assembled (rebuilt or converted M1 rifles) at various arsenals and depots on an "as needed basis" by both the Army and the Marine Corps. A USMC museum piece in this case, the Springfield Armory rifle (serial no. 282929) was fitted with an "SA 1-53" M1D barrel, M2 flash hider, T4 leather cheek pad (MRT 2-52), and M84 telescopic sight (no. 10002). A number of M1 sniper rifles were known to have been assembled at the larger USMC base depots through the years. The conversion of a standard M1 to a sniping rifle was readily accomplished by any competent armorer. When earmarked for sniper use, the weapons were chosen with no regard for their origins. The M1D in particular was based on M1 rifles manufactured by Springfield Armory, Winchester, Harrington & Richardson, and, to a lesser extent, those made by International Harvester. M1C and M1D sniper rifles assembled by Marine Corps armorers were often referenced as "depot Garands." (Peter R. Senich.)

The M84 was designed to replace M81 and M82 telescopes as they became unserviceable, but the proximity of its standardization with the end of the war found only a handful produced for testing and evaluation. The M84 was not available in quantity until the Korean War when Libby-Owens-Ford (L.O.F.) became the prime contractor.

In final production form, the scope was finished in black oxide and issued with a web carrying case. The overall length with rubber eyepiece and extended sunshade was 13.188 inches, with a tube diameter of .870 inch. An identification plate, attached to the right side of the sight, bore the designation:

Telescope
M84
Serial No. 34502

Even though commercial telescopic sight development would attain a highly sophisticated level in the years following the Korean War, the M84 sight was to remain as the principal sniper telescope for both the Army and Marine Corps until the early 1960s, when U.S. military involvement in Southeast Asia emphasized the upgrading of existing sniper equipment. Nevertheless, with a total of "well over forty-thousand" M84 telescopic sights manufactured before production finally ended, and with the U.S. policy of "surplus disposal" such as it is, the 2.2-power scope will undoubtedly remain "in service" someplace on this globe for years to come.

In order to compensate for the offset position of the telescope on the M1 rifle, it was necessary either to make special stocks for the sniping variants, modify regular issue stocks, or develop an adaptor that would permit the sniper to see through the telescope and still keep his face supported by the stock. The final solution: the T4 cheek pad consisting of a leather cover with a pocket containing three removable felt inserts. This enabled the sniper to adjust the thickness of the cheek pad to suit himself. The pad was laced to the left side of the stock to bring the right eye in line with the telescope.

Since some sniping was expected during periods of semidarkness (dawn-dusk), a funnel-shaped flash hider was provided. The flash hider (M2) was fastened to the muzzle of the rifle by means of a bracket similar to that used with the M7 Grenade Launcher, utilizing the bayonet stud as a point of anchorage. Ordnance studies indicated that this device would eliminate approximately 90 percent of muzzle flash at 100 yards, but it did not reduce the smoke emitted from the barrel and, in fact, could reduce accuracy due to its relatively loose fit and method of attachment.

According to Springfield Armory records dated 23 May 1945:

> Tests are in progress for determining the effect of loose and tight flashhiders on the accuracy of U.S. Rifles, Caliber .30, M1C. Test results thus available show the accuracy of the M1C tends to fall off with the increase in longitudinal play between the hider and the rifle. As further noted, eccentricity in the mounting of the flash hider, due not only to looseness but to the lack of symmetry of the cone or mounting bearing, may have an adverse effect on accuracy.

Further experiments conducted some years later found the M2 design to be definitely inferior. As it was then stated:

> For best suppression of flash, the compression wave of powder gas which follows the bullet out of the muzzle must be "broken-up." A group of rods extending in front of the muzzle was found most efficient in diffusing the hot gases. Vertical and horizontal rod groupings have been tried, but the most efficient results were obtained with the horizontal pattern.

This resulted in the adoption of the "prong-type" T-37 flash hider following the Korean War (1958). The T-34 device replaced the M1 gas cylinder lock and became an integral part of the gas cylinder assembly. If the rifle was zeroed with the flash hider, its removal and replacement with a conventional gas cylinder lock could cause a change in zero. It was recommended that the flash hider be left on the sniper rifle and kept tight at all times. The T-37 device was not manufactured or issued in quantity.

Apart from the accuracy problems directly attributed to the early M2 "funnel" or "cone-type" flash hider, an inordinate amount of M1C production failed to meet accuracy requirements through the early months of 1945 (M1C acceptance levels over weekly periods were approximately 40 percent, and approximately 20 percent on reworked rifles).

Springfield Armory came under fire from the Office of the Chief of Ordnance (Washington) for various reasons, including what was deemed to be "inadequate targeting practices and the questionable selection of components used in producing and assembly of the M1C Sniper's Rifle."

As further stated:

> The office fully appreciates not only the desirability but also the necessity of selecting not only components with preferable dimensions within the drawings, but eliminating from possible assembly into M1C Rifles all components that are not within drawing dimensions. This weapon should represent the best artisan skill of the Armory and it must live up to all the expectations of the soldier receiving it. In the case of the flash hider as well as the other components, it may be necessary to use selective assembly in order to obtain the high quality weapon required and this procedure should be followed when necessary.

In retrospect, if there was any question regarding the importance of the M1C at the official level, this statement by the Chief of Ordnance certainly removed any doubts. The Ordnance Department was obviously committed to fielding the best sniper equipment possible.

Though expected to perform a specialized task, at that point, the M1C was being assembled with no more care than was used for a standard M1 rifle. According to Ordnance Department records:

> There had been no selection of parts for the M1C Rifle. When they were assembled, the assembling of the barrel, receiver and headspacing were done on the standard production line. The rest of the assembly for the Sniper's Rifle was performed by their best men on day rate, not piece work, and these assemblers selected or fitted stocks to give the desired fit on the receiver, and hand guards were selected or fitted to eliminate bending of the barrel. In addition to this, trigger and sear components were selected or fitted to provide a trigger pull not to exceed 6 1/2 lbs. In all other instances, M1C Rifle components are identical with the production M1.

As a matter of interest, in addition to the mechanical work necessary to assemble the rifle, the receiver base, mounts, and telescopic sights were fitted and the work inspected at predetermined intervals.

According to Springfield Armory records cited by Scott A. Duff in the "Garand Collectors Association Newsletter" (Vol. 3, No. 1):

> The scope mounting system adopted for use on the M1C was of a two piece design with one part attached to the rifle's receiver [base] and one part attached to the scope [mount]. Several mounting systems had been designed but, interestingly, the mount adopted was not the one proposed by Springfield Armory.
>
> The method of assembling the mount to the receiver involved sending the unheat-treated receiver to the Griffin & Howe Company in New York for installation of the mount [base]. The receiver/mount assembly was then returned to

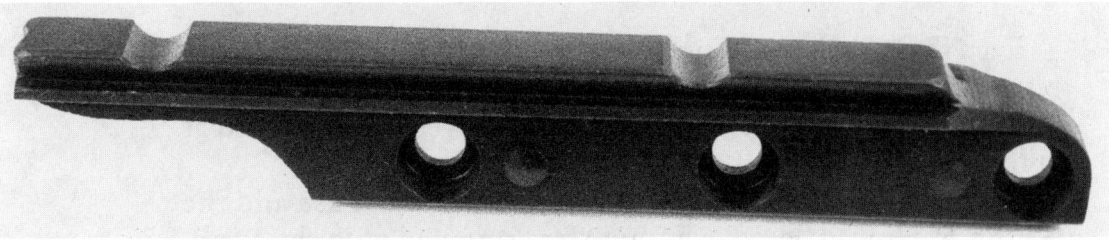

The M1C dovetail receiver base was part of the telescope mount assembly furnished by Griffin & Howe. The two base alignment pins were not a part of the original design proposal; these were added when M1C pilot production began in late 1944. The rifle serial number was stamped on the left side or directly beneath the base (narrow flat) when the rifle was assembled. A part of the original specifications, the telescope mount and base numbering matched the rifle serial number when the weapon left Springfield Armory during World War II. (Peter R. Senich.)

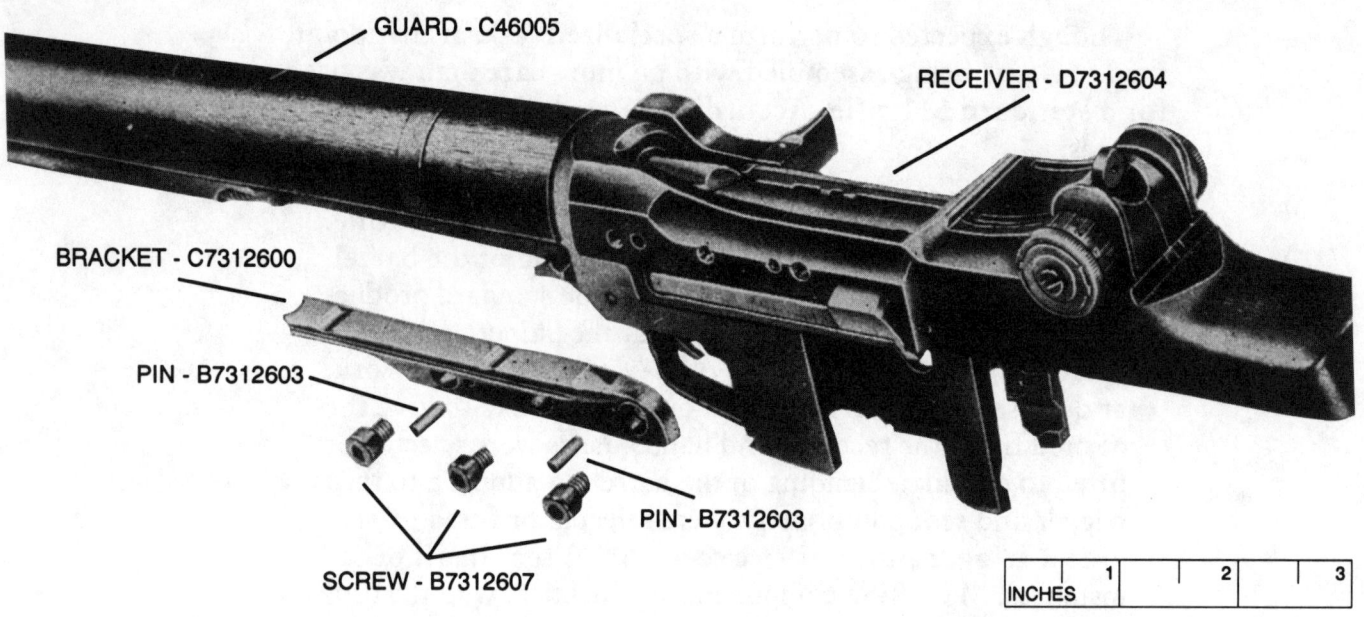

An excerpt from a 1945 Army Technical Manual illustrates the base, screws, pins, and receiver mounting area of the typical M1C sniping rifle. (U.S. Army.)

the Armory for heat treating. . . . Several factors which contributed to decreased accuracy of the M1C were discovered as the result of much research and experimentation. One of the problems discovered was in heat-treating the receiver and mount as one unit. This procedure was changed. The new method involved removing the mount from the receiver upon return from Griffin & Howe and heat-treating them separately. The parts were then reassembled.

The final targeting procedure involving use of either the M81 or M82 Telescope was stated, in part, as follows:

> Rifles that shoot an acceptable group then have the index plates for windage and elevation zeroed and the number of clicks available for extreme adjustments of windage and elevation then checked for compliance with requirements.

Even though telescopic sights, receiver bases, and mount assemblies for the M1C were manufacturer-inspected and Ordnance-accepted at their source, these components were also checked at Springfield Armory prior to use.

When originally fabricated, both the receiver base and the Griffin & Howe telescope mount were stamped with the corresponding rifle serial number. Telescopes, however, were not numbered to the rifle (stamped or etched), but were instead hand numbered with white paint on the underside of the tube using the last four digits of the rifle serial number.

By design, when the weapon was accepted following satisfactory targeting, the M1C Sniper's Rifle represented a complete package.

AO
-4-als

PROCESS SHEET
MCEB TEST REPORT - PROJECT # 395   11 August, 1945
                                     2 August, 1945

From: G-4 (Ordnance)
To: Chief of the G-4 Section

Subject: Rifle (Sniper's), M1C.

References: (a) Ltr CMC, Ser MC-408084, to Pres, MCEB, dtd 19Feb45.
(b) Ltr Pres, MCEB, Ser 000747, to CMC, dtd 3Aug45.
(c) Ltr CMC, File 1540-60, to QMG, dtd 10Aug45.

I. TEST INITIATED BY AND REASON FOR:

Test initiated by G-4 (Ordnance) in order to determine the suitability of the M1C Rifle for Marine Corps use.

II: RESUME AND CONSIDERATIONS OF CONCLUSIONS OF EQUIPMENT BOARD

The accuracy of the M1C Rifle when aimed with the M81 Telescopic Sight is approximately the same at all ranges as that of the same rifle when aimed with the standard iron sight when the target is plainly visible; however, the accuracy of the M81 Telescopic Sight is superior at all ranges when aimed at indistinct targets. The M81 Telescopic Sight is superior when fired in poor or failing light. The M81 Telescopic Sight is inferior to the standard iron sight when fired during a rain. The mechanical elevation and deflection adjustment mechanism in the M81 Telescopic Sight is reliable. The durability of the M1C Rifle with M81 Telesopic Sight is satisfactory.

G-4 (Ordnance) concurs with the Marine Corps Equipment Board's conclusions.

III: ACTION TAKEN:

Reference (c) authorized the issue of M1903A1 Rifles (Sniper) w/Telescope, Sighting, Unertl, 8X, on a basis of 108 per Marine Division and directed that the Commandant be notified when present stocks of this Sniper Rifle are depleted in order that another rifle could be authorized. It is expected that the M1C Rifle will be authorized.

Copy of test report forwarded to Office, Chief of Ordnance, War Department.

H. V. HIETT.

Process Sheet, Marine Corps Equipment Board (MCEB) Test Report, Project No. 395, Rifle (Sniper's) M1C (11 August 1945). (U.S. Marine Corps.)

Describing this package, Scott A. Duff related:

> Another interesting facet of M1C production was the method employed to package the completed rifle/scope combination. As a result of the scope being serial numbered to the rifle upon which it had been targeted, it was considered crucial that the scope be kept with that rifle.
>
> The Armory report from the first half of 1945 indicated that the matching serial number scope and mount, a sling, flash hider, and grenade launcher were packed with each rifle. The stock and receiver group were separated and each was placed in a standard rifle bag. Each of the accessories was wrapped separately and all of the aforementioned were placed in a carton. Five such cartons were placed in a wooden crate, three on edge and two on their sides.

Whereas Springfield Armory attributed its problems to a variety of sources, including the flash hider, mount, telescope, ammunition and, admittedly, to existing targeting facilities and procedures, in response to the Chief of Ordnance, the Commanding General of Springfield Armory replied (21 May 1945):

> Certain unsatisfactory conditions of the M1C Rifle have been successfully corrected; redesign of certain features of the M1E7 mount has eliminated for the most part its loosening under firing, and a change in design of the trigger has brought the trigger pull within specifications. The problem of its inaccuracy, however, still remains, and although much has been investigated, no final solution has been reached.
>
> Certain observations relative to the accuracy of the M1C Rifle have been made which may be of interest to your office:
>
> a. Many rifles are rejected for one flyer in a five shot group and upon the firing of a sixth shot, it has been found that in more than 60 percent of the cases that shot will fall with the four good shots and be well within a 2 1/2 inch group.
>
> b. The effect of the flash hider on the M1C Rifle definitely tends to increase inaccuracy.
>
> c. M1C rifles compared as a group to M1 rifles are not as accurate and it is only by selection and reworking that M1C rifles can approach the specified accuracy.
>
> d. Partial investigation on standard and special bullet seats has indicated that the relationship of present quality of ammunition used for targeting to standard

bullet seat is an important factor influencing accuracy. Ammunition has been gaged and found to be quite irregular, sometimes failing even to pass the acceptance gage. Present bullet seats, however, will receive this questionable ammunition without exerting any correction upon it.

e. Tests conducted on some specially made barrels have indicated that by a change in diameter and location of the present bullet seat, accuracy may be improved. However, this will further change the M1C from the standard M1.

To date, investigation of the problem has caused the Armory to believe that the combination of design of mount and design of rifle is such that a consistent conformance to specification will not be obtainable even though manufacture is changed to come within closer tolerance than now allowed.

It is the opinion of the Armory that two changes may now be made to increase the acceptance of M1C rifles. One is permission to fire a sixth shot when one of five is not within the group and the other is the change in requirement from a 2 1/2 inch group to a 3 inch group, which is the accuracy specified for the standard M1. (It may be noted that the accuracy requirement for the M1903A4 Sniper's was not changed from that of the M1903A3—a 3 inch group). However, these two changes, although increasing the output of acceptable M1C rifles, will in no way improve the quality of this weapon.

Only by using the M1E8 mount (M1D Sniper's) can a Sniper's weapon with a standard range of M1 components be produced that has better than average accuracy. This type of mount permits the selection from standard production of especially accurate weapons for conversion to Sniper's rifles. Because of this, the Armory is expediting manufacturing and development program number 35.

Based on these conclusions, the Ordnance Department made the following recommendations to Springfield Armory (1 June 1945):

The M1C Rifle as presently manufactured and accepted at Springfield Armory apparently will not meet the accuracy requirements of specifications.

The need for reference rifles assembled from components known to be within the drawings and specifications is very great.

There is a great need for checking each M1 and M1C Rifle, by actual firing, before acceptance to make sure that no rifles can leave the Armory of the type fired on the open range and referred to in this report.

The Armory's firing ranges for targeting and accuracy are inadequate and should be supplemented by outside range facilities. The design of the Armory's machine rest can be improved.

It is hereby recommended that each M1 rifle at the Armory be accepted only after the targeting and accuracy requirements of the specifications have been met and tested by actual firing.

That each Sniper's Rifle be tested for targeting and accuracy by firing and that a final test be made using the telescope sight and that this target be packed with each rifle.

That all accuracy and target firing be done outdoors until such time as the Armory can provide itself with adequate facilities.

That instructions covering specifications, drawings, particularly engineering changes and manufacturing, inspection procedure for the M1 and M1C Rifles be furnished the Armory so as to obtain uniformity and gain close coordination of this work. Such letters of instruction have now been furnished the Armory.

That immediate steps be taken to provide adequate and efficient targeting and accuracy ranges at the Armory for rifle and other needed work.

That steps be taken to provide and maintain standard reference rifles and ammunition so that reference standards can serve to eliminate unknown factors.

That steps be taken to improve the targeting equipment now available at the Armory, particularly the machine rest and lighting installations.

That targeting and accuracy requirements of specifications be met at the earliest possible date. (Instructions to the Armory have been issued.)

That a liberal sampling of those M1C Rifles in Field Service stock at the Armory should be checked by firing on an adequate range to determine whether it will be necessary to recheck and rework the entire quantity for compliance with specification requirements. Immediate action should be taken in this recheck so as to keep to a minimum the quantity of M1C Rifles shipped from Springfield Armory for Field Service stocks until the rifles are of known satisfactory quality.

In view of the problems with the M1C at Springfield Armory during the early months of 1945, it is understandable why so few M1 sniping rifles reached the front lines before the war ended.

Reviewing the situation then at hand, it is important to note that both the Office of the Chief of Ordnance and Springfield Armory shared the same viewpoint regarding the desirability of the then emerging M1D (M1E8) over the M1C.

According to the Chief of Ordnance:

In lieu of the accuracy problems with the M1C, it was hoped that the M1D mount, when developed, will enable the Armory to select an accurately shooting rifle from normal production and then attach the scope.

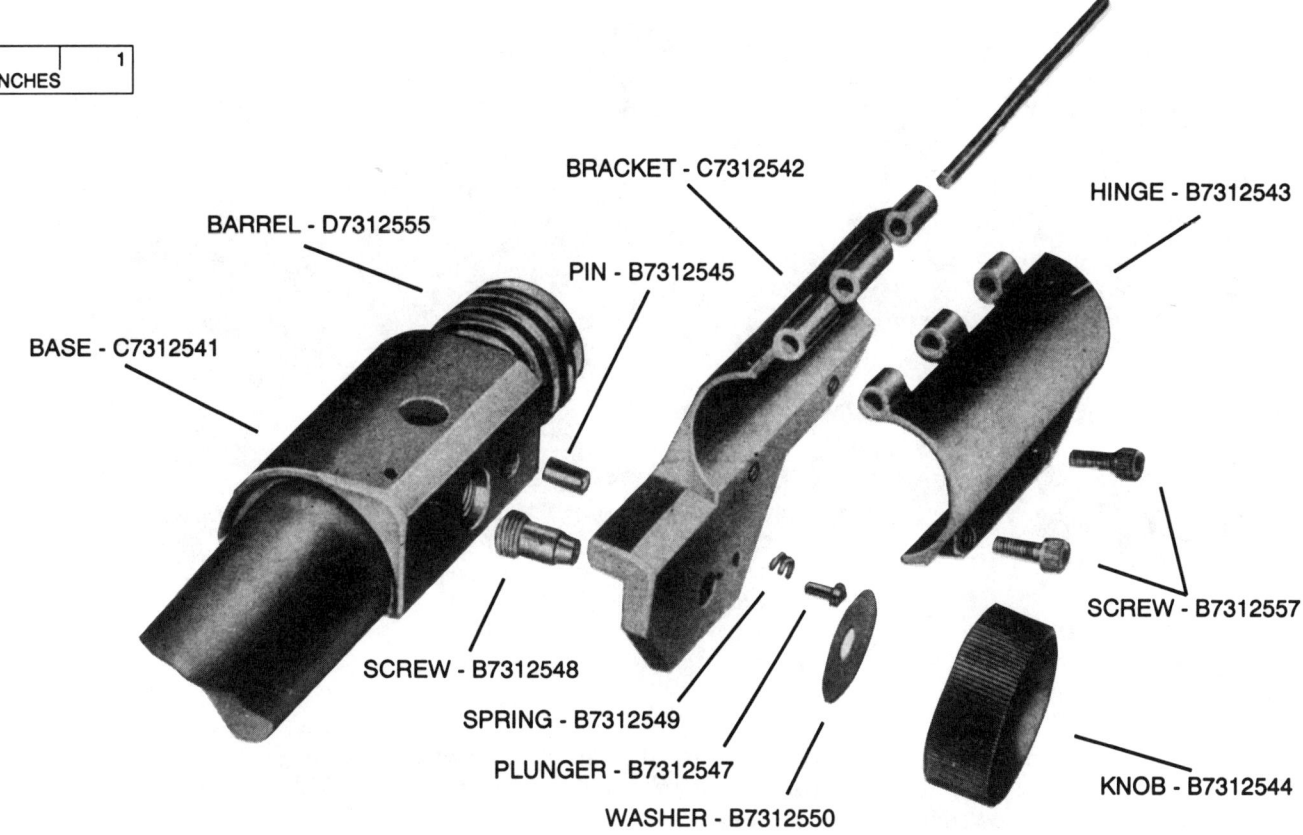

Army technical manual illustration with the principal components of the M1D sniper system. The telescope mounting block required use of a shortened handguard. (U.S. Army.)

Though difficult to determine beyond all question, experts believe somewhat less than 8,000 M1C rifles were fabricated at Springfield Armory before production ended. According to "official" government production figures dating from World War II, however, a total of "6,896 M1 sniping rifles" was manufactured at Springfield Armory from late 1944 through August 1945.

Considering the development status of the M1D in mid-1945, this total is thought to represent the M1C in entirety, inasmuch as available records indicate only a few M1Ds were produced for testing purposes during this period.

Even though an unspecified number of M1Cs were apparently manufactured after the war was officially ended, so far as it is known, M1C sniper rifle production had been terminated by mid-1946.

While it appears that all M1 sniper rifle production during World War II took place at Springfield Armory, evidence strongly suggests that had the war lasted longer, Winchester Repeating

Arms (W.R.A.) would have been involved with M1 sniper rifle production as well. Beyond developmental work (prototype receivers), however, the extent of Winchester participation in the semiautomatic sniper rifle program remains unconfirmed.

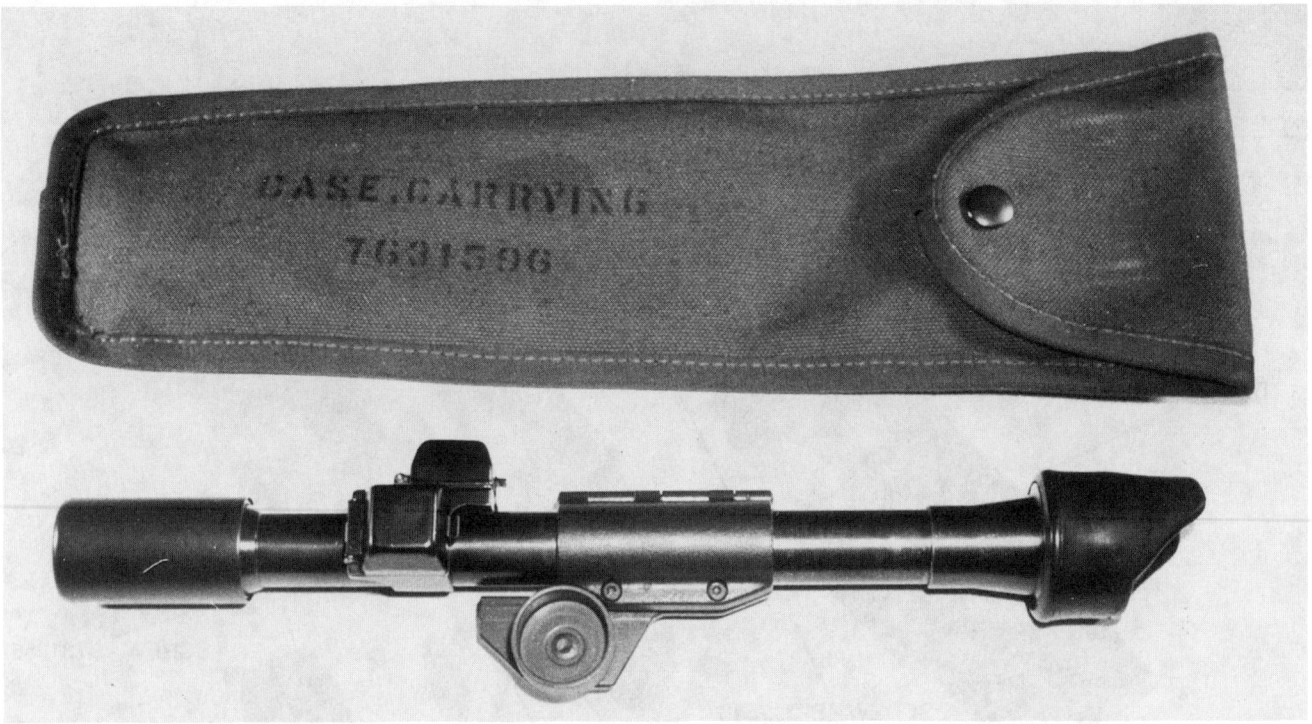

Korean War M84 telescope and M1D mounting with an issue carrying case. The ordnance drawing number for the M84 case was listed as "D7631596" in various technical manuals. The telescope carrying case for the M1 sniper rifle was referenced as a "Small Arms Item." (Peter R. Senich.)

Precious few M1C rifles reached the front lines by war's end, particularly in the European theater, where the M1C was heard of but never encountered. Even though the war lasted an additional three months in the Pacific, the scarcity of the M1C prevailed there as well.

Roy F. Dunlap, commenting on this in *Ordnance Went Up Front*, stated:

> They were beautiful outfits and I would have given anything to have one during the war, but they arrived in the Philippines just before the Japanese surrendered. The rifles were selected, the best-finished and tightest M1s I ever saw, and of course sights and rifle came together as a unit.

Consequently, little opportunity existed to judge the combat effectiveness of the M1 sniping system until it was reissued for the Korean War.

Drawing attention to the importance of providing snipers with rugged equipment, Roy Dunlap further related:

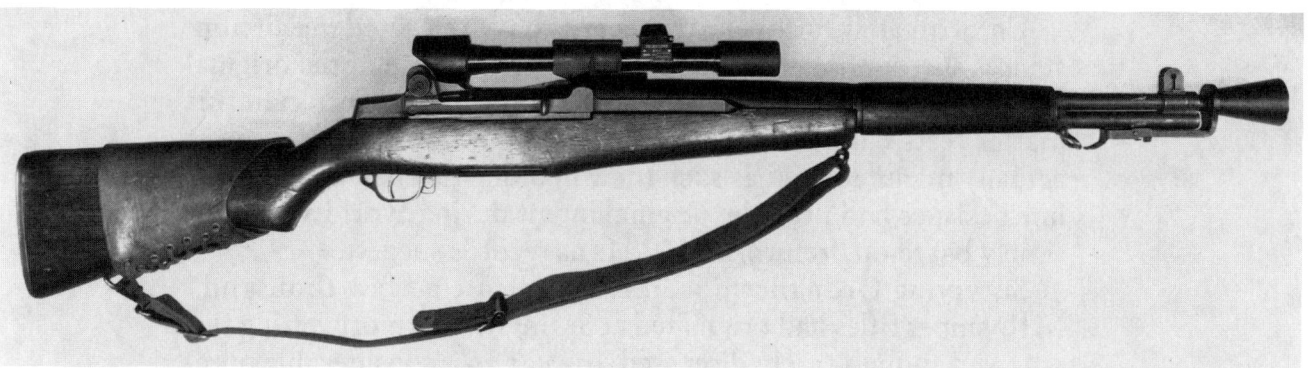

Springfield Armory M1D sniper rifle, serial no. 3602284, with an "SA 3-53" M1D barrel and early-manufacture M84 telescopic sight (no. 5618). An "original issue" sniper rifle, the M1D is part of the West Point Museum collection. Although M1D sniper rifles are considered fairly common, authentic, original rifles with documented military origins are not. (West Point Collection.)

Only a man who has been in war can appreciate the rough treatment a rifle must undergo and still be serviceable. While the sniper arm will no doubt in most cases be treated as gently as possible, the rain won't stop when it is in the field, and the sniper must use the same transportation hither and yon as any other soldier. If you've ever ridden around front areas in jeeps, half-tracks, and GMC trucks, in the dark, almost to the front line, you know how difficult it is to keep your face from getting dented in, let alone a three and a half foot rifle.

Although the M1C was to remain as a principal sniping arm for American combat forces during the Korean War, efforts to field additional sniper equipment included Springfield Armory's manufacture of "D" barrels and the subsequent assembly of M1D sniper rifles from about mid-1951 until the end of hostilities in Korea in July 1953.

Unfortunately, inconclusive records have relegated the circumstances surrounding the manufacture and issuance of the original Springfield M1Ds to obscurity. The point of contention in this matter rests with whether the Korean War-era M1Ds were ever actually manufactured as such (new manufacture) on an assembly line basis, as had been the original intent during World War II, or simply based on "refurbished" M1s as records suggest.

Surviving Ordnance documents indicate a "few thousand" M1D sniper rifles had originated at Springfield Armory during this era. And though rarely discussed, insofar as a considerable number of M1 rifles were also rebuilt at Rock Island Arsenal, a major ordnance facility, during the Korean War, the level of Rock Island involvement with M1D assembly, as some experts contend, remains subject to speculation.

In any case, however, drawing from information provided by M1 Garand authority Scott A. Duff in his work, *The M1 Garand: Post World War II*, a total of 21,380 M1D and 4,796 M1C sniper rifles were "rebuilt" by the Maintenance Branch at Springfield Armory between 1 July 1951 and 30 June 1953. Of further interest at this point, Duff related the following:

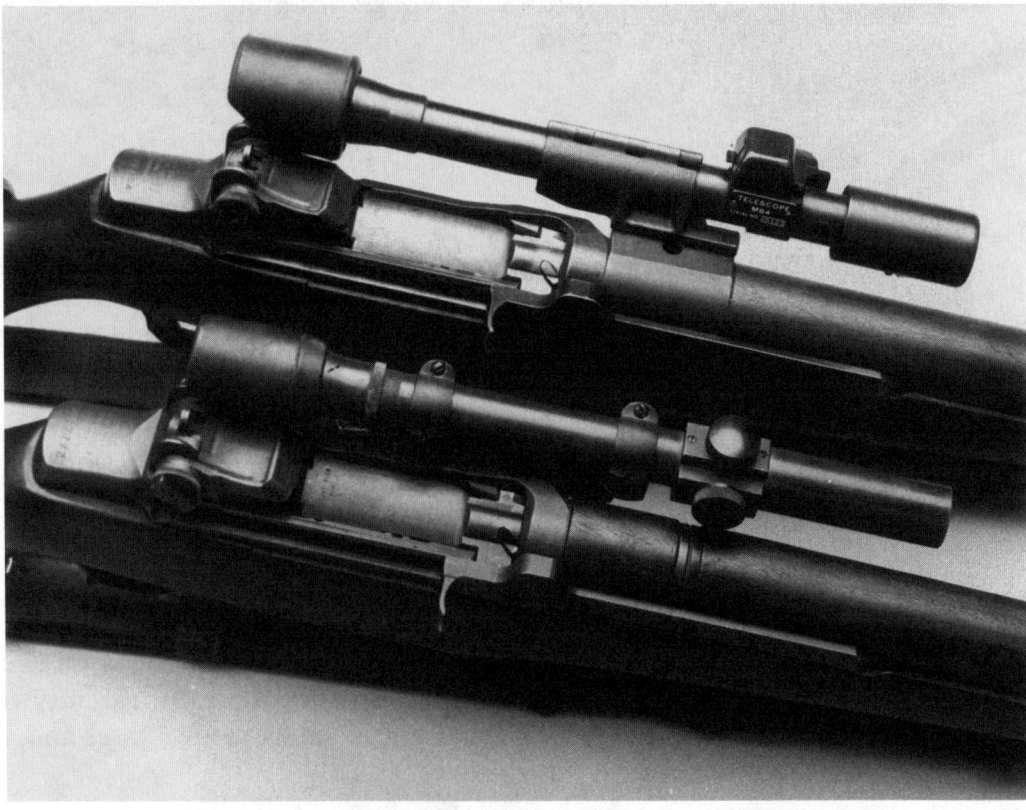

A comparison of the offset telescope mounting of an M84 telescopic sight fitted to an M1D (top) and an M82 sight with a Griffin & Howe mount on an M1C. Despite the difference in telescope mounting, the sights were in the same relative position on the rifle. An original design requirement, the mounts were positioned to permit clip loading of the rifle with the scopes in place. (Canfield Collection.)

Many other additional items of interest took place during this period, some of which have been little known to date. The Armory records indicate that the Manufacturing Development Section began salvaging 4,000 M1C receivers by plugging the scope mounting holes. This activity began in November 1952, and by 31

Although semiautomatic sniping rifles proved to be more than satisfactory in Korea, combat sniping reports indicated the maximum effective range as 600 yards. Despite ranging limitations attributed to the 2.5-power telescopic sights, the M1 sniper rifles performed as well as could be expected. (U.S. Marine Corps.)

December 1952 it was reported that approximately 1,500 M1C receivers had been plugged.

Whether this represented the culminative total of M1C receivers rejected in times past for one reason or another—including manufacturing defects—is not known. However, if the figure 4,000 represented M1C sniper rifles previously accepted as believed, though speculative perhaps, this may account for the abundance of original Springfield Armory-marked (rifle serial numbers) M1C receiver bases and scope mounts available on the surplus market some years ago. Unfortunately, many of these same components were subsequently used to produce M1C rifles for the collector's market long after the last authentic M1C sniper rifle left Springfield Armory.

In retrospect, although a rather large number were apparently assembled and readily available for combat purposes, the M1D was to serve only as a supplement and did not see extensive issue or use during the Korean War. At the time M1 rifles were superseded by the M14 some years later, the M1D was again officially classified as a "Substitute Standard."

Though difficult to manufacture, the M1C scope-mounting was decidedly superior to the "single-point" M1D mount. Problems with the Griffin & Howe mounting centered on burrs or nicking of the male dovetail (receiver base) when the scope was removed. If this occurred, it became virtually impossible to slide the mount onto the base until the upset metal was removed with a fine grain stone or file. On the other hand, excessive tightening of the M1D mount frequently resulted in stripped threads. These were not insurmountable problems, however, since from all indications, snipers chose to leave their telescopes in place on the rifle more often than not.

Although M1 sniping variants were favored by Army and Marine Corps snipers over the "bolt-action rifles" in Korea, the length, weight, and thickness of the M1C and M1D made an awkward package for a sniper who was expected to do a lot of crawling or climbing during his work day. Complete with telescope, mount, sling, cheek pad, and flash hider, the rifle weighed a good 12 pounds, and the overall length, with flash hider attached, ran a shade over 46 inches. The thickness of the M1 receiver made it difficult to carry in one hand, particularly in heavy brush or rough country. If any rifle required a sling, it was certainly the M1 in sniping configuration.

As it had during the war years, the M1 again proved reliable even through the bitter, sub-zero Korean winters. Functioning was rarely a problem, provided that lubricating oil was used sparingly.

Winter sniping activity taxed even the most proficient marksmen when accurate shooting became no small task. The necessity of "getting off a quick shot" was further emphasized during periods of extreme cold. It was nearly impossible for a sniper to maintain a long period of observation to detect a target with a cold gunstock pulling the heat from his cheek as it rested on the stock. Efforts to overcome this included covering the leather cheek pad with G.I. socks to prevent the face from literally freezing to the pad.

Although M1 sniping variants proved to be more than satisfactory, combat sniping reports from Korea indicated the maximum effective range as 600 yards, with rather consistent results between 400 to 600 yards.

In deference to the M1, limitations of the telescopic sights and ammunition used with this system did little to increase the chance of long-range hits. While adequate at short to medium ranges, the resolving power of the issue telescopes made long-range target definition extremely difficult.

At this juncture, special or match grade ammunition was not available or even considered for sniping purposes. USMC snipers drew regular .30-caliber ball ammunition that showed up fairly well at shorter ranges, but was not reliable at 500 and 600 yards. When obtainable, .30-caliber armor-piercing ammunition was employed since its heavier bullet provided increased stability over longer ranges.

RESTRICTED
MC-521362　　　　　　　　　　　　　　　　　　　AUG 1 6 1945

From: Commandant of the Marine Corps.
To: The Commanding General, Department of the Pacific.

Subject: Rifle M1, scope mounted.

Reference: (a) Conf 1st end DofP Ser. 045268, dtd 28Jun45 on ltr DQSF to CMC, dtd 26Jun45, w/7 enclosures.

　　1.　Reference (a) forwarded the test report of the Pachmayr telescope mount for use with the M1 Rifle and set forth pertinent comments concerning the mount.

　　2.　It is the general opinion of personnel of this Headquarters that the Pachmayr Mount is superior to the Griffin and Howe Mount which is used on the M1C Rifle. However, it is not deemed sufficiently superior to warrant its adoption since the M1C Sniper Rifle is presently available to the Marine Corps.

　　3.　The issue of the M1903A1 Rifle, with Telescope, Sighting, Unertl, 8X has been authorized on the basis of 108 per Marine Division. It is expected that the M1C Rifle will be adopted when present stocks of the M1903A1 Rifle are depleted.

　　4.　In view of the above, it is believed that further study of the Pachmayr Mount is not warranted. No further action will be taken by this Headquarters.

　　　　　　　　　　　　　　　　　　A. A. VANDEGRIFT

Official correspondence regarding the testing of the commercial Pachmayr Mount with the M1 rifle and the intent to issue the USMC M1903A1/Unertl on the basis of 108 per Marine Division (16 August 1945). The Marine Corps Commandant at that time, General Alexander A. Vandegrift, had commanded the 1st Marine Division during the campaign in the Solomon Islands. (U.S. Marine Corps.)

As a matter of interest, Marine Corps snipers had made extensive use of armor-piercing ammunition during World War II and continued to do so in Korea as well. According to various USMC marksmen then active, the M1903A1/Unertl system "really worked well" with the heavier bullet armor-piercing ammunition.

Equipped primarily with the Springfield 03A1/Unertl combination, Marine Corps snipers also employed a number of M1Cs originally intended for Army use. Even though the Marine Corps had thoroughly evaluated the M1C in 1945 and had recommended its adoption, the M1C had not been procured in any appreciable quantity.

Consequently, when the 1st Provisional Marine Brigade entered action in Korea on 7 August 1950, the M1 sniper rifle was not a viable part of the Marine Corps small-arms inventory.

Reviewing late World War II efforts, however, the Commandant of the Marine Corps had requested that the Marine Corps Equipment Board (MCEB) evaluate the sniping version of the M1 rifle "to determine the suitability of the M1C Rifle for Marine Corps use" (19 February 1945). Acting on this request, the test report generated by the MCEB on 2 August 1945 stated in part:

> The durability of the M81 Telescopic Sight and of the M1C Rifle as equipped with the M81 sight is satisfactory. It is expected that the M1C Rifle will be authorized.

Under the circumstances, however, with the war in the Pacific all but over by that time, the M1C sniper rifle was not formally adopted by the Marine Corps.

As a point of interest, in this case the MCEB test report had made specific mention of the rifles and sights used for its evaluations. A unique example, as it was then stated in the "general notes":

> The two rifles tested in this project are Rifle, U.S., Caliber .30, M1C (Sniper's), No. 3251852 with telescope serial No. 31586 which will be referred to in this report as Test Rifle No. 1, and Rifle, U.S., Caliber .30, M1C (Sniper's), No. 3309877, with telescope serial No. 31590, which will be referred to in this report as Test Rifle No. 2. Both rifles were new at the beginning of the test.

Concurrent with MCEB testing of the M1C at Quantico, while not clearly defined, a "Pachmayr telescope mount for use with the M1 Rifle" had also been evaluated by the Marine Corps in the final months of the war.

According to official correspondence dated 16 August 1945 between the Commandant of the Marine Corps and the Commanding General, Department of the Pacific:

> It is the general opinion of personnel at this Headquarters that the Pachmayr Mount is superior to the Griffin & Howe Mount which is used on the M1C Rifle. However, it is not deemed sufficiently superior to warrant its adoption, since the M1C Sniper Rifle is presently available to the Marine Corps.

A comparatively simple commercial design, the Pachmayr mount positioned the telescope over the bore but could be swung aside (rotated to the left) to permit clip loading of the M1 magazine. A similar design, the Pachmayr "Lo-Swing Mount," was tested and approved for Army sniper use with the M1 rifle in 1953.

When the first in a succession of what became known as "limited wars" brought American combat forces to the forefront of the world stage in mid-1950, a part of the harried efforts to blunt the North Korean invasion included activating a Marine brigade at Camp Pendleton, California, along with "makeshift" American advance units drawn from the Eighth Army's occupation forces in Japan.

From the onset, the mobilization of the 1st Provisional Marine Brigade (later absorbed by the 1st Marine Division) was beset by problems. Comprised of elements of Marine units serving in both the Atlantic and Pacific, as well as a large number of reservists, most of its equipment was of World War II vintage and had to be taken from depots throughout the United States and brought to a satisfactory state of combat readiness.

Whereas the Marine Corps had entered the Korean conflict with only "a token number of M1C sniping rifles," according to USMC ordnance personnel then active, the M1Cs originally fielded for scout-sniper use in Korea were drawn from Army inventory and shipped overseas. So far as it is known, however, the small arms allocated to the Marine Corps at this juncture were not marked in any unique manner as such, but rather, simply transferred from one equipment list to another.

During early Korean involvement, Marine Corps stocks of sniper rifles were being depleted. Before additional procurement was undertaken, it was considered desirable to examine existing sniper materiel to ascertain whether a more suitable sniper rifle was available or should be developed.

As a result, on 9 February 1951, the Commandant (Headquarters) directed the Marine Corps Equipment Board to establish a project to examine and evaluate both military and commercial sniper materiel to determine which would meet Marine Corps requirements. Efforts to arrive at a satisfactory conclusion involved a series of exhaustive studies conducted through the balance of 1951. Based on its "Study of Sniper's Rifles, Telescopes and Mounts," it was the opinion of the Board that:

(1) The U.S. Rifle, Caliber .30 M1C with the Griffin & Howe mount (fixed receiver base), is suitable for interim and long term Marine Corps use as a sniper's rifle.

(2) The Stith (Bear Cub) 2 3/4X Telescope is suitable for interim Marine Corps use after modification of the range and windage adjustment to include click adjustments.

(3) The Griffin & Howe removable mount as issued with the U.S. Rifle, Caliber .30, M1C is suitable for interim Marine Corps use after modification of the telescope holding bracket to accept the Stith (Bear Cub) Telescope.

(4) There is no requirement for the development of a sniper's rifle to meet long term Marine Corps requirements.

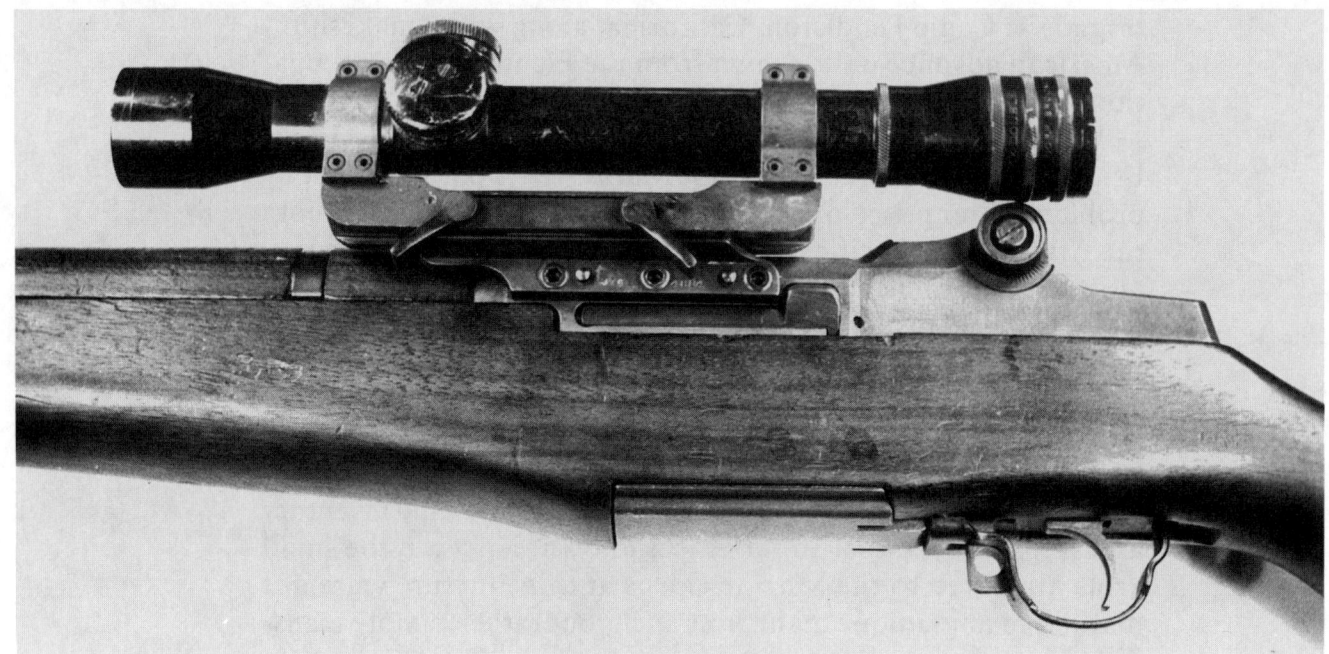

A close-up view of a USMC M1C sniper rifle with a 4-power Kollmorgen 4XD telescope (MC 750-P) and Griffin & Howe mounting. Rifle no. 3718018, 6-52 barrel date, is part of the Marine Corps small-arms collection. The receiver base number (3764884) does not match the rifle. The vast majority of M1C rifles rebuilt for USMC use during the Korean War have Springfield Armory barrels dated 1951, 1952, or 1953. Most of the Marine Corps M1C rifles were sold as "excess property" (surplus) some years ago. (Peter R. Senich.)

An original factory carton for the USMC Stith-Kollmorgen Model 4XD telescopic sight. An excellent rifle scope adopted by the Marine Corps "between wars," the Kollmorgen sight is considered to have been one of the best telescopic sights the Marine Corps ever fielded. (Douglas Collection.)

(5) There is a requirement for development of a telescope to meet long term Marine Corps requirements.

(6) It is recommended that the U.S. Rifle, Caliber .30, M1C as outlined, be standardized in the Marine Corps for interim use.

Of all the military and commercial telescopes evaluated, the MCEB considered the Stith "Bear Cub" as the most suitable at

Comparative view of the Griffin & Howe telescope mounts used with the Army M1C (left) and the USMC Kollmorgen 4XD scope. The levers on both mounts are in the unlocked position. The standard mount has 7/8-inch scope rings; the larger rings are 1 inch. (Peter R. Senich.)

that point. However, as cited by point five of the aforementioned, the sight was to be modified to conform to Marine Corps requirements. Therefore, in 1952, the Stith Company, in conjunction with the Kollmorgen Optical Corp. (the actual manufacturer of this sight), submitted a fixed-focus, 4-power telescope with audible click, range, and windage adjustments.

When accepted by the USMC on an experimental basis, the Stith-Kollmorgen Model 4XD was considered by most scope-wise men to be the "best" telescopic sight then available. This sight was not developed strictly for military use, however, as commercial variants were available for sporting purposes as well.

The USMC 4XD scope tube was produced from heavy Dural stock (aluminum alloy). Both elevation and windage assemblies were equipped with graduated scales with each graduation corresponding to a 1-inch shift of the line of sight at a range of 100 yards. The windage scale was stamped "L" and "R" to indicate left and right corrections. The elevation scale was stamped "UP" to indicate elevation correction. The adjustment dials were 1.125 inch in diameter and, in comparison to other military telescopes, adjustments were effected quite easily. The lenses, coated and ground, were clear and free of color right out to the edges and afforded excellent light-gathering power in subdued light.

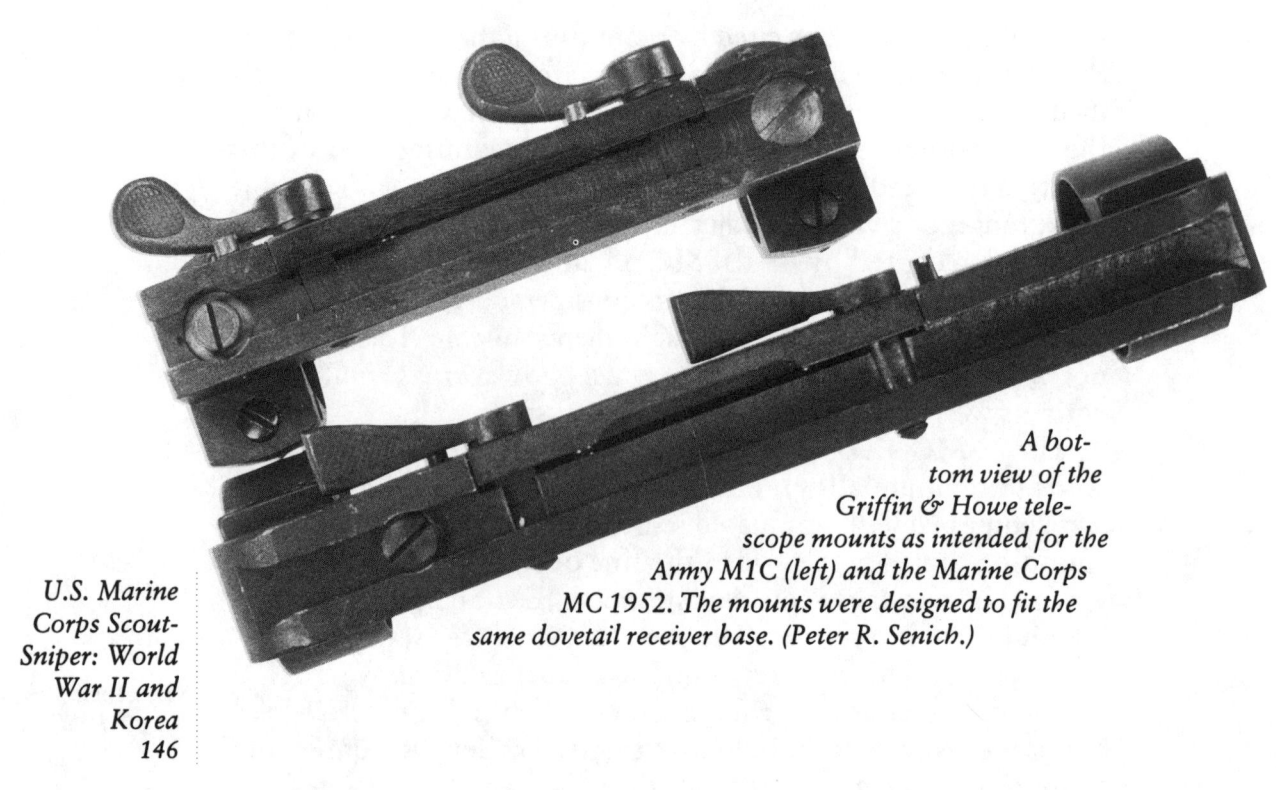

An M1C-equipped "Fifth Marine Regiment sniper somewhere in Korea" during August 1952. (U.S. Marine Corps.)

A bottom view of the Griffin & Howe telescope mounts as intended for the Army M1C (left) and the Marine Corps MC 1952. The mounts were designed to fit the same dovetail receiver base. (Peter R. Senich.)

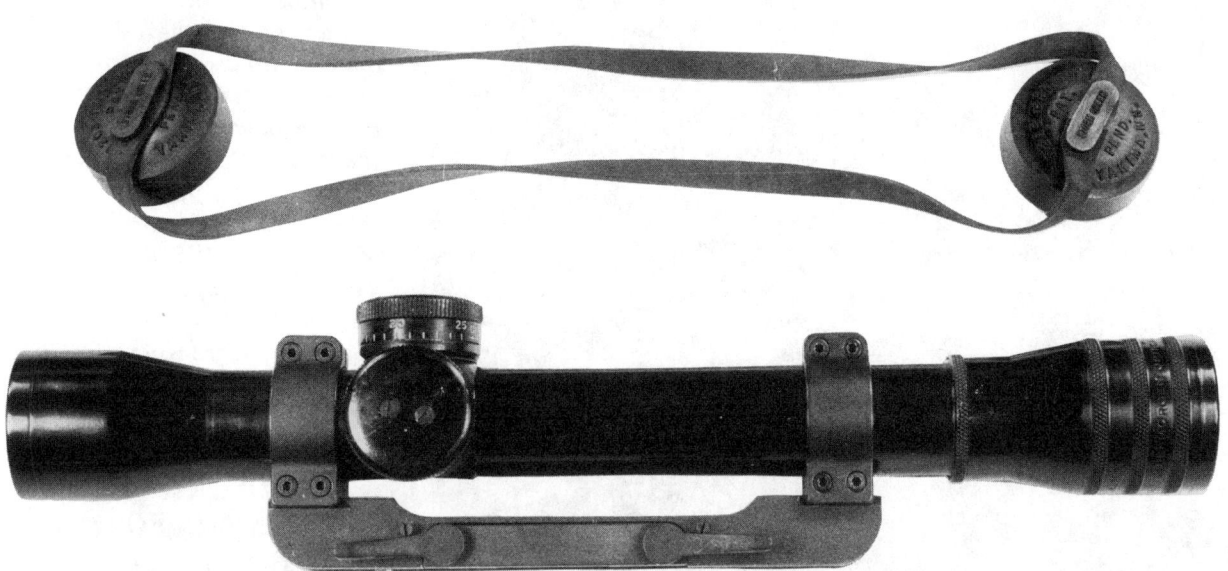

USMC Stith-Kollmorgen Model 4XD telescope, Griffin & Howe mounting, and issue Storm Queen molded rubber lens covers. The 4-power scope was slightly over 11 inches long with a main tube diameter of approximately 1 inch. The unusually large elevation and windage adjustment knobs (1 1/8-inch diameter) were designed to meet Marine Corps specifications. Kollmorgen 4XD rifle scopes were manufactured for the Marine Corps on a contract basis and bear appropriate markings. The acquisition of "unmarked" 4XD type sights with a black- or green-anodized finish has not been confirmed. (Peter R. Senich.)

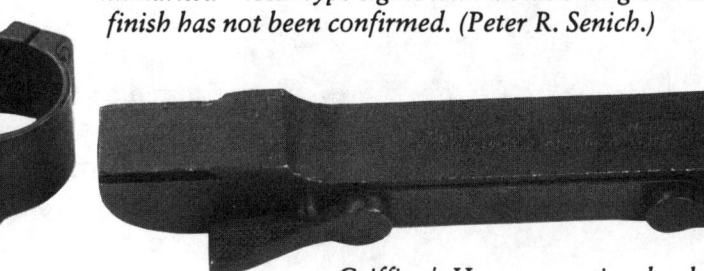

Griffin & Howe mounting developed for Marine Corps use with the M1C and Kollmorgen 4XD telescopic sight. Mount locking levers were furnished with both round and flat ends as illustrated. Allen-head screws were used to tighten the two-piece rings to the telescope and mount. A rugged assembly, the Griffin & Howe USMC telescope mount was considered an optimum design for the M1C. (Peter R. Senich.)

USMC Griffin & Howe mounting for the Stith-Kollmorgen Model 4XD telescope (top view). The Federal Stock Number (FSN 1240-647-1107) appears above the item identification (Mount Telescope) and manufacturer's legend. Note the locking-levers with rounded ends. (J.B. Anderhub.)

A Marine rifleman shown "scoping the area." With the rifle positioned as it is, the marksman was using the telescopic sight for observation purposes (2nd Battalion, 1st Marines, May 1952). The flak-vest (upper-torso body armor) became standard issue during the Korean War. (U.S. Marine Corps.)

Overall telescope length ran slightly over 11 inches, tube diameter 1.023 inch, and objective and ocular ends approximately 1.250 inch in diameter. Cross-hair reticles were furnished to the Marine Corps and eye-relief was cited as being 3 to 4 inches. Commercial "Storm-Queen" lens covers consisting of molded rubber cups connected by narrow stretch bands were issued for protective purposes. In addition to the manufacturer's legend, located on the ocular end of the telescope, there was the inscription:

Stith Mounts S.A., Tex.
4X Double
Kollmorgen Optical Corp. Brooklyn, N.Y.
Pat Pend.

A Marine Corps serial number appeared on the top or side of the tube: MC 750-P. Variations stamped "U.S." with a Federal Stock Number (FSN) have also been noted. Inasmuch as the telescope tube was made from aluminum, conventional metal finishing methods could not be employed. Therefore, an extremely durable finish ("black hard-coat") compatible with this material was used instead.

Griffin & Howe ultimately furnished the telescope mounting used with the Marine Corps M1C. The "double-lever" side mount made for

NOVEMBER 1959　　　　　　TM-OR-02407A-15

MARINE CORPS
TECHNICAL MANUAL
ORDNANCE

OPERATION AND MAINTENANCE,
FIRST THROUGH FIFTH ECHELON

FOR

TELESCOPE, RIFLE, 4xD,
MC-1

UNITED STATES MARINE CORPS

Marine Corps Technical manual (Ordnance) for the 4XD, 4-power telescope. The 54-page manual was used for field and depot maintenance of the Kollmorgen rifle telescope. (Cors Collection.)

the Stith-Kollmorgen sight was, in effect, a scaled-up version of that originally adopted for the Army's "C." Although it was designed to fit the standard M1C receiver base, the USMC mounting was substantially stronger and 5.125 inches in length, as compared to the 3.875-inch mount utilized with Army issue telescopes.

The original Griffin & Howe M1C mount had .875-inch rings secured to the slide (rail) by means of retaining screws running upward from inside the slide which engaged the lower half of the ring assembly. The USMC mount, on the other hand, had 1-inch "full-split" rings which attached to the slide by the lower portion of the ring being dovetailed (female) to correspond with a male dovetail located on top and at either end of the slide. Tightening eight allen-head screws (four on each ring) secured the scope within the rings, and, in turn, tightly clamped the rings to the slide.

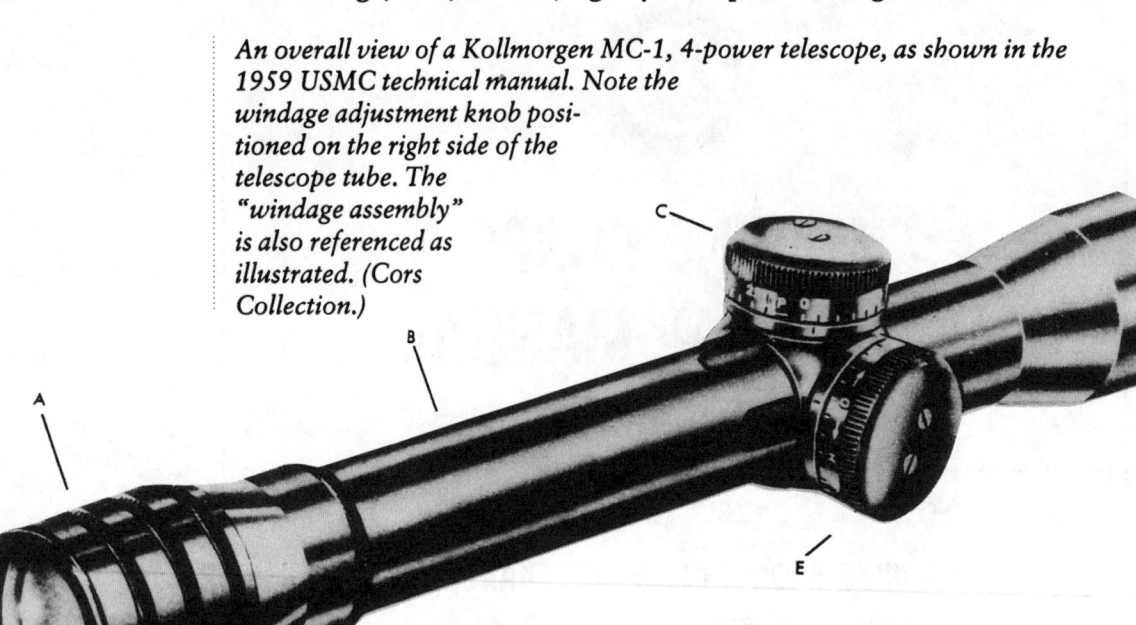

An overall view of a Kollmorgen MC-1, 4-power telescope, as shown in the 1959 USMC technical manual. Note the windage adjustment knob positioned on the right side of the telescope tube. The "windage assembly" is also referenced as illustrated. (Cors Collection.)

A – Eyepiece Assembly – MCD-4138-2
B – Main Body Tube – MCD-4138-5-1
C – Elevation Assembly – MCD-4138-1
D – Objective Lens Assembly – MCD-4138-3
E – Windage Assembly – MCD-4138-1
F – Lock Ring – MCD-4138-6

Whereas the Army mount locking levers were rotated approximately 90 degrees clockwise from a horizontal position to lock the slide on the receiver base, those on the USMC variant were both turned down and inward to lock the slide in place. In both cases, however, the mounts were slid rearward from the front of the receiver base until they rested against a stop within the slide. The purpose of this was to counteract the recoil force of the rifle.

Unlike those of the Army, USMC mounts were not numbered (stamped) to the rifle on which they were issued. Mounts were fitted carefully to the receiver base, and serial numbers were either taped to the telescope or simply noted in stock (supply) records. In some cases, however, late-issue Marine Corps M1Cs were noted with the last four digits of the rifle serial number applied to the Kollmorgen telescope tube using red or white paint.

So far as combat use in Korea, there were at least three types of M1C sniper rifle employed by the Marine Corps during this era. These were the original M1C "Army rifles" manufactured as such by Springfield Armory late in World War II or shortly thereafter; those weapons rebuilt at Springfield Armory from approximately mid-1951 until mid-1953, from which an unknown number were allocated to the Corps for combat use in Korea (this in advance of the formal adoption of the M1C-USMC [MC 1952] as a mounting platform for the Kollmorgen

MARCH 1962

SL-3-00544A

MARINE CORPS STOCK LIST

COMPONENTS LIST

FOR

RIFLE, CALIBER .30 AUTOMATIC:

MC 1952, SNIPER, WITH TELESCOPE AND MOUNT,

WITH EQUIPMENT

FSN 1005-678-2758

Marine Corps Stock List (March 1962) references the M1 sniper rifle as the "MC 1952." Apart from the official MC 1952 or MC-1 designations variously applied to the M1C, the "D Model," on the other hand, was simply referenced as the M1D by the Marine Corps. (Peter R. Senich.)

4XD riflescope); and, in addition to those mentioned, though believed to have been few in actual number, "select M1 rifles were modified to M1C specifications at various USMC ordnance depots on an as-needed basis."

Despite their acceptance by the Marine Corps, the Stith-Kollmorgen 4XD telescope reportedly did not see combat use in Korea, being in service from about 1954 through 1962 when the M1C-USMC rifle was made obsolete by the Marine Corps. Even though the M84 telescope was manufactured during the Korean War, Model 81 and 82 scopes were used almost exclusively with the M1C by both Army and Marine Corps marksmen. Though unconfirmed, M1D sniper rifles originating at ordnance depots

First Marine Division sniper-spotter team tracking targets in Korea. Although observation telescopes were available, field glasses were used most frequently. According to one combat veteran, "Binoculars were less of a bother to carry." With a capability for engaging multiple targets in rapid succession, the M1C was favored by many USMC snipers during the Korean War. (U.S. Marine Corps.)

U.S. Marine Corps Scout-Sniper: World War II and Korea

and arsenals were reportedly "coming through" fitted with M84 telescopic sights.

Contrary to the definition of obsolete—that is, no longer in use—the M1C and M1D remained as quasi-official sniping arms of the Army and Marine Corps through the mid-1960s, when combat requirements in Southeast Asia necessitated the upgrading of sniper equipment. Even though the M1 sniping rifle has been long removed from "Standard Type" classification, a substantial number of these rifles still repose in National Guard armories across the United States and in ordnance base depots throughout the world.

In addition to protracted military use for special applications by indigenous forces in low-intensity conflicts, the venerable .30-caliber sniping rifles (M1D) were drawn from base depots in Europe to supplement the long-range sniping capability of American combat forces in the Kuwait Theater of Operations (KTO) during the Persian Gulf War in 1991.

CHAPTER 9

Scout-Sniper: Training the Specialist

When the armed forces of the United States were finally committed to the European conflict by declaration of war on 6 April 1917, adequate as U.S. sharpshooting weapons were for the task at hand, by no stretch of the imagination were American personnel ready to do combat with the Germans in this capacity. Consequently, specialized training attuned to combat conditions on the western front was conducted at various "schools of sniping" by experienced British and Canadian instructors in order to thoroughly prepare American sniper candidates prior to their actual involvement in the trenches. As the British and Canadians had learned painfully early in the war, there was a great deal more to mastering the extremely efficient German snipers than pointing telescopic sighted rifles in their direction.

Unprepared as they were initially, by the summer of 1918 when the total weight of the American Expeditionary Force was finally brought to bear, American snipers, while employed only in limited numbers, proved to be as effective as their British and Canadian counterparts. The methods employed by the highly successful "Scouts, Observers and Snipers" would serve American military forces for the next 20 years.

An extension of the state of the art as it existed in 1918, the Marine Corps view of training snipers after 1920 was based on tactics developed by the British during the "Great War." An example is noted in the U.S. Navy *Landing Force Manual* (1927), whereby the recommended use of snipers is directly related to the principles of trench warfare. As the manual stated in part:

> Sniping fire may be delivered from specially constructed sniping posts, from shell craters, sapheads, or other positions outside the trenches, through loopholes in the parapet or over the parapet.

While not defined as such in the 1927 manual, at some point, the Marine Corps made a clear distinction between "sniper" and "telescopic sight rifleman." According to the 1935 Marine Corps manual *Rifle and Pistol Marksmanship*, the "Old Corps" method of precision shooting:

> Long distance firing practice (800 to 1,000 yards) is advanced training for men qualifying in the higher grades,

who are to enter competition. It develops skill above and beyond that developed by qualification firing, as certain factors enter here which have no place in short-range firing. It is a necessary foundation stone for those who are to be trained as snipers or telescopic sight riflemen.

Sniping—A specialized type of training for only the most expert of riflemen, to make him the equal of a big-game hunter in stalking his prey and defending himself against enemy snipers.

Many of the precepts established during World War I would serve as the foundation for training Marine Corps snipers during the war with Japan. Yet with the advent of jungle warfare in the South Pacific in 1942, an entirely new chapter in the art of fieldcraft and marksmanship as it related to the Marine sniper would necessitate formulating new and more efficient tactics necessary to effectively eliminate the enemy and remain alive in the process.

As a part of the overall effort to field satisfactory sniper equipment beginning in late 1940, in addition to evaluating sniping rifles, telescopic sights, and related hardware, the Marine Corps set about to determine the best course of action for training and fielding a new breed of combat specialist: the scouts and snipers, or simply "scout-snipers," as they would be known in the Corps.

Members of the 2nd Marine Brigade, the first American expeditionary force in the Pacific following Pearl Harbor, fasten tropical vegetation to helmet nets and to their uniforms during maneuvers intended to "warn off" the Japanese in the Samoan Islands (American Samoa, January 1942). The prospect of an extended campaign against the Japanese prompted the hasty development of suitable jungle camouflage techniques for use on the Pacific islands. Tropical camouflage and concealment for men and equipment had received little attention before World War II. (U.S. Marine Corps.)

In conjunction with the presentation of the report, "Equipment for the American Sniper" to the Commandant, HQMC, by the Marine Corps Equipment Board (27 March 1941), the president of the board, E.P. Moses, in addition to recommending that the Winchester Model 70 and the Unertl Sniper Telescope be adopted, offered the following:

> It is further recommended that a Board be appointed without delay to study the training and employment of Sniper-Observer Scouts, and to prepare a policy to govern the training and employment of Snipers, the distribution and care of equipment, and the establishment of Scouts and Snipers Schools under the Inspector of Target Practice, Headquarters, U.S. Marine Corps.

Nevertheless, amidst the ebb and flow of the general prewar indecision with regard to adopting new equipment and training personnel to use this equipment, apart from token procurement and the reallocation of existing equipment to test new theories (or as some suggest, to placate certain factions), when the Japanese made their fateful move against the United States in late 1941, the Marine Corps was not prepared to field or equip snipers.

However, with the realities of total war helping to clarify and establish priorities, by mid-1942 the need for "specially trained snipers" was outlined in an official memorandum from the Director, Division of Plans and Policies (USMC) to the Commandant, HQMC (19 July 1942). As the memorandum stated in part:

> It is believed that sniper training should be initiated in the Marine Corps in the near future; that a suitable course be tentatively adopted for this purpose; and that after the adoption of such course, snipers schools should be established at Training Centers for the purpose of furnishing combat units with trained snipers.

In conjunction with "Action Recommended," the memorandum, directed that:

> ... when the above recommendations are received, a snipers course be adopted and promulgated for use in snipers schools to be maintained initially at the Training Center, Marine Barracks, New River, North Carolina, and at the Training Center, Camp Elliott, San Diego, California.

As a result, the Commandant, HQMC, in a directive to Capt. E.O. Swanson, USMCR, Marine Barracks, Quantico, Virginia (4 August 1942), via the Commanding General, specified the following:

IN REPLYING
REFER TO No.

AO-347-alm

10798

HEADQUARTERS U. S. MARINE CORPS
DIVISION OF PLANS AND POLICIES
WASHINGTON

19 July 1942.

MEMORANDUM:

From: The Director, Division of Plans and Policies.
To   :   The Commandant, U. S. Marine Corps.

Subject: Snipers' Schools.

References: (a) Approved DP&P Study No. 8090, dated
                 8 April 1941.
             (b) Ltr. CMC to CG, 1stMarDiv and CG,
                 2dMarDiv, AO-283-gjf, dated 16
                 April 1941.

   I.   DISCUSSION:

        1. The importance of having specially trained snipers in combat organizations is widely recognized in all armies, and reports indicate that it has proved of great value, especially by the Russians and the Japanese. The British also stress sniper training.

        2. Reference (a) recommended as follows:
   (a) "That forty M-1903 rifles be equipped for employment of Lyman 5A sights, and that twenty rifles with serviceable telescopic sights be furnished each Marine Division for test and training."

   (b) "That the Commanding Generals, First and Second Marine Divisions, be directed to initiate a training program for snipers and to make recommendations after a suitable period as to the type of equipment required and as to a suitable training program." (Reference (b)).

        3. The forty (40) rifles equipped with telescopic sights were shipped to the 1st and 2d Marine Divisions about May 1941. No reply has as yet been received to reference (b).

Recommendation from the Director, Division of Plans and Policies, USMC (A.H. Noble), that a "sniper course be adopted" for Marine Corps use at New River, North Carolina, and Camp Elliott, California (19 July 1942). (U.S. Marine Corps.)

Subject: Snipers' Schools.
- -

4. It is understood that a snipers' course has been worked up by Major Van Orden, and an outline of this course is now on file with the Weapons School at Quantico. It is further believed that a snipers' course is now being conducted by the Second Marine Division. There is also available in the Gunnery Section an outline of a British Snipers' Course which has been employed in Bermuda.

5. It is believed that sniper training should be initiated in the Marine Corps in the near future; that a suitable course could be tentatively adopted for this purpose; and that after the adoption of such course, snipers schools should be established at Training Centers for the purpose of furnishing combat units with trained snipers.

6. The Infantry School at Fort Benning is now preparing a Snipers' Manual for use in training snipers for the Army.

7. There are available at the Quartermaster Depot at Philadelphia approximately 1,000 star-gauged rifles which are the property of the Marine Corps Rifle Team and which could be used for equipping snipers. Suitable telescopic sights would have to be provided for these rifles.

II. ACTION RECOMMENDED:

1. That a Board of three (3) officers be appointed, consisting of Captain C. A. Lloyd, U.S.M.C., and two other officers to be nominated by the Commanding General, The Training Center, Quantico, Virginia, for the purpose of drawing up a snipers' course for use in Marine Corps Snipers' Schools, and that the Board also make recommendations as to the following:

    (a) Equipment desired.
    (b) Number of snipers to be furnished
        various combat units.
    (c) Length of course.
    (d) Number of students per class.
    (e) Allowance of ammunition for training.

(Action: A&I).

2. That when the above recommendations are received, a snipers course be adopted and promulgated for use in snipers schools to be maintained initially at The Training Center, Marine Barracks, New River, North Carolina, and at The Training Center, Camp Elliott, San Diego, California.
(Action: DP&P, GS.)

1240-10
AH-85-efc
1975-60
1530-30-175

AUG 4 1942

From: The Commandant, U. S. Marine Corps.
To: Captain Emmet O. Swanson, USMCR,
Marine Barracks, Quantico, Virginia.

VIA: The Commanding General.

Subject: Board to draw up a sniper's course.

1. A board, consisting of yourself as senior member and of Captain Calvin A. Lloyd, USMC, and Captain Walter R. Walsh, USMCR, as additional members, is hereby appointed to convene at the Rifle Range, Marine Barracks, Quantico, Virginia, as soon as practicable and at the call of the senior member, for the purpose of drawing up a sniper's course for use in Marine Corps Sniper's Schools. The board will also make recommendations as to the following:

(a) Equipment desired.
(b) Number of snipers to be furnished various combat units.
(c) Length of course.
(d) Number of students per class.
(e) Allowance of ammunition for training.

2. The junior member will act as recorder.

T. HOLCOMB

Copies to: Director, Division of Personnel
Director, Division of Plans & Policies
CO, Hdqrs. Co., Hdqrs., USMC
CG, MB, Quantico, Va.
CG, Training Center, Quantico, Va.
Each officer named

Official authorization to "draw up" a sniper's course of instruction for use in Marine Corps sniper schools (4 August 1942). (U.S. Marine Corps.)

A board, consisting of yourself as senior member and of Captain Calvin A. Lloyd, USMC, and Captain Walter R. Walsh, USMCR, as additional members, is hereby appointed to convene at the Rifle Range, Marine Barracks, Quantico, Virginia, as soon as practicable and at the call of the senior member, for the purpose of drawing up a sniper's course for use in Marine Corps Sniper's Schools.

As then followed, in addition to determining a suitable course of instruction, two "official" specialist schools for training USMC scout-snipers were initiated in the latter part of 1942. The "East Coast" school directed by Capt. Walter R. Walsh, USMCR, at New River, North Carolina, near Camp Lejeune, and the "West Coast" facility commanded by Lt. Claude N. Harris, USMC, at Camp Elliott (Green's Farm) near San Diego, California.

According to "A Training Center Chronicle," an article by F.R. Jones, USMCR (Camp Elliott, 1943):

> The Scout and Sniper School and Officer Candidate Detachment are located at Green's Farm, an outpost camp five miles northeast of the main encampment, in the heart of Camp Elliott's most rugged boondock country.
>
> Scout and Sniper School was activated in January 1943, by Marine Gunner (now 1st Lt.) Claude N. Harris. It is charged with the mission of teaching men the technique of scouting and sniping; of developing in them self-reliance and combat initiative; and of instructing them in the knack of jungle living.

Even though Green's Farm would serve as the training site of record, it is of interest to note that a location for training "scouts and snipers" had been established some months earlier.

In discussing the naming of various camp sites at Camp Elliott "to facilitate their use in correspondence within the 2nd Marine Division," according to the 9 May 1942 issue of *Chevron*, the "River Camp" was designated as the location of the "Scout-Sniper School," and while included in the listing, Green's, or as it was also known, Oliver's Farm, was not noted or mentioned in conjunction with the scout-sniper school. Of further interest, scout-sniper training had apparently taken shape long before the "official sites" were established. Although the locations and extent of this early activity remains unknown at present, according to World War II-era 2nd Marine Division historian Richard W. Johnston:

> A part of the overall specialized training then taking place, schools for scouts and snipers were operating in the San Diego area as early as March 1942.

Additional insight on the West Coast scout-sniper school (Green's Farm) was provided by Frank X. Tolbert in the October

IN REPLYING
REFER TO NO.

2445-45
MHK-rmh
Serial No. 1416

UNITED STATES MARINE CORPS

HEADQUARTERS, TRAINING CENTER,
CAMP ELLIOTT, SAN DIEGO, CALIFORNIA.

February 13, 1943.

From: The Commanding General.
To: The Commandant, U.S. Marine Corps.

Via: The Commanding General, Fleet Marine Force,
San Diego Area.

Subject: Scout-snipers.

Reference: (a) CMC Ltr to CG,FMF,SDA, 2385/70-5090,
Serial MC 13769, dated 3Feb43.

    1.   In connection with paragraph one (1) of reference (a), it is the intention of this Headquarters to assign six (6) scout-sniper teams to each replacement battalion.

    2.   Authority is requested to transfer scout-sniper teams with replacement battalions equipped with caliber .30 model 1903 rifles.

    3.   It is believed that scout-snipers will be more effective if armed with the same rifle used during their course of training and which they are familar.

M. H. KINGMAN

069/130 1975
CG,FMF,SDA--Fwd, approved.

3766

19Feb43

H. M. SMITH.

Correspondence from the Commanding General, Camp Elliott, to the Commandant, USMC, regarding scout-sniper teams (13 February 1943). (U.S. Marine Corps.)

1943 issue of *Leatherneck* magazine. Commenting on the activities of Lieutenant Harris and his training program in "Deadly Teams Emerge from this Academy," Tolbert stated in part:

> Harris, a veteran of 15 years' service in the Corps and one of the greatest of Marine riflemen, has been C.O. of the school since its start in January of this year. The lieutenant, then a Marine gunner, was brought from an island outpost in the Pacific to organize and command this new academy.
>
> As a rifleman, Harris was one of the proudest proteges of Colonel Merritt A. Edson, the Raider chief. Harris won the national rifle championship in 1935 and he fired on seven championship Marine Corps teams....
>
> All of the students are volunteers. The school takes 15 expert riflemen out of each replacement battalion at Camp Elliott. Many of the men have had experience as rifle or pistol range coaches. But most of them are fresh from Boot Camp. The course lasts five weeks and the top five men of each class are given three additional weeks of training with a Raider battalion at nearby Camp Pendleton. However, these five men do not necessarily become Raiders. On graduation, all men are advanced one rank.
>
> Three graduates are allotted to a company, but they are not attached to any platoons or squads. They work unattached at their specialties as the company commanders see fit to use them. They operate in pairs, one man equipped with an '03 rifle with telescope sights and the other man having an M-1. In sniping, one man acts as rifleman and the other as spotter.
>
> One of the chief tasks of the instructors is to form smoothworking "teams" for assignment to the companies. The third member of this scout and sniper team is a sort of utility man who is ready in the event one member of a team becomes a casualty or is replaced....
>
> There are lectures on camouflage, individual concealment, the making of spider traps, map reading, compass reading and many other subjects....
>
> There are no rifle ranges at the school. In the third week of instruction, the boys start firing—always at field targets. The ranges are 200, 300, 400, and 500 yards. The students have to figure out their ranges for themselves....
>
> The final week concerns telescopic firing, for the most part, with the students estimating their range and changing their own sights. There's considerable instruction in other infantry weapons, including the B.A.R., the carbine and the Reising gun.

As noteworthy as the credentials of Lieutenant Harris were, his counterpart at New River, Captain Walsh, prior to his involvement with the scout-sniper program, had earned an impressive reputation as a competitive marksman and intrepid FBI agent dur-

An example of early camouflage "battle dress" (1942). As then stated, "No single color is as effective as properly designed multi-colored patterns, particularly against close observation. Camouflage suits are now receiving final service tests by all branches of the armed forces." (September 1942.) A developmental "jungle combat uniform," the camouflage pattern illustrated is similar to the original Marine Corps issue. Note the use of face painting ("skin tonedown") and the early style World War I helmet. The rifle is a standard M1903 Springfield. (U.S. Army.)

ing the 1930s. Acknowledged by many as one of the "top" Marine marksmen of all time, Captain Walsh would go on to become the first Marine to be "Triple Distinguished," winning the Distinguished Rifleman Badge, the Distinguished Pistol Shot Badge, and the International Distinguished Badge for his exploits with United States teams in international competition.

The following is the culmination of personal interviews conducted by Capt. Mark K. Edmondson, USMC (Ret) with Col. Walter R. Walsh, USMC (Ret), on 28 July, 1 August, and 23 August 1990, regarding the activities of the East Coast training program and Marine Corps sniping in general during World War II.

According to Colonel Walsh, the officer chosen to establish and command the USMC scout-sniper school at New River:

A principal West Coast training facility for USMC scout-snipers during World War II, the specialist school at Green's Farm (Camp Elliott, San Diego) was established in 1942. (Leatherneck magazine.)

Considered the most readily identifiable part of Marine Corps combat gear during World War II, the camouflage helmet cover with its characteristic camo pattern saw extensive use during the war in the Pacific and again in Korea. (Peter R. Senich.)

Typical World War II Marine Corps issue two-piece herringbone twill "mottled-pattern" jungle camouflage top. (Otoupalik Collection/Schulz photo.)

In the early part of World War II, a board decided that the Marine Corps needed snipers and what a sniper school should consist of. They directed that there should be one sniper school on the East Coast and one on the West Coast. I was directed to organize and run the one on the East Coast. This school opened in the latter part of 1942.

There were excellent range facilities there, but absolutely no sniper school materials. Although a course outline was supposedly available from the rifle range detachment at Quantico, we had to develop the course from scratch. We had to improvise a great deal, but that is exactly what you have to do in those situations to get things moving.

Rifles began arriving from Philadelphia almost immediately, about the same time, as I remember. They came in huge green boxes and had scopes with them. These were the same scopes we had used on the USMC rifle team in the matches. By the time I left the school in mid-1943, there were about 100 '03 sniper rifles with scopes there. I'm certain the scopes were mostly Unertl, although we had also used Lyman and Fecker scopes on the rifle teams. Some of these could have been in the sniper program since much of the rifle team equipment and people were involved with the program at large.

We began processing students thereafter with about 20 per class and approximately three weeks for the course. The quality of the students varied; some were picked out of boot

Marine Corps jungle camouflage trousers. As the war in the Pacific moved from the jungles to more open terrain, the use of camouflage clothing became less prevalent. In many cases, it was not uncommon to see a mixture of camouflage and standard green twill battle dress uniforms on USMC combat personnel during the later stages of the island campaign. (Otoupalik Collection/Schulz photo.)

camp or rifle qualification elsewhere because they had shown aptitude for rifle shooting. Others, a minority, were sent just to fill the quota for sniper school.

Once these people left our school and went into the line units during the war, their use was not always what they had been trained for. The snipers had to be given a time and place to zero their rifles and plan their movements. This was not always provided them, and they were not able to function to full effectiveness.

To begin with, ammunition was supposed to be the "white box" National Match ammunition used in match competition, which was supposed to be the best military ammo in consistency of performance. However, this special ammo was not always available in the field, and other types, such as regular ball or AP, would be substituted with varying results, depending on the shooter.

(*Note*: The term "white box" ammunition refers to special .30-06 Springfield match ammunition supplied to the military rifle teams on a contract basis, so-called because the labels were typed or printed on white boxes, unlike normal commercial match ammo. Cartridge headstamps were either typical commercial or military style. While there was no comparing the performance of hand-loaded match ammunition with standard "ball" service ammo, the .30-caliber armor-piercing (AP) M2 cartridge with its 168 grain (+ -) "heavy" bullet was frequently employed by USMC marksmen during World War II and again in Korea.)

The same situation existed with the care and maintenance of the sniper rifles in the user units. The rifle/scope combinations were held in unit inventories and maintained there. Maintenance was not always of the highest quality; thus any reports about sniper effectiveness have to be weighed against these variables, if known. Also, care given the rifles and scopes in the field varied with the individual, some giving better care than others. Obviously, the level of performance was directly affected by this factor.

The school at New River had its own armorers, but they performed only basic routine maintenance on the sniper rifles. Major, higher echelon maintenance was performed at Philadelphia if required. During my short tenure there, no rifles were returned to Philadelphia, however.

Having been an integral part of the Marine Corps sniping program during its formative stages during World War II, Colonel Walsh continued with a description of the early USMC sniper issue:

> The sniper rifles were USMC Rifle Team National Match '03s made at Springfield Armory and used by the team in the 1930s. They all had polished bolts and most had "C" stocks, although some team rifles still had straight "S" stocks, since some of the older shooters, having started with the straight stocks, preferred to stay with them even after the pistol-grip "C" stock became standard.
>
> The one consistent characteristic seemed to be the way the handguard was modified. They all had been milled, or planed down and provided with a small rectangular opening for the front scope block.

Of further interest was the insight Colonel Walsh provided on the USMC team rifles of that era—the basis for the "Springfield Sniper Rifle":

> The rifle team stopped receiving '03s in 1940 when Springfield Armory ended their production. The rifles were held at the Philadelphia Quartermaster Depot where they were maintained by the armorers. All team rifles were carefully worked over with the major effort expended on getting the bedding correct. As I recollect, correct bedding of the barreled action was a "6 o'clock bed," where the barrel touched the stock only at the forend at the 6 o'clock position.
>
> Another important job of the armorers was to star-gauge barrels as they arrived from Springfield Armory. As a matter of course, barrels were checked before the shooting season began, and after the match season ended.
>
> The rest of the time the rifles were traveling with the rifle

team out of Quantico. Usually, team rifles could have 5,000 to 7,000 rounds through them before their performance would fall off and the star-gauge was used to verify excessive wear if any. These rifles were then removed from the team inventory by the armorers based in Philadelphia.

The rifle team would carry two rifles per man with another complete set as backup. The team would travel with approximately 200 rifles.

Among the first scout-snipers trained by the Marine Corps during World War II. The marksmen are equipped with Springfield rifles mounting Lyman telescopic sights. The improvised supports for the spotting scopes served the same purpose as the "shooting stools" used by the USMC rifle teams during match competition. According to the original caption, "Marine Gunner Emmett W. Orr is the instructor" (center, standing). An "Old China Hand" and distinguished marksman, Emmett Orr was well known in the Marine Corps. (U.S. Marine Corps.)

In addition to providing a remarkable first-person account of the early Marine Corps sniper program, Colonel Walsh revealed certain aspects of the USMC Springfield sniper rifle that were previously unrecorded, including the intended use of "white box" match ammunition at the field level, the mixed use of both Style "S" and Style "C" stocks, and the attention to "correct-bedding," then a basic accurizing technique that would not be used with sniper rifles in general until years later.

A Marine Corps sniper candidate receives instruction prior to "firing the combat range" in July 1943. The Model 1903A1 Springfield is fitted with a Lyman 5A (5-power) telescopic sight, an improved version of the early Winchester A5 target model. The helmet was painted to alter its form. A variety of camouflage clothing was issued during the island campaign. The pattern shown saw extensive use during World War II. (U.S. Marine Corps.)

In response to the question invariably asked of all Marine Corps personnel having firsthand experience with the '03A1/Unertl system, Colonel Walsh replied:

> As for the effectiveness of the USMC '03A1/Unertl sniper rifle, I never used it in combat so I can't say for certain. However, years after the war I talked to a fellow who had used the rifle in combat against the Japanese on Peleliu. He stated it had proved very satisfactory for sniping and he had used it successfully during that campaign.

IN REPLYING
REFER TO NO.

UNITED STATES MARINE CORPS
SCOUT SNIPER SCHOOL
RIFLE RANGE BATTALION, TRAINING CENTER,
CAMP LEJEUNE, NEW RIVER, N. C.

28 April, 1943.

From: Officer in Charge.
To: The Commandant, U.S. Marine Corps.

Via: The Commanding Officer, Rifle Range Battalion.

Subject: Graduates, Scout Sniper School.

1. The First Class of the Scout-Sniper School was graduated on 24 April, 1943, and all members were returned to the organizations from which they were temporarily detached for duty at this school.

2. The graduates, listed in order of merit, and their organizations, Camp Lejeune, New River, N. C., are as follows:

Pfc Clarence W. DUFFIELD	23rd Marines	(Reinforced) (3-K-23).
PlSgt William KELLER	Parachute Bn., TC, (H & S Co).	
Pfc Harold P. KEVILLE	23rd Marines	(Reinforced) (3-K-23).
Pfc William H. VAN WIE	23rd Marines	(Reinforced) (2-E-23).
Pfc Raymond P. PARNITZKE	23rd Marines	(Reinforced) (1-C-23).
Pvt Emil A. CATALANO	23rd Marines	(Reinforced) (2-E-23).
Pfc Nicholas J. COSENZA	23rd Marines	(Reinforced) (F-20th Eng.-23).
Pvt Carl R. KINCAID	23rd Marines	(Reinforced) (2-G-23).
Pvt Joseph J. DWORNIK	23rd Marines	(Reinforced) (1-B-23).
Pvt John J. BYK	23rd Marines	(Reinforced) ("C"20th Eng.-23).
Pfc Richard V. YOUNG	23rd Marines	(Reinforced) ("C"20th Eng.-23).

-1-

Graduation roster for the "First Class" of the East Coast USMC Scout-Sniper School at New River (Camp Lejeune), North Carolina (28 April 1943). (U.S. Marine Corps.)

Subject: Graduates, Scout Sniper School. (Contd)

    Pfc Leo J. VAKULCHIK   23rd Marines (Reinforced)
                                                        ("C"20th Eng.-23).
    Pfc Clarence F. THIBEAULT   23rd Marines (Reinforced)
                                                          (2-F-23).
    Pfc Everett HAMPTON   23rd Marines (Reinforced)
                                                          (3-L-23).

3.   The following men are non-graduates:

Corp Joseph J. PURCELL   Parachute Bn., TC.
Pfc Leslie T. BAXTER   23rd Marines (Reinforced)
                                              (1-A-23).
Pvt Clarence E. HALL   23rd Marines (Reinforced)
                                              (F-20th Eng.-23).
Pvt Dighton T. KETCHAM   23rd Marines (Reinforced)
                                              (2-G-23).
Pvt John L. BLACKWELL, Jr. 23rd Marines (Reinforced)
                                              (3-L-23).
Pvt Louis R. KLINS   23rd Marines (Reinforced)
                                              (1-C-23).
Pvt J. J. MC GRATH   23rd Marines (Reinforced)
                                              (1-B-23)
Pfc Kenneth R. MAHAR   23rd Marines (Reinforced)
                                              (2-F-23).
Pvt Robert Lacey NALLEY   23rd Marines (Reinforced)
                                              (3-I-23).
Pvt Anthony S. BORASKI   23rd Marines (Reinforced)
                                              (3-I-23).

Walter R. Walsh
WALTER R. WALSH

RTP-jws   1st Endorsement   29 April, 1943.
    RIFLE RANGE BATTALION, TRAINING CENTER,
      CAMP LEJEUNE, NEW RIVER, N. C.

From: The Commanding Officer.
To: The Commandant, U.S. Marine Corps.

    1.   Forwarded.

R. T. PRESNELL

A 1st Marine Division scout-sniper instructor is shown making an adjustment to the Unertl scope (June 1952). With exceptions for terrain and the enemy they were now facing, Marine snipers in Korea were trained essentially the same as they were during World War II. An interesting example of "parts swapping" at the field level, the M1903A1 rifle has a one-piece (stamped) trigger guard normally found on M1903A3 rifles. (U.S. Marine Corps.)

Korean War-era Marine Corps photo with caption that reads, "Sniper School Class—a group of 18 Marines pose with their diplomas after completing snipers school in Korea" (5th Marines, 1st Marine Division, June 1952). Depending on the availability, Marine sniper candidates were often given their choice of weapons. Though most were equipped with the M1 Garand, in addition to an M1903A1 Springfield Rifle, note the Remington M1903A4 sniper rifle (front row). The telescopic sights are removed from the rifles. (U.S. Marine Corps.)

A classic illustration considered by many to have captured the very spirit of the unique Marine Corps combat specialists. A 1st Marine Division scout-sniper is pictured with his equipment during the Korean War. (U.S. Marine Corps.)

Korea presented a formidable battleground for American combat forces and even for the most proficient snipers, since the rugged terrain, in most cases, necessitated long-range shooting that rested beyond the resolving power of the issue telescopes. A Marine marksman prepares to fire on the enemy from "Siberia Hill" in Korea. The sniper is working from a fortified position typical of those stretching across the Korean Peninsula during the later stages of the war. In time, combat in Korea would evolve into an almost endless series of bitter hand-to-hand struggles and fire fights in and around the trench lines. As any combat veteran of Korea will attest, the action there was no less difficult than any that had preceded it. (U.S. Marine Corps.)

Sniper: The Japanese Approach

CHAPTER 10

By the time American combat forces began their long march toward Japan in 1942, the Imperial Japanese Army (IJA) had literally dismantled major elements of long-established European, British, and American military forces during its conquest of the Orient. As a result, the Japanese soldier had earned a reputation as a tough, resourceful foe with no other purpose than to die if need be, in service to his Emperor.

Whereas early war combatants were intimidated by the reputation of the Japanese soldier, this would later change. Nevertheless, among those candid enough to treat the matter with some objectivity, the average Japanese soldier was highly respected.

During the early weeks of the long struggle for the Solomon Islands, Marine Corps "brass" readily admitted that, during the early going in particular, "the jungle belonged to the Japanese."

Experienced in jungle warfare as they were, the Japanese would create a great deal of consternation among American forces during the initial phases of the island campaign. Of all the unique tactics employed by the Imperial Japanese Army at that time, the use of snipers would prove especially troublesome.

Although a great deal has been written about the Japanese sniper of World War II, first-person accounts and observations have, for the most part, been largely ignored in contemporary offerings. With this in mind, in an effort to present the reader with the best possible insight, a compilation of firsthand accounts and personal narratives of "people" who were actually there is presented as follows:

Hanson W. Baldwin, correspondent, New York Times (Guadalcanal)

The Japanese are full of tricks, deceit and cunning; the unorthodox is their rule. Hard, ruthless, brave, well-equipped, they are the best jungle fighters in the world—judging from their operations in the Solomons and elsewhere in the Pacific. And many of our fighting men in the South Sea area—particularly those who have faced the Japanese—agree they are the toughest of our foes.

The Japanese are never content with defense; they always try to attack. And to confuse and destroy their foes they try

everything, from the strategy of terror to sniping, according to Marines who have fought them on Guadalcanal.

The "devil personified" to countless veterans of the war in the Pacific. A Japanese sniper takes careful aim with his telescopic sighted "97—Shiki Sogekiju" (Type 97 Sniper Rifle) from his vantage point in a coconut palm. Though most Japanese snipers were ineffective, combat veterans always knew when they were facing a dangerous marksman. (Max Crace illustration.)

In jungle fighting opposing forces are often only a few yards apart, hidden from each other by a thick, leafy screen. Camouflage and concealment are of prime importance; if the enemy sees you before you see him you will probably never know what hit you. The Japanese, therefore, use all sorts of tricks—particularly at night—to entice the enemy to reveal his positions and to deceive him as to his opponents' whereabouts.

The Japanese are good at bird calls and animal cries, which they use at times to cover their rustling progress through the jungle or to distract the Marines' attention. When they want to be, the Japanese jungle fighters can be almost completely noiseless and invisible. Carefully camouflaged, they inch their way through the tall grass or wait motionless and supremely patient for hours, lashed to treetops or almost neck deep in swamps.

Many of the Japanese are equipped with tree spurs made of strong steel wire, which they use to shinny up the smooth boles of the palms to the fronded tops to get into position for sniping.

A camouflage suit or cape (top left) typical of those employed by Japanese snipers in the Solomon Islands (1942). A unique form of individual camouflage, the special suits were woven from a coarse, fibrous material found on coconut palms. (U.S. Army.)

According to Intelligence reports, Japanese sniper training placed considerable emphasis on jungle camouflage techniques. An example of these efforts, the unique suit at top right is shown ready for use. By all accounts, Japanese snipers were all but impossible to detect when positioned in a tall tropical palm. (U.S. Army.)

John G. Dowling, correspondent, Washington Post (Matanikau)

One feels like a fool when there are snipers about. You recognize they are not too much of a menace and yet they make you nervous. There is always a chance they will let one fly at you and there is always a chance that—for a change—their aim will be true. It is beneath your dignity to fall on the ground and crawl, yet standing there you feel like a balloon in a shooting gallery.

Richard Tregaskis, correspondent, International News Service; author, Guadalcanal Diary

I was sitting on the side of the ridge that looks over the valley where our tents are located. A throng of Zeros were dogfighting with our Grummans in the clouds and I was trying to spot the planes.

Suddenly I saw the foliage move in a tree across the valley. I looked again and was astonished to see the figure of a man in the crotch of the tree. He seemed to be moving his arms and upper body. I was so amazed at seeing him so clearly that I might have sat there and reflected on the matter if my reflexes had not been functioning—which they fortunately were. I flopped flat on the ground just as I heard the sniper's gun go off and the bullet whirred over my head. I knew then that his movement had been the raising of his gun.

Capt. John Monks, USMC, 3rd Marine Division (Bougainville)

And the men on watch were tired, too. But tired men can become dead men, for tired men grow careless. And they knew it. They strained to pierce the blank scrim of the jungle night, and listened intently to the million jungle noises—ground noises particularly, for they must learn to distinguish the sound of a lizard or a rat or a toad, or any one of the hundred little ground animals in the jungle, from the even belly-slide of a crawling Japanese jungle fighter. The men in the Third Marines were used to the jungle; but every jungle is different, and for the first time after their training they were playing for keeps.

Among the earliest official attempts to familiarize the American serviceman with Japanese snipers and IJA jungle tactics in general, a series of intelligence bulletins were published by the Military Intelligence Service (U.S. War Department) during the Solomon Islands campaign.

"Intelligence Bulletin No. 1," September 1942, provided the following information:

Camouflage was widely used, and all movements were made as silently as possible. Some of the Japanese who acted as snipers painted their faces and hands green to conform to the leaves of the trees and covered their clothes with leafy branches.

Many of them climbed trees and tied themselves with ropes so they would not fall out if they went to sleep or were wounded.

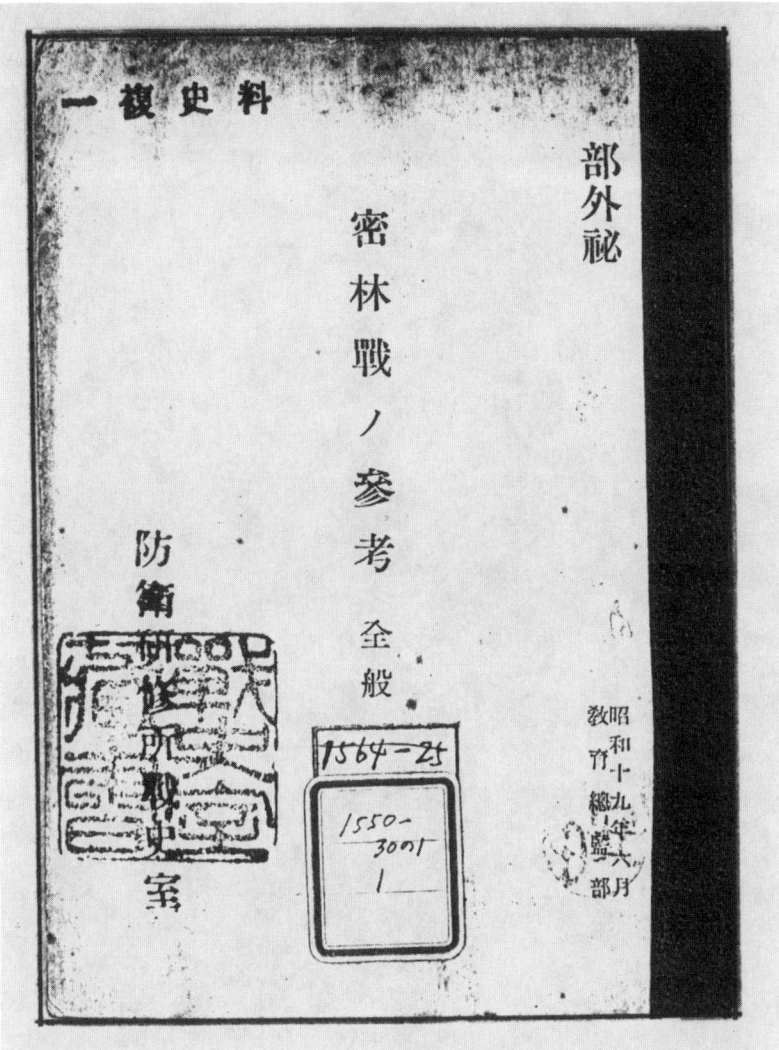

A principal World War II Imperial Japanese Army training manual dealing with jungle warfare (1944). According to Japanese military historians, a specific manual for individual camouflage "was not issued during the war." The use of camouflage was considered an integral part of jungle warfare in the Japanese Army. (Peter R. Senich.)

Experienced in jungle warfare as they were, the Japanese would create a great deal of consternation among American forces during early phases of the island campaign. The average Japanese soldier made efficient use of camouflage appropriate for his area of operations. In this case, corded net garnished with tropical vegetation was used to cover the helmet and uniform. (Donald G. Thomas.)

An original Marine Corps photo made at Guadalcanal (December 1942) depicts a "U.S. Marine garbed in a Japanese sniper outfit." A unique example of typical Japanese sniper combat dress (circa 1942), note the coconut fiber cape and the use of "climbing spikes," a simple method employed by the Japanese to climb trees. (U.S. Marine Corps.)

Following the initial bulletin, there was further mention of the Japanese sniper in Bulletin No. 2, October 1942, and again in No. 3, November 1942. According to "Intelligence Bulletin No. 3":

> Cleverly hidden Japanese snipers proved very troublesome to the U.S. Marines. A Marine sergeant reported that our biggest problem was in locating and destroying snipers.
> They were well concealed in trees, bushes, and buildings. Time and again, our forces passed through an area and were shot at from the rear. A second Marine officer said that the Japanese used a large number of snipers, well camouflaged. "They shot at us from the tops of coconut trees, slit trenches,

garden hedgerows, from under buildings, from under fallen palm leaves," he explained. "One sniper, shot down from a tree, had coconuts strung around his neck to help conceal him. Another in a palm tree had protected himself with armor plate. Our Thompson and B.A.R.s proved to be excellent weapons for dealing with snipers hidden in trees."

The snipers sought especially to pick off officers and non-commissioned officers who wore insignia or markings indicating their rank.

The Japanese placed snipers on the flanks of their positions and weapon emplacements.

A large number of the Japanese wore green uniforms and painted their faces and hands green so they would be hard to see among the green vegetation on the islands. They also wore camouflage nets with wood fiber strands and garnished with vegetation. Japs wearing these were hard to see, even at 50 yards, if they were still.

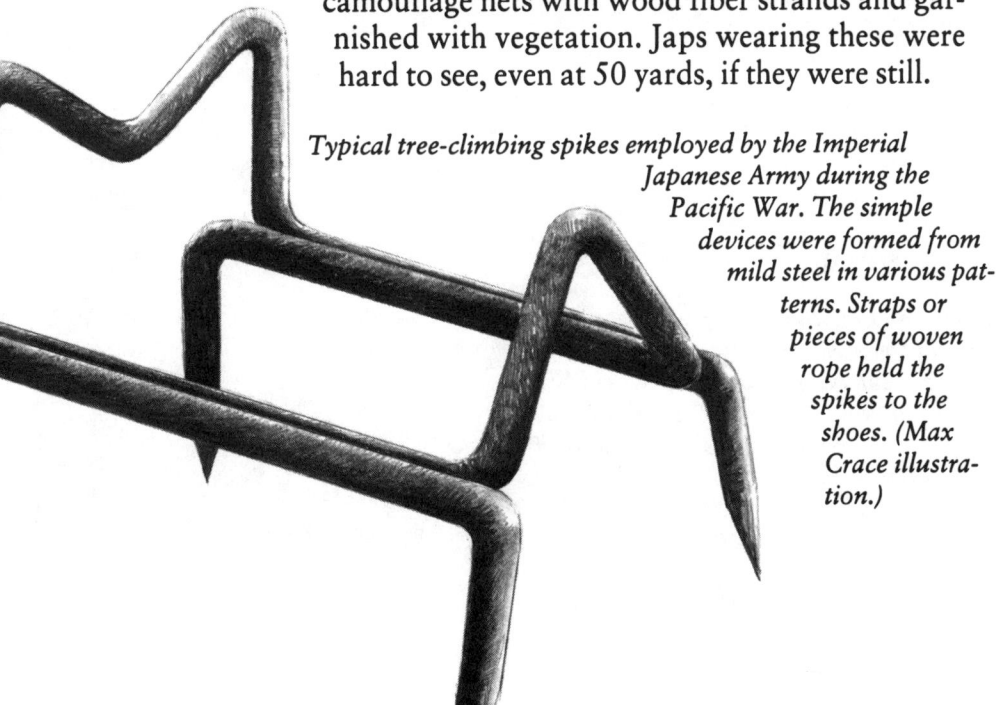

Typical tree-climbing spikes employed by the Imperial Japanese Army during the Pacific War. The simple devices were formed from mild steel in various patterns. Straps or pieces of woven rope held the spikes to the shoes. (Max Crace illustration.)

Adding to our perspective on Japanese snipers, Master Gunnery Sergeant Lou Diamond, USMC, in his magazine article "SNIPER!," in *American Rifleman* (August 1944), provided the following:

You've heard stories of Jap snipers tying themselves in trees. Well, they do that. Usually, though, they use a contrivance like a boatswain's chair which is hauled up into the fronds of a palm or into the crown of a conifer tree, the sniper himself being equipped with climbing spikes. Sometimes, too, they work in pairs. Such teams search out an American, make him disclose his position, then try to keep him pinned down until a grenade can be heaved into his lap.

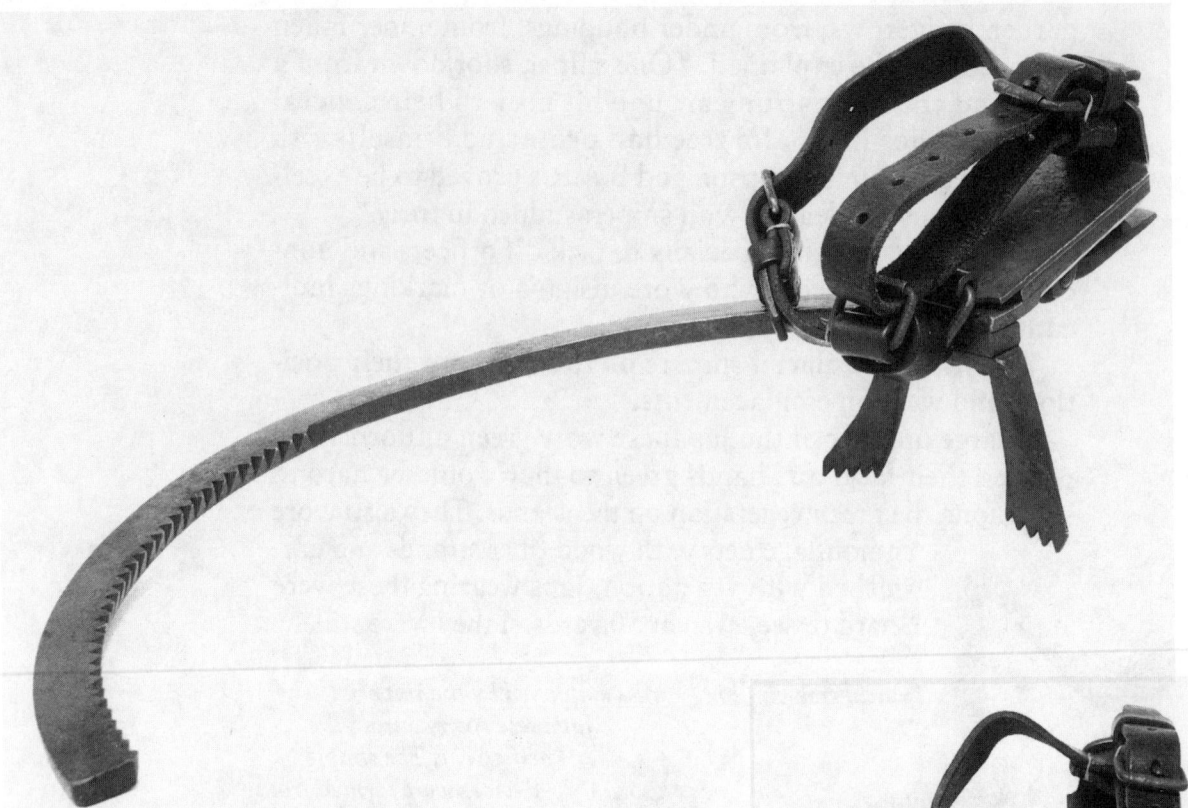

Unique and relatively rare, an elaborate form of tree-climbing device issued to Japanese combat forces during World War II. In addition to sniper use, climbing hardware was employed by observers and ordinary riflemen as well. (Doss H. White.)

An alternate view of the IJA tree-climbing device. Intended primarily for use on palm trees in this case, the leather straps were placed over and behind the climber's shoe. (Doss H. White.)

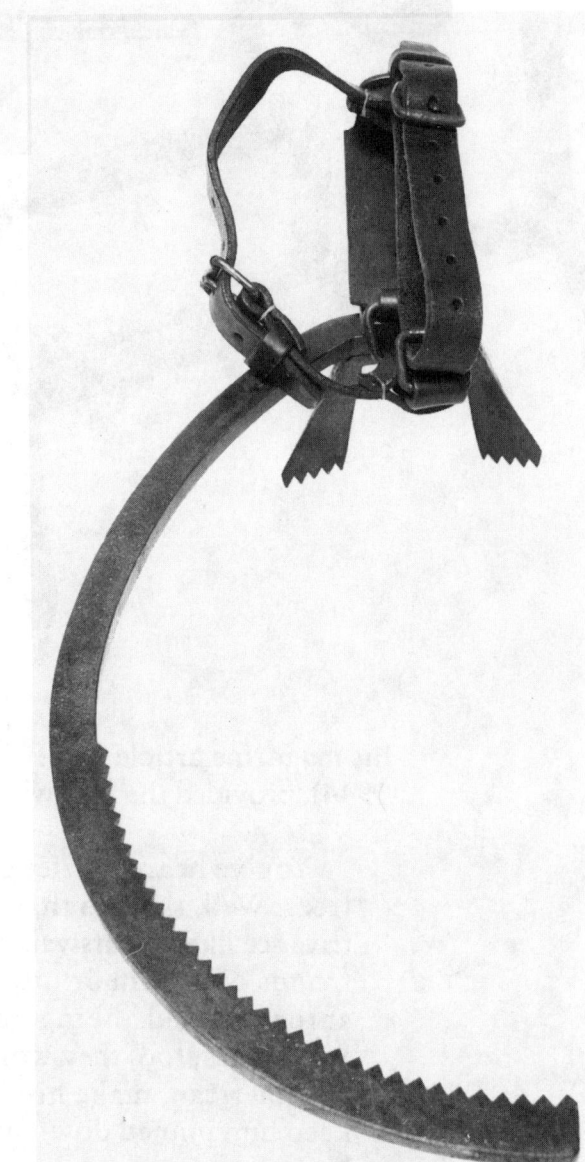

A Jap sniper will concentrate on his job of firing, from a tree for instance, even when some of our men are cutting the tree from under him. He won't change his ordered field of fire, even to make you lay off his tree.

Strange things happen, sometimes, to Jap snipers. I saw one, lying at the base of his tree, wearing his climbing irons and all tangled up in the wreckage of his boatswain's chair, who had been stabbed

A Marine rifleman demonstrates another means by which Japanese combat personnel scaled palm trees. In addition to using climbing spikes, an appropriate length of rope running from one foot to the other enabled a climber to "shinny up" a coconut tree at a fairly rapid pace. The coconut palm illustrated is typical of those used by Japanese riflemen for harassing American forces during the early stages of the war in the Pacific. (U.S. Marine Corps.)

to death with a knife. Some Marine must have spotted him, must have lain in wait for him, and caught him as he came down out of his tree, probably to return to his unit.

With regards to jungle warfare in general, the following

excerpts from the January 1945 issue of the *Marine Corps Gazette* are particularly noteworthy:

> There are certain advantages in jungle warfare which are almost invariably entered on the black side of the defender's combat ledger. The defender is usually able to select the position he will defend, dig in, get up his supplies, site and camouflage his weapons, conceal his personnel, establish his security, and wait for the attacker, all according to a previously prepared plan. The attacker is burdened with the problem of locating the defender, feeling out the position, and blasting his way through it. In the process of doing so, he cannot expect to employ cover and concealment as effectively as the defender because he must move. In moving, he must expose his personnel. Thus the well concealed enemy sniper is automatically provided with an abundance of targets without exposing himself.
>
> The Japs are now showing a tendency toward .30 caliber small arms in an effort to secure penetration and "brush cutting" qualities. However, the majority of Jap soldiers and practically all snipers still use .25 caliber weapons. Snipers are usually equipped with rifles, carbines, or Nambu light machine guns.
>
> The .25 caliber weapon will not cut brush or penetrate like a .30 caliber weapon. It will, however, penetrate our helmet at ranges of 150 yards or more. This is penetration enough in most cases. Its most annoying characteristic is that for all practical purposes the Japanese small arms power is actually smokeless and generates little muzzle blast when used in a .25 caliber weapon. Thus a sniper can "hole up" or "tree up" with any of his three small arms, and although he may fire considerably, we will seldom, if ever, locate him by smoke or muzzle blast.
>
> At the beginning of hostilities (and in many cases even now) the Jap was generally a better woodsman than our Marines. He had been meticulously trained and equipped for jungle warfare long before Pearl Harbor and he had received the training and used the equipment in the jungle. The training had been realistic and tough. Jungle techniques had been developed and proven while we were parading in blues at the Marine Corps Base. The Jap sniper had learned to live as successfully as an animal in the jungle while our boys were enjoying a standard of living they had been raised to regard as a right, rather than a privilege.

Without question, one of the most important documents pertaining to Japanese snipers generated during World War II appeared in the March 1945 issue of *AIM*, the official publication of the British Middle East Command. The article, "How The

Japanese Train Snipers," was based on information obtained directly from Japanese combatants. As it was then stated:

> Candidates for sniper training are selected, without an examination of any kind, by the respective platoon leaders of each company. However, it is customary to select only those men who have superior marksmanship records. The men do not consider it a special honor to be selected to attend sniper training classes; instead, the work is looked upon as just another phase of the training program.
>
> Short men are preferred to tall men. The Japanese reason that small men present less conspicuous targets to hostile fire. The wearing of glasses does not necessarily disqualify a soldier from becoming a sniper. When troops are distributed over a wide area, each battalion trains its own snipers.
>
> The snipers use either the 6.5mm rifle, Model 97, or the 6.5mm rifle, Model 38. The former is regarded as distinctly superior. In addition, the snipers are supplied with a telescopic sight, Model 97. After receiving his rifle, a marksman determines its individual characteristics by firing it from a fixed mount.

(*Note*: The Type 97 sniper rifle represented a slight modification of the standard Type 38 Japanese service rifle. In sniper trim, the Type 97 was provided with a telescope mounting base on the left side of the receiver, a turned-down bolt handle, and a 2.5-power telescopic sight.)

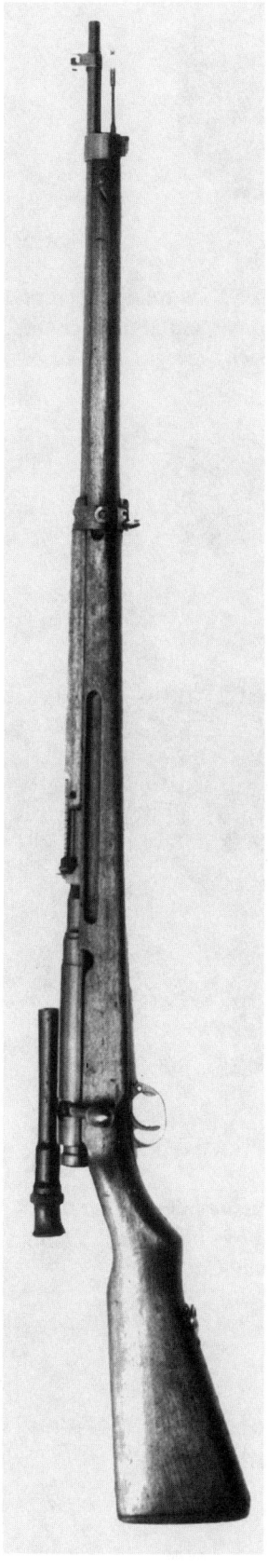

The Japanese Type 97 sniper rifle (97—Shiki Sogekiju) represented a slight modification of the standard 6.5mm (.256-inch) Arisaka Type 38 Japanese service rifle. In sniper trim, the Type 97 was provided with a telescope mounting base on the left side of the receiver, a turned-down bolt handle, and a 2.5-power telescopic sight. Some, but not all, Type 97 rifles were provided with a monopod attached to the rear barrel band. (Fred L. Honeycutt, Jr.)

Japanese snipers are taught that their missions, in order of importance, will be: (1) to kill or capture hostile personnel—especially unit leaders and snipers;(2) to neutralize or destroy hostile installations which may obstruct the successful completion of a Japanese unit's mission; (3) to destroy the enemy heavy weapons and the personnel manning them; and (4) to deal effectively with all tar-

A top view of the Type 97 (6.5mm) sniper rifle illustrates the turned-down bolt handle and the positioning of a typical scope on the left side of the receiver. The markings at the rear of the tube indicated the power, manufacturer, and scope serial number. The rotary locking lever rotated 180 degrees (counterclockwise) to unlock the sight. (Fred L. Honeycutt, Jr.)

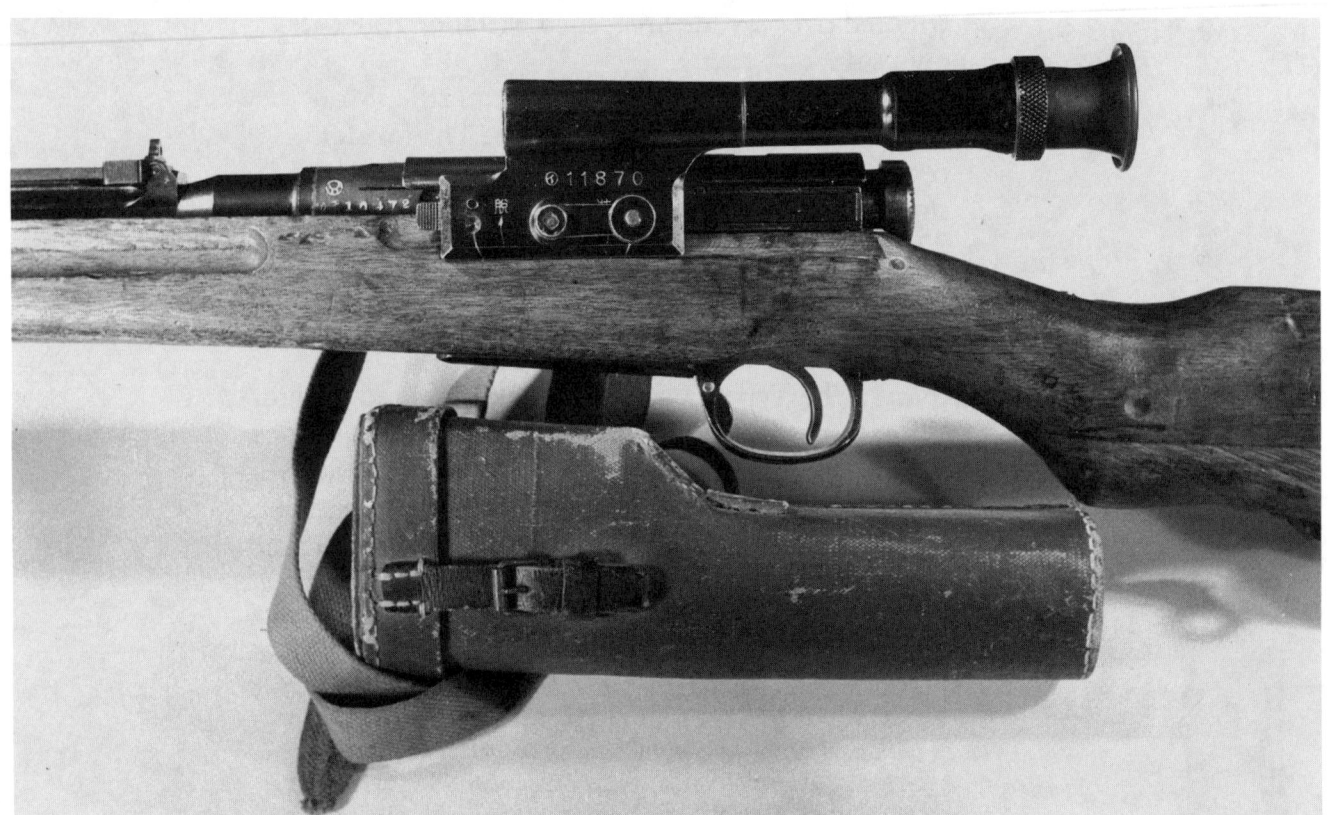

A close-up view, Type 97 (6.5mm) Japanese sniper rifle with 2.5-power telescopic sight and issue carrying case. A nonadjustable sight (no external windage or elevation adjustments), the telescope was aimed by aligning a graduated reticle on the target. A lense-cleaning brush and cloth were furnished with each sight. (Conway Collection.)

gets of opportunity which may come within range.

As a rule, an officer personally supervises each sniper's firing. For firing at targets at ranges of 300 yards or more, telescopic sights are sometimes used. When soldiers fire rifles without the aid of these sights, they are instructed to aim without closing either eye.

The men are taught to estimate ranges with the naked eye. The instructors place objects at measured distances, varying from 200 to 600 yards, and the men then estimate their ranges. Excellent eyesight and continual practice are necessary for accurate estimation. The men are not required to judge the distance of objects over water.

According to one prisoner, every light machine gun squad has a sniper; however, not all snipers are equipped with the Model 97 rifle and the Model 97 telescopic sight. In one company of a representative infantry regiment there are only three Model 97s.

A thorough course in individual camouflage is provided. Men are taught that camouflage of the upper half of the body is especially important. Helmet nets and body nets are issued to all men for camouflage purposes. For additional camouflage, the nets are garnished with foliage. A prisoner remarked that although all men strictly observe such measures during training, they do not actually carry them out during combat, especially in the jungle. The nets become entangled with the shrubs and vines and hinder movement.

Often, instead of using nets, the men cut small branches and twigs and stick these into their pockets and buttonholes.

Another prisoner told us that his particular unit had never heard of the use of camouflage suits, straw hoods, or fiber capes. In localities where the background is not green, appropriate camouflage measures are taken, such as using dry branches and leaves and dry bark to blend with the color of the background.

When fighting in open terrain, a Jap sniper usually fired at a range of 500 yards. There is no established range for firing in the jungle, since trees and other vegetation are so likely to obscure the sniper's vision.

As a precautionary measure, the safety catch of the rifle is always set when the squad is deployed near the front lines. This is especially true in the jungle, where the trigger may become entangled in the undergrowth and tripped accidentally.

Methods of muffling the sounds of ejecting and reloading rounds are not taught. If a sniper wishes to do so, he can take the expedient of moving the bolt slowly.

Japanese soldiers are inclined to regard only those men equipped with Model 97 rifles as being true snipers; it was felt that men equipped with the Model 38 rifle could not hope to perform as effectively.

Although snipers recognize the distinct advantages offered by high ground, it was said that Japanese training makes no mention of firing from trees. Since so much is left to the discretion of the individual sniper, this may be true. It must be remembered, however, that Japanese snipers have

The Type 99 Japanese sniper rifle (99—Shiki Sogekiju) with a 2.5-power (nonadjustable) rifle scope. A telescopic sighted version of the 7.7mm Type 99 infantry rifle, the sniper model was provided with a turned-down bolt handle and a telescope mounting base on the left side of the receiver. Though similar to the 6.5mm Type 97 in many respects, Type 99 sniper rifles were issued with 2.5-power, 4-power nonadjustable, and 4-power externally adjustable telescopic sights. A monopod was also fitted to some of the Type 99 rifles. (Fred L. Honeycutt, Jr.)

A top view of the Type 99 sniper rifle (7.7mm) with the 2.5-power nonadjustable sight. The similarity between the Type 97 and Type 99 sniper rifles is readily apparent. The 2.5-power telescope issued with the Type 99 was essentially the same as those furnished with the Type 97. The 2.5-power model was the only scope issued with the 6.5mm Type 97 rifle, however. (Fred L. Honeycutt, Jr.)

repeatedly posted themselves in trees, especially to fire on targets of opportunity.

From a practical standpoint, it is interesting to note that even though the actual combat use of telescopic sights by the Japanese was from all indications, negligible, by their definition "a true sniper" was a specialist equipped with a telescopic sighted rifle. An infantryman using the standard service rifle, though trained and employed in much the same way as his counterpart was, for the most part, simply an ordinary rifleman on a harassing mission.

A postwar U.S. Army paper, "Tasks Trainfire III AND IV," 14 September 1955, in discussing military sniping techniques at large, placed the Japanese sniper of World War II in the correct context:

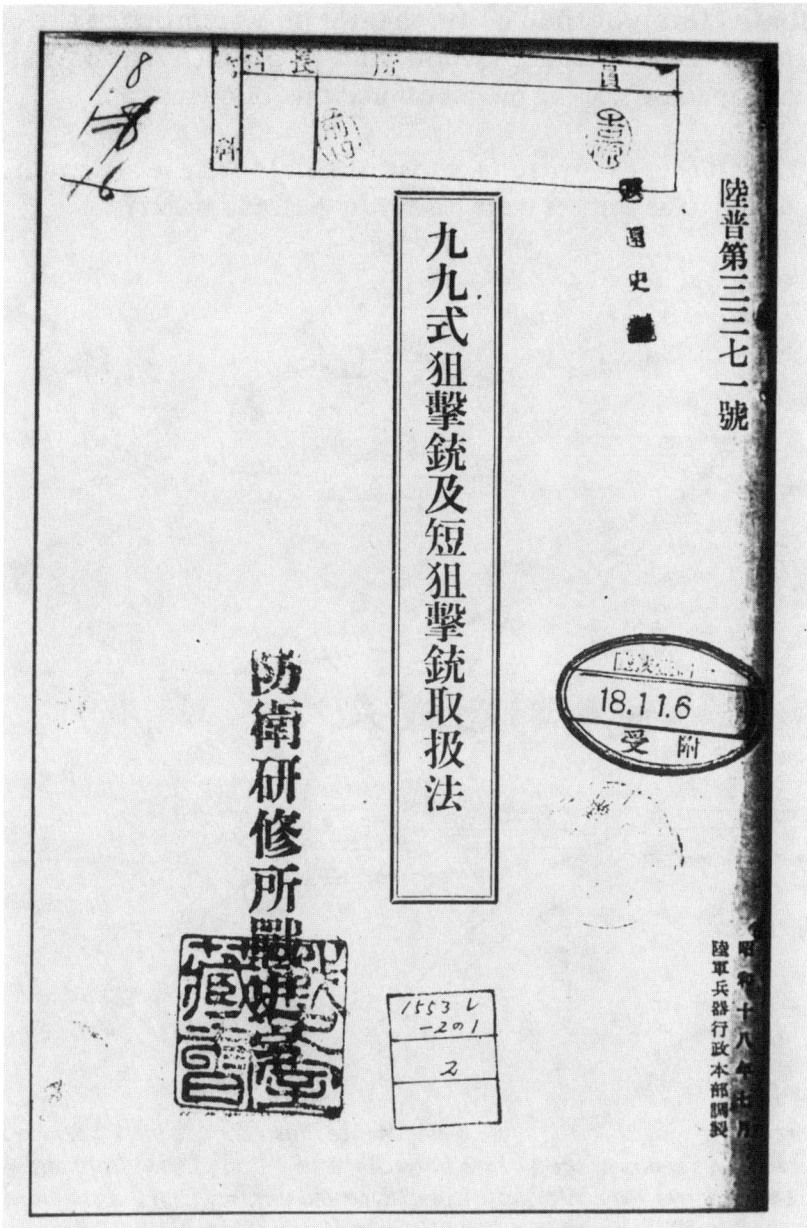

Imperial Japanese Army (IJA) manual for the 7.7mm (.303-inch) Arisaka "Type 99 Sniper Rifles." The figures "18.11.6" shown on the cover indicate the date, and read "18th Year of Showa, November 6th" (1943). (Peter R. Senich.)

Some Japanese riflemen were referred to by many of our troops in the Pacific as "snipers" although these riflemen lacked many of the characteristics traditionally associated with snipers. These "snipers" operated in jungle areas, remaining behind retreating Japanese forces, or in front of defensive forces. These snipers were experts at camouflage and were frequently stationed in trees where they simply waited for targets to appear.

Though difficult to substantiate or determine at the field level in a combat environment, as a matter of interest, Otto Hebel, a combat veteran of the Pacific theater as a member of the 6th Regiment Scout-Sniper Platoon, 2nd Marine Division, in discussing Japanese sniping tactics offered the following:

> With few exceptions, most of the Japanese riflemen referred to as snipers were simply by-passed infantry.

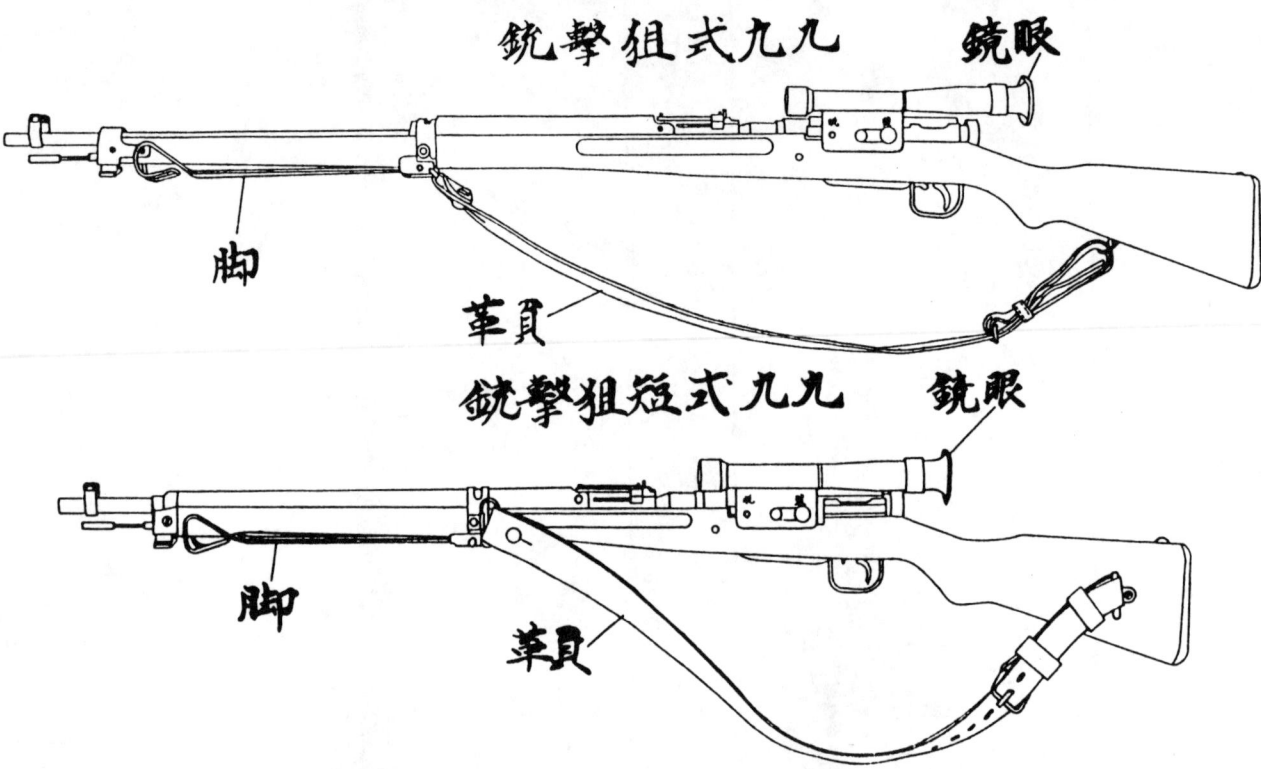

An interesting World War II Japanese ordnance illustration depicts a developmental sniper version of the 31-inch barrel Type 99 "Long Rifle" (top) and the 25 1/2-inch barrel Type 99 "Short Rifle." Deemed unsatisfactory in standard form, the Type 99 long rifle was only produced in limited numbers. The Japanese caption above each weapon reads, "99—Shiki Sogekiju" (Type 99 Sniper Rifle) and "99—Shiki Tan-Sogekiju" (Type 99 Short Sniper Rifle). Even though the 7.7mm Arisaka Type 99 "short rifle" would emerge as the principal Japanese infantry rifle in standard and sniper trim, so far as it is known, no sniper versions of the Type 99 long rifle are believed to have been issued. Both rifles are shown with the 4-power nonadjustable "Type 99 Telescopic Sight." (Peter R. Senich.)

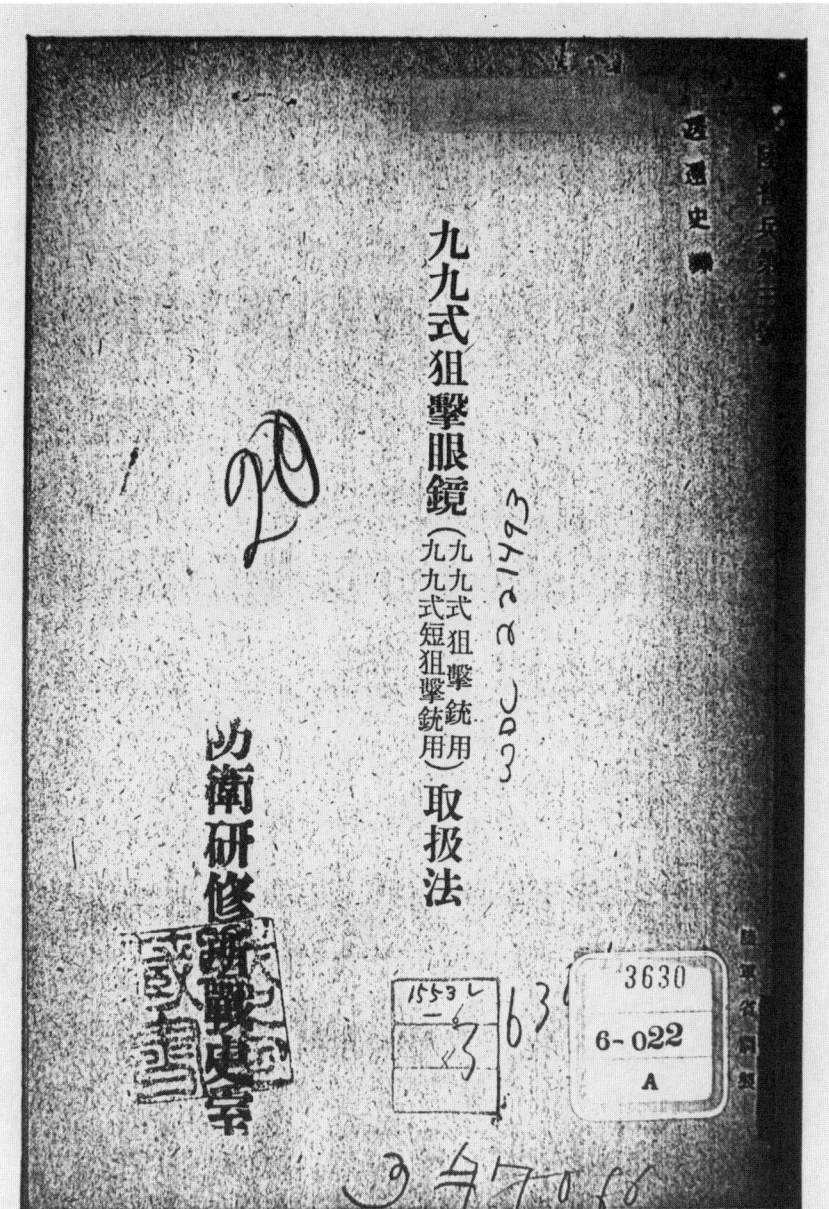

Japanese Army manual detailing the workings of the "Type 99 Telescopic Sight," the 4-power (nonadjustable) rifle scope, one of three models issued with the 7.7mm Type 99 sniper rifle. (Peter R. Senich.)

Scout-Sniper: Combat Experiences

CHAPTER 11

Apart from the fact that the "stateside" USMC scout-sniper schools at New River near Camp Lejeune and Green's Farm at Camp Elliott are acknowledged to have been the first "official" Marine Corps sniper training facilities of World War II, as the combat strength and size of the Marine Corps increased in the months following the opening of the island campaign in the South Pacific, scout-snipers were trained at various "overseas" locations as well.

Although it was not a part of their early training and combat involvement on any large scale, scout-sniper training was to be provided in due course to personnel from specialized units such as the Marine Raiders and the Parachute Battalions.

Consequently, by the time the Japanese surrendered in August 1945, all of the Marine combat divisions active during the Pacific campaign (1st, 2nd, 3rd, 4th, 5th, and 6th Marine Divisions) had, to some extent, trained scout-snipers in one form or another, in one place or another.

From all indications, however, few of the combat personnel so trained were ever utilized to take full advantage of their special schooling. Regardless of official doctrine and recommended use, the role of the scout-sniper in the Marine Corps has always been widely interpreted.

According to Marine Corps personnel then active, in addition to serving as combat infantrymen in most cases, scout-snipers were employed as "teams" in strength ranging from platoon and squad levels to "twos" or "threes," as circumstances warranted. The specialists were tasked with varied duties involving scouting, patrolling, reconnaissance, demolitions, sniping, and countersniping. Scout-snipers were also used for "mopping-up" behind advancing troops—a task many considered one of the most dangerous in the Corps—and as a reserve force to "plug-holes" in the line.

As a matter of interest, even though most, if not all, of the scout-sniper candidates were thoroughly trained in the use of telescopic rifle sights, of all the diverse weapons employed by men trained as scout-snipers during World War II, the telescopic sighted sniper rifle, in any form, appears to have been used least of all. Contrary to popular belief, the war in the Pacific did not include the wholesale Marine Corps use of snipers. In fact, as many Marine combat veterans insist, "men with sniper rifles were rarely encountered."

Nevertheless, where snipers were effectively deployed, in addition to sniping and countersniping measures, telescopic sighted rifles, particularly those fitted with target scopes, were used to direct machine gun and mortar fire and for observation purposes in general.

As a residual benefit provided by the ranging capability of the target scope, the sniper rifles served to spot targets beyond the range of ordinary field glasses (binoculars). This was especially true during the later stages of the war, when combat moved from the confines of the jungle to more open terrain.

The Second Regiment Scout-Sniper Platoon, 2nd Marine Division, would earn a rightful place in Marine Corps history with its actions at Tarawa Atoll (Betio), which were among the most notable examples of organized scout-sniper use in the Pacific.

United Press International's Richard W. Johnston, unofficial historian of the 2nd Division and eyewitness to the landings at Tarawa, in describing the events of the first day (20 November 1943), related:

> Out of the crazy chaos of bobbing boats near the line of departure—an imaginary line 6,000 yards out, marked by the sweeps, which had found no mines—a few craft loaded with specialists headed in toward Betio. They were about fifteen minutes ahead of the first assault wave of forty-two amtracs, carrying the storm troops of 2/2, 3/2 and 2/8.
>
> These specialists were marines of the Second Regiment Scout and Sniper platoon, under Lieutenant William Deane Hawkins of Texas, and engineers under Lieutenant Alan Leslie of Oregon. Their mission was to land on the end of the pier that reached 500 yards into the lagoon and clean out all Japs—Japs who might enfilade the assault waves. They made the pier, at 0855—the first Americans to land in the Gilberts, the first men ashore in the Central Pacific Offensive.

As Johnston continued:

> The scout-snipers and engineers were a major factor in blasting enemy forces out of the beach emplacements.

(*Note*: Lt. William D. Hawkins, USMC, would receive the Congressional Medal of Honor, posthumously, for his actions at Betio Islet.)

Responding to specific questions some years after the war, Stan Deka, a member of the 34-man regimental scout-sniper platoon named by Robert Sherrod in his book, *Tarawa: The Story of a Battle* (1944), and a part of the advance landing party led by Lt. William D. Hawkins, provided valuable insight on his activities as a scout-sniper during the Pacific War:

Q *When did you first volunteer for scout-sniper training?*
A The unit was organized in New Zealand in February 1943. I volunteered at this time. The main function of the unit was scouting and patrolling.

Q *What was the official unit designation, and to what division were you attached?*
A 2nd Marine Scout and Sniper Platoon, 2nd Marine Division.

Q *What were the requirements for those men volunteering? Were they expert riflemen?*
A All were considered good rifle shots. Most important, all were volunteers and interested in scouting and patrol assignments.

Q *To your knowledge, what other divisions were actively employing scout-snipers?*
A I was only aware of the 2nd and 6th Marine Regiments of the 2nd Marine Division.

Q *When did your scout-sniper unit first see action as a combat team? Where did this take place?*
A 20 November 1943, Tarawa Atoll.

Q *Were you active as a scout-sniper for the balance of the Pacific Campaign?*
A I had participated in the operations at Guadalcanal. It was during this campaign that we found a need for scouting units. I was a scout-sniper at Tarawa, Saipan, and Tinian.

Q *Did you consider yourself a better-than-average marksman?*
A Yes!

Q *After becoming a scout-sniper did you receive any special training in the use of camouflage or in the use of your telescopic sighted rifle?*
A Much of the training emphasis was placed on scouting, patrolling, map reading, use of demolitions, camouflage, and the telescopic sighted rifle.

Q *You were issued the Springfield Model 1903 bolt-action rifle with a telescopic rifle sight. Were all men in your unit equipped with the same rifle/scope combination?*
A We operated in three-man teams, one man with the Springfield, one with an M1, and one with a Thompson submachine gun. The '03 had the scope. The other men furnished protection for the man with the scope.

Marine Corps sniper team during action on Okinawa. Trained as snipers and observers, while one scans the area with field glasses, the other stands by ready to fire on targets of opportunity. With Japanese combat personnel dug into caves as well as they were on Okinawa, Marine snipers would use .30-caliber armor-piercing ammunition "to bounce their shots" off of the inside walls in an effort to flush the occupants. (U.S. Marine Corps.)

A weapon considered to be indispensable for eliminating hidden enemy snipers, the .45-caliber Thompson submachine gun emerged as a favorite weapon among Army and Marine Corps combat personnel in the South Pacific. As one Marine veteran stated, "You could really mess up a coconut tree with a top-cocker." The reference "top-cocker" applied to the earlier Thompson SMG with the bolt-actuator knob positioned at the top of the receiver (3rd Marine Division, Bougainville, November 1943). (U.S. Marine Corps.)

Marine Corps scout-snipers (2nd Marine Division) following action on Tinian in 1944. The men are armed with Thompson submachine guns, a carbine, and the USMC M1903A1/Unertl sniping rifle. (Stan Deka.)

Members of the scout-sniper platoon, 6th Marines (2nd Marine Division), following a training exercise on the big island of Hawaii in 1944. The rifles are "Marine Corps Springfields" (M1903A1) with Unertl scopes. (Otto Hebel.)

(*Note:* The use of three-man sniper teams had evolved from the lessons learned during the early stages of jungle warfare. Although circumstances normally dictated the course of action, in many cases, the man who was to function as the sniper would select a suitable position. The second man, acting as an observer, would search the area for targets while the third member of the team placed himself in a position to act as security. Two-man teams had been tried, but it was found that the man not firing could not observe and provide security at the same time.)

The scout-snipers tasked with landing at Tarawa Atoll (Betio) in advance of the main assault force. The remnants of the 2nd Regiment scout-sniper platoon, 2nd Marine Division, during reorganization at Camp Tarawa, Hawaii, in December 1943. (Stan Deka.)

Q. *At any time during your activity as a scout-sniper did you or any member of your unit use a scope-equipped rifle other than the Model '03 with the Unertl sight? Did you ever see the M1 Garand in use with a telescopic sight?*

A. No to both questions!

Q. *Did any members of your unit employ civilian hunting rifles with or without telescopic sights at any time?*

A. No.

Q. *Did you consider the Unertl telescopic sight adequate? Did you experience any unusual problems with this sight?*

A. We found it quite adequate; we found no faults with the scope.

Q. *Was training in the use of the telescopic sight adequate?*

A. Yes.

Q. *Were you responsible for taking care of your weapon, or was it taken to a unit armorer for repair or adjustment?*

A. We maintained our own weapons; very few repairs were needed.

A Marine marksman credited with "two 1,000-yard kills" maintains his equipment during a lull in the action on Okinawa in May 1945. Japanese combat personnel had developed a healthy respect for the marksmanship of Marine Corps snipers long before the end of hostilities in the Pacific. (U.S. Marine Corps.)

Q *Were you issued a telescope carrying case to protect your sight?*
A No. The scope was never removed from the rifle.

Q *What measures were taken to protect your sight during landings?*
A We only had a cover for the front and rear of the scope.

Q *While involved in sniping, were binoculars or special observation telescopes used for spotting targets?*
A We used only conventional binoculars.

Q *What was the shortest range ever encountered for sniping; also the longest?*
A We did some shooting at less than 100 yards on Tarawa. Some hits were made at 400 yards on Saipan.

Q: Were you issued standard ball or armor-piercing rifle ammunition? Was tracer or incendiary ammunition used in the field?

A: Standard ball ammunition was used. Tracer ammo was only used in practice.

Q: Did you ever engage in countersniping against the Japanese at any time?

A: Yes, on Tarawa, in defense of Colonel Shoup's command post.

Q: Did you ever encounter a Japanese sniper equipped with a telescopic sighted rifle?

A: No, those we had contact with used standard rifles.

Q: Did scout-snipers record their "hits"?

A: We only discussed our hits in the unit. No record was kept.

Q: In your opinion, were the scout-snipers effective as a combat team?

A: Yes, very effective! They were called on to handle many of the tough assignments because they worked so well as a team.

Q: Of all the actions you were engaged in, which one do you consider the most difficult?

A: Tarawa! Due to the size of the island, shooting was done at a very close range. It was very difficult to establish a solid beachhead and penetrate the Japanese emplacements. The reef had hampered the landings.

On 4 December 1943, Gen. Julian C. Smith turned over command of Tarawa Atoll to the Navy. The 2nd Marine Division returned to Hawaii for reorganization and rehabilitation. In retrospect, the assault on Betio would stand as one of the bloodiest battles in Marine Corps history.

Severely criticized for what stateside observers regarded as "reckless assault," the savage struggle for Tarawa Atoll forced strategic planners to review their tactics for the assault of heavily defended islands.

At a time when virtually everything associated with island assault was placed under close scrutiny, the M1903A1/Unertl system was arbitrarily rejected by the 2nd Marine Division. As it was then stated:

> 11 February 1943, G-5 (Div. of Plans and Policies) says Unertl scope 8X is not desired by 2nd Division. They have recommended adoption of the Weaver 330-C.

Whereas recommendations by a top combat division to adopt the Weaver scope were duly noted in Washington, despite official moves to have the "Army Standard" (M1903A4/Weaver 330C) replace the Springfield/Unertl combination, the M1903A1 sniper rifles mounting Unertl target scopes were still in use when the war ended. The Army M1903A4 was not adopted officially.

Whether or not the true potential of scout-snipers during World War II was ever fully recognized by the field commanders largely responsible for their combat use remains the subject of some debate. At the "official level," however, a place had been made for the "scout-sniper" in the United States Marine Corps.

The early USMC *Manual of Military Occupational Specialties* (June 1945) prescribed the following:

SCOUT-SNIPER

> An especially trained RIFLEMAN (SSN745) who engages in scouting and patrolling activities to obtain information concerning strength, disposition, and probable intentions of enemy forces; disrupts enemy communications; destroys enemy personnel by rifle fire. May perform supervisory duties involving the control, coordination, and tactical employment of other SCOUT-SNIPERS. Must possess all the qualifications of SSN745 (Rifleman). Must be particularly skilled in employing the principles of camouflage to conceal himself. Must know how to move over various kinds of terrain without being detected. Must be skilled in the use of the rifle, with and without telescope sight. Must know techniques of searching terrain for signs of enemy activity. Must be able to read maps, make sketches, and use compass and field glass.

Despite the lessons learned during World War II, when the Korean People's Army (KPA) sought to reunite North and South Korea under the Communist banner in 1950, scout-sniper training and sniper weapon development or procurement in the Marine Corps was virtually nonexistent.

Even though the need for snipers would manifest itself later when the war of move and countermove settled into a series of bitter struggles for strategic hills and fixed positions, sniper use among American forces would remain minimal at best.

With the main line of resistance (MLR) stretching 155 miles across the Korean peninsula, the two sides fashioned trench lines and fortifications reflecting their different strengths and weaknesses. Consequently, with changes necessary to fit the circumstances, terrain, and the enemy they were now facing—the KPA and the Chinese People's Volunteers, or Chinese Communist Forces (CCF) as they were called by the UN Command—scout-sniper training would be organized along the same lines as it existed at the close of World War II.

Marine Corps combat personnel "sniping at the Chinese Communists from a trench-line in Korea." Even though the use of standard sights reduced the maximum effective sighting range, "a good rifle" in competent hands was just as deadly as a weapon with telescopic sights. Many Marine marksmen preferred using standard rifle sights for sharpshooting purposes in Korea. Firing multiple shots with an M1 rifle increased the chances of a "hit." (U.S. Marine Corps.)

While the weapons fielded in Korea were essentially the same as had been used against the Japanese, rather than the close-quarter, limited-range situations experienced in the Pacific, combat in Korea, with target opportunities of 1,000 yards or more in many cases, offered the Marine sniper a chance to test the limits of his marksmanship and equipment.

One of a series of X Corps "Combat Notes" circulated among United Nations forces during the Korean War, the following material represents an official outline of the techniques employed by the scout-snipers of the 1st Marine Division during the latter part of 1951:

> In view of the recent highly successful operations of scout-sniper patrols as used by the 1st Marine Division, it is believed profitable to outline the techniques employed. The scout-sniper patrol can be quickly organized and used as a flexible, direct means of striking the enemy; by harassing and unnerving him and continuously inflicting casualties we reduce his strength and seriously impair his morale.
>
> The essential unit of the scout-sniper patrol is a two-man team equipped, one with a pair of 7 X 50 field glasses and

First Marine Division sniper directing machine-gun fire, Korea, May 1951. According to the original caption, the .30-caliber machine-gun crew was "attempting to clear the ridges of Chinese Communist Forces along a main supply route." (U.S. Marine Corps.)

the other with a sniper rifle; both have received dual training as snipers and observers. The equipment is interchangeable. While one scans the area with glasses, the other stands by ready to fire on sighted target of opportunity. Glasses and rifle work as a team in much the same manner as HMG fire is directed by an observer at the gun position.

Coupled with the observer-sniper unit is a four-man team which provides security. The scout-sniper patrol is a light, fast, compact, self-sustained group, capable of moving swiftly, and striking the enemy with deadly accuracy.

The scout-sniper patrols have been stationed on prominent ridges 800 to 1,100 yards forward of the MLR from which they are able to view the terrain occupied by the enemy. The patrols move quietly along concealed routes of

Another view of the Marine sniper in support of a machine-gun crew in Korea. In some cases, snipers were known to use tracer ammunition for spotting purposes. Note the M1 Garand resting beside the marksman. Even though the '03/Unertl was more than satisfactory for sniping purposes, many snipers chose to carry the semiautomatic rifle for added security. (U.S. Marine Corps.)

approach to their positions, generally during the hours around sunset and dawn. The teams are most efficient in the early morning hours when they remained concealed in the shade from a morning sun shining into the eyes of the enemy.

On occasion they have been able to see and direct fire on the enemy under a blanket of fog which obscured observation from higher points and gave the enemy a false sense of protection.

Snipers have been able to operate with success at ranges up to 1,000 yards; however, 600 yards is considered optimum range.

Alternate positions are prepared so that the patrol may shift if its positions are discovered; to date, because of careful attention to stealth and camouflage, only one of these patrols has received countersniper fire.

A Marine sergeant credited with nine kills poses for a combat photographer during a break in the action in July 1952. Note the extremely worn finish on the telescopic sight. (U.S. Marine Corps.)

As employed by the 1st Marine Division, the scout-sniper patrol serves a dual mission. First, direct action against the enemy, as described above: second, and possibly more important, the sighting and reporting of enemy targets of opportunity to the battalion's supporting arms. From their advance positions, the scout-sniper patrols are able to observe deep into valleys and cover ridges where observation from OPs located on the MLR is restricted.

Targets, sightings, and intelligence information gained through these observations are relayed instantly to the rifle company CP by means of a sound power telephone line from the patrol positions. All supporting arms (artillery, 4.2 mortars, 81mm mortars, 75mm recoilless rifles, 60mm mortars and .50 caliber MGs) have wire communications with the company CP and can quickly and effectively fire as directed, making corrections from the patrol's sensing.

Attached .50 caliber machine guns have been used as a section and have proven a deadly dual sniper team. The two guns fire single shots simultaneously at the same target from separate points and in this way double the probability of a hit while confusing the enemy as to the weapon's positions. As a long-range sniping weapon the .50 caliber machine gun is found to be valuable for enfilading enemy trenches.

Of further interest, Maj. Norman W. Hicks, USMC, in his article, "Team Shots Can Kill," from the December 1963 issue of the *Marine Corps Gazette*, recounted the experiences of a Marine colonel nearly "taken out" by a Communist sniper in Korea (1952):

> The battalion commander (3d Bn, 1st Marines) was only scratched, but he reflected that is was a helluva situation when the CO could not even take a look at the ground he was defending without getting shot at. Right then and there he decided that something had to be done about that enemy sniper.... As he made his way back from the outpost, his mind mulled over the problem of enemy snipers. A decision was made before he reached his command post. He would form a sniper unit.
>
> Sending for the S-4, the colonel learned that within the supply section there was an adequate number of rifles and telescopic sights. In addition, there were "snooper" scopes, an infrared device which enables a man to see in the dark.
>
> The colonel next sent for an experienced gunnery sergeant who had spent considerable time firing with various rifle teams. He told the gunny what he wanted; and then sat back and waited. His expectations were to be completely fulfilled.
>
> The gunny visited each company to pick candidates. He outlined his requirements to the company commander. He wanted riflemen who possessed the characteristics of good infantrymen. But above all, he stressed the quality of patience. This trait is absolutely essential, for a sniper must remain still and alert for long hours, waiting for the enemy to show himself.
>
> Each company sent a number of candidates, and the gunny selected approximately six 2-man teams per company. Next he picked his sniper range, an area in the battalion rear. He got necessary target supplies, issued weapons and 'scopes to the five dozen Marines, who commenced setting up a training range.
>
> Soon the range was ready, and the gunny began an intensive 3-week course on sniping. Fortunately, there was no shortage of either .30 or .50 caliber ammunition at that time, so the students were able to practice until proficiency was attained.
>
> Each student trained not only with the .30 caliber M1

rifle (or the '03 Springfield, depending upon his preference), but with the .50 caliber machine gun, fired single shot. Scopes were mounted on the machine guns and they proved to be effective for ranges up to and beyond 1,200 yards.

Lying for hours with their rifles sighted up the draws, the sniper teams trained together daily, learning their new roles well. When they finished the gunny's sniper course, they were qualified snipers in every sense of the word, and their future performance readily proved it. Returning to their respective companies, the men occupied camouflaged bunkers, which protruded only a foot above the ground's surface. These were artfully concealed, and the occupants entered or left only during darkness. The enemy found them extremely difficult to spot.

At the time the snipers finished their special training, enemy artillery and mortars were daily peppering both the MLR (Main Line of Resistance) and the outposts. Enemy snipers seemed to be in control. The whole area of the 1st Marines was a hot spot of sniping.

Then, the Marine sniper teams were sent out to the various outposts. All hands turned to helping the rifle experts in spotting the enemy snipers. The change in the situation was fantastic.

"In nothing flat there was no more sniping on our positions," remembers the Battalion CO. "Nothing moved out there but what we hit it."

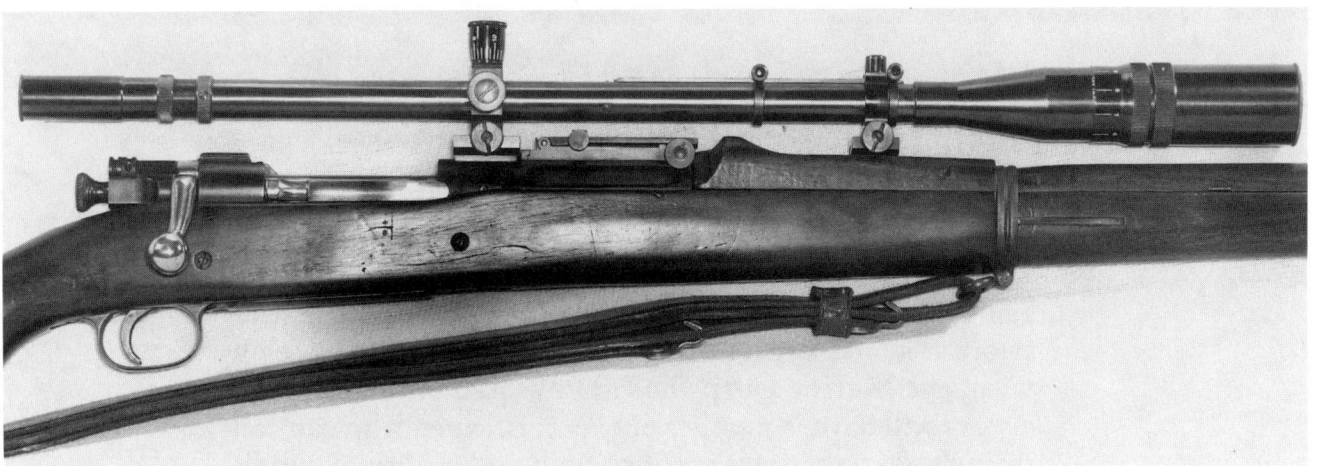

USMC Springfield sniper rifle serial no. 1529585, 3-39 barrel date. A rifle with a known history in this case, the M1903A1/Unertl combination saw combat duty in Korea. The Marine rifleman tasked with using this weapon was killed in action; the rifle was sent home to his family. (Cors Collection.)

Among the more comprehensive accounts of Marine Corps sniper training in Korea, the classic, "They Call Their Shots," by Lt. Col. Glen E. Martin, USMC (*Marine Corps Gazette*. April 1953) described the organization and effective use of a scout-sniper platoon:

First Marine Division marksmen at Bunker Kill, Korea, in August 1952. According to the original caption, "Marine snipers keep the enemy busy while new positions are being prepared. The seesaw battle for the strategic position has seen the enemy make seven unsuccessful attempts to retake it." (U.S. Marine Corps.)

The controversial sniper platoon is up for discussion again. There have been those who swore by it, those who swore at it, and a vast throng who just didn't care. To begin with, the Marine Corps has always had, and probably always will have, a number of expert riflemen who can call their shots to the fraction of an inch under normal conditions. These experts can be used as a nucleus for the training of sniper platoons—tremendous assets for infantry units in action. This is no innovation. Sniper platoons have been employed before. Rather, this is a presentation of the case in favor of their use, and a concrete example of the use of one such unit in Korea.

In the month of April 1951, the 2d Bn, 5th Marines was notified that enough additional sniper rifles would be on hand shortly to bring the battalion total up to eighteen. This information was brought to the attention of the battalion staff by the S-4 who was concerned about the care of the sights. He had found from previous experience that the sights were subject to fogging and that if men were not properly trained and supervised initially, the sights would be in for repairs before they could be used in combat.

The S-3, well informed on the subject, stated that the battalion lacked men with sniper experience, but he stated further that we did have a few men with limited experience with telescopic sights.

We all agreed the weapons could be used effectively if we could get men qualified to operate them, and then get these men to the right place at the right time. Frequently targets at medium ranges and greater could not be handled effectively. They were often beyond effective small arms range and too limited in size for economical expenditure of larger caliber ammunition.

In selecting personnel for this group it was decided they should be men who had qualified as experts on the rifle range, could adapt themselves to the use of telescopic sights, and would volunteer for the duty.

An alternate view of the USMC sniper-spotter team operating at Bunker Hill in Korea. The rifle is an M1C; the binoculars (6x30) are typical of those issued to American combat forces during World War II and Korea. Though barely visible, the rifle telescope is a 2.5-power Lyman Alaskan commercial sight without the combination rain and sun shield. A military issue rubber eye guard was used with the scope. (U.S. Marine Corps.)

They would train in the battalion rear area until such time as they were well qualified. They would set up their own range and the materials would be those the S-4 could requisition—actually, field expedients were the mainstays of the entire operation.

The call went out for the experts, and the "Exec" interviewed the men individually as they reported to the battalion command post. It should be pointed out that this entire program was set up under combat conditions. The men in the platoon built their own range and set up their training problems and lectures despite the situation to the front. . . .

In the instructional phase we were fortunate. The Exec had commanded a reconnaissance company during World War II, and was well versed in both the theory and the application of scouting and patrolling and those things necessary to keep a scout effective. While some of the prospective snipers were shooting, the others were being schooled. All the knowledge and experience the Exec had was being fed to the future snipers as rapidly as time would permit. After a week of this dawn-to-dusk routine he again talked with the men individually. As a result of these talks, some were returned to their units due to their own preference, others because they weren't suited to be snipers.

After the sorting process, the sniper platoon was placed in Weapons Company. The men were organized into three squads, four teams to a squad, and two men to a team. Each team was issued a pair of field glasses. . . .

The snipers were accurate up to 600 yards, but beyond that not too reliable. (It was felt that this was due to the ammunition.) Therefore, we reasoned, we could get support by firing through the gaps of assaulting squads at ranges 600 yards and under, and in an attack situation they would be used in this manner. We had not anticipated that they would be used as conventional scouts; but they were on occasion, and strangely enough they ate it up and were very efficient.

In the defense, the snipers would be used with patrols, attached to a squad or a platoon in the strength necessary—they proved to be extremely effective in this role. Further, they would be used on outposts during the day, but withdrawn inside the lines at night.

It was felt that due to the terrain (which permitted easy isolation), the enemy situation (massing), and the limited firepower of the sniper groups, it would be best to attach them to a unit no lower than a squad.

On 21 May, in compliance with a 5th Marines fragmentary order, the snipers went on their first big patrol. The patrol proved that snipers could be used effectively in this type of work. . . .

In surveying our sniper platoon program we found that

some of our theories worked, others were workable with minor modifications, and some just wouldn't hold water. As time went on some of the snipers came up with innovations of their own which were better than our carefully planned theories.

The Browning Automatic Rifle (BAR) and the M1903A1/Unertl provided an effective combination for the Marine Corps in Korea. Though considered awkward, the BAR was a favorite support weapon for the scout-sniper teams. Automatic weapon fire was often used in "street-fighting" to flush the enemy, with a marksman waiting "to nail the target." (U.S. Marine Corps.)

A M91/30, 7.62mm sniper rifle with a 3.5-power PU telescopic sight is typical of those employed by North Korean and Chinese Communist forces during the Korean War. Although most weapons were supplied by the Soviet Union, other Communist-bloc countries were known to furnish sniping equipment as well. A simple, durable weapon, the Mosin-Nagant M91/30 sniper rifle was extremely effective in capable hands. (West Point Collection.)

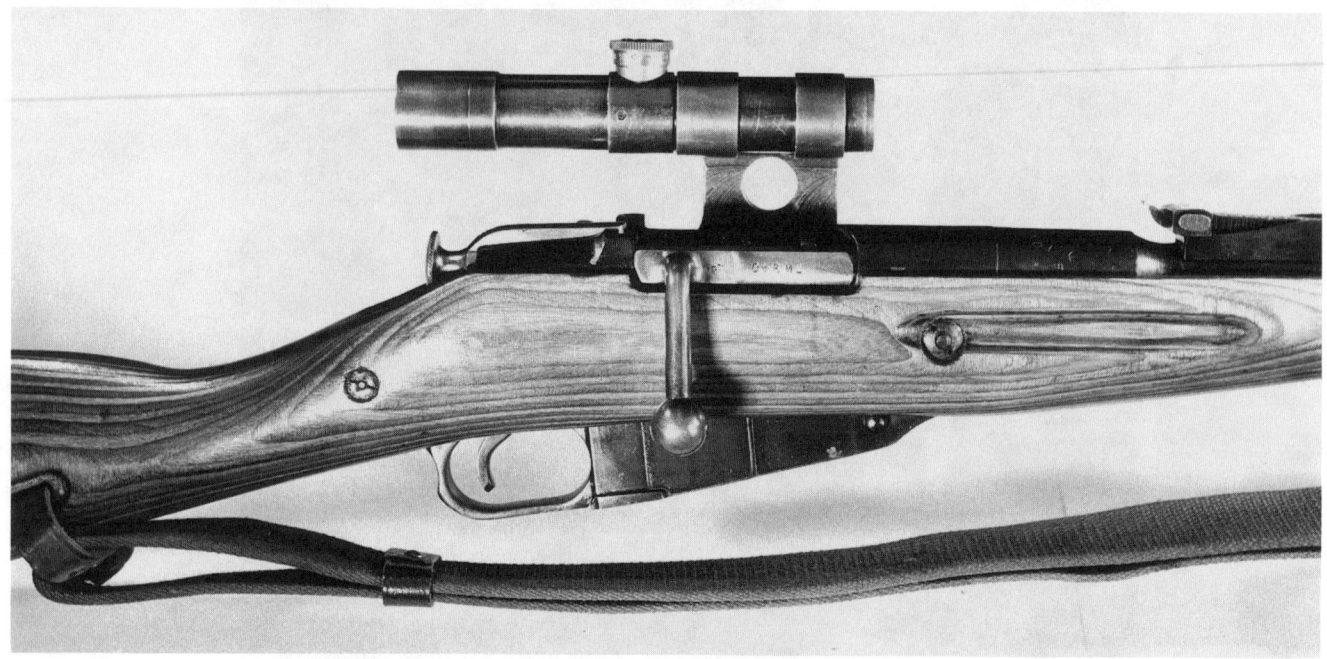

A typical Soviet-manufacture Mosin-Nagant M91/30 sniper rifle with 3.5-power PU telescopic sight. An adaptation of the basic Soviet infantry rifle, a turned-down bolt handle was used to clear the sight. Fitted with either PE or PU telescopic sights on various mountings, the M91/30 served as the principal sniper issue for the Communist-bloc countries following World War II. (Conway Collection.)

We found, for instance, that the '03 rifle gave better results than the M-1, probably because the sights mounted on the '03 were more powerful. (It is realized that this statement is subject to debate.) However, neither the range of the M-1 nor of the '03 was sufficient for all types of sniper work in Korea.

If the range could be stretched to 1,200 yards or a little more, the sniper unit could have been used more than it was.

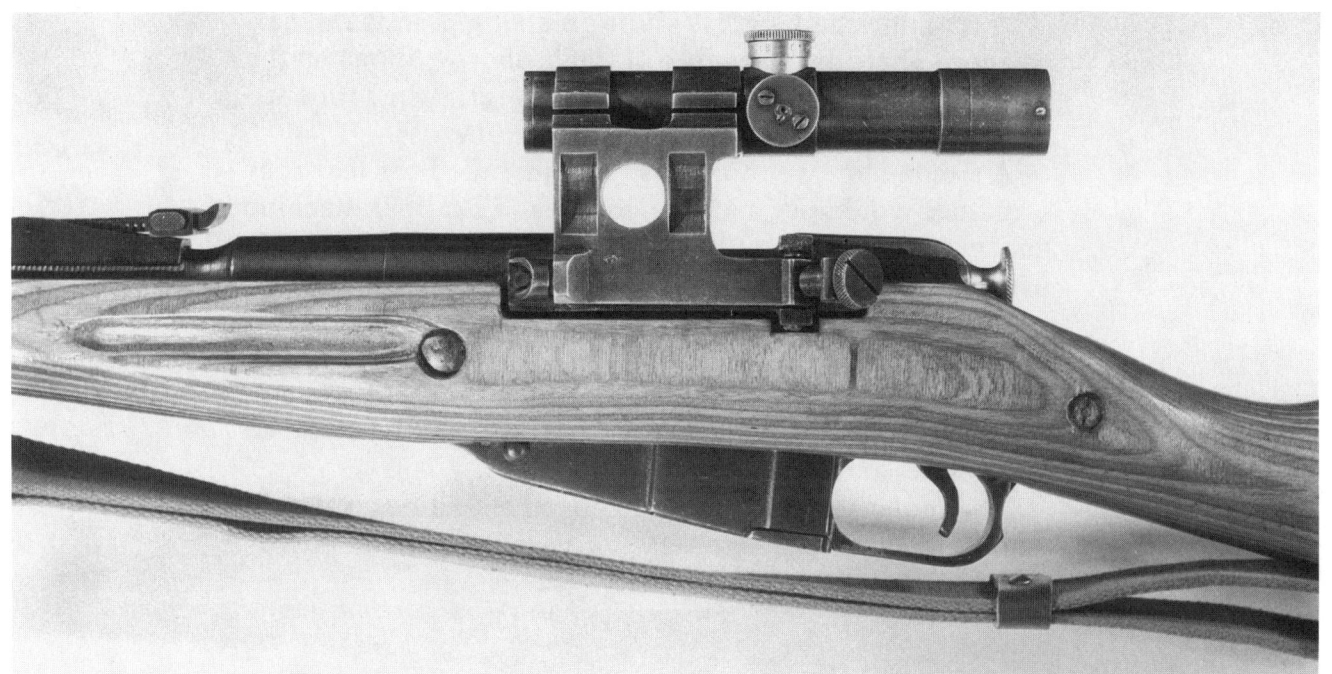

Another view of the Soviet Mosin-Nagant M91/30 sniper rifle. In some cases, Communist snipers were trained by Soviet advisers according to proven Red Army doctrine. Though unconfirmed, Soviet advisers were said to "try their hands" at picking off American troops whenever the opportunity presented itself. (Conway Collection.)

One of the more unusual "posed" Marine Corps combat photographs dating from the Korean War. According to the original caption, "A private acts as a decoy to lure Red troops from cover while a crack Marine shot waits for the best target." A matter of time in any case, as the caption continued, "The Commanding Officer of the unit made the Marines stop this practice" (July 1952). (U.S. Marine Corps.)

We recommended a glass sight on a single-shot .50 cal. weapon. There are a number of single-shot weapons on the foreign markets today (used by other governments for anti-tank weapons) that could be used for the purpose.

A single-shot weapon was recommended for fear that ordnance would put a glass sight on a .50 caliber machine gun, ground mount, and say it was the answer to our problem. This weapon is far too bulky for sniper work in Korea.

We decided three of these .50 caliber rifles to a sniper platoon would be about right since they could be used as additional weapons when the occasion demanded. Other equipment needed by the platoon to operate efficiently would be field glasses and SCR-300 radios....

The sniper platoon can be an effective unit but it should be pointed out right here—as you train them, so shall they produce results.

A Special Equipment: The Combat Edge

CHAPTER 12

Among the myriad examples of innovative infantry weapons and tactics developed and fielded from World War II through Korea, from the standpoint of value to combat personnel and particularly men trained as scout-snipers, especially noteworthy are the emergence of night vision equipment that made it possible to detect and fire on the enemy in total darkness and the application of telescope-sighted .50-caliber machine guns for relatively accurate long-range firing.

The infrared night vision sights, first conceived in 1943 by the Army, were developed for the express purpose of neutralizing the night infiltration tactics of the Imperial Japanese Army.

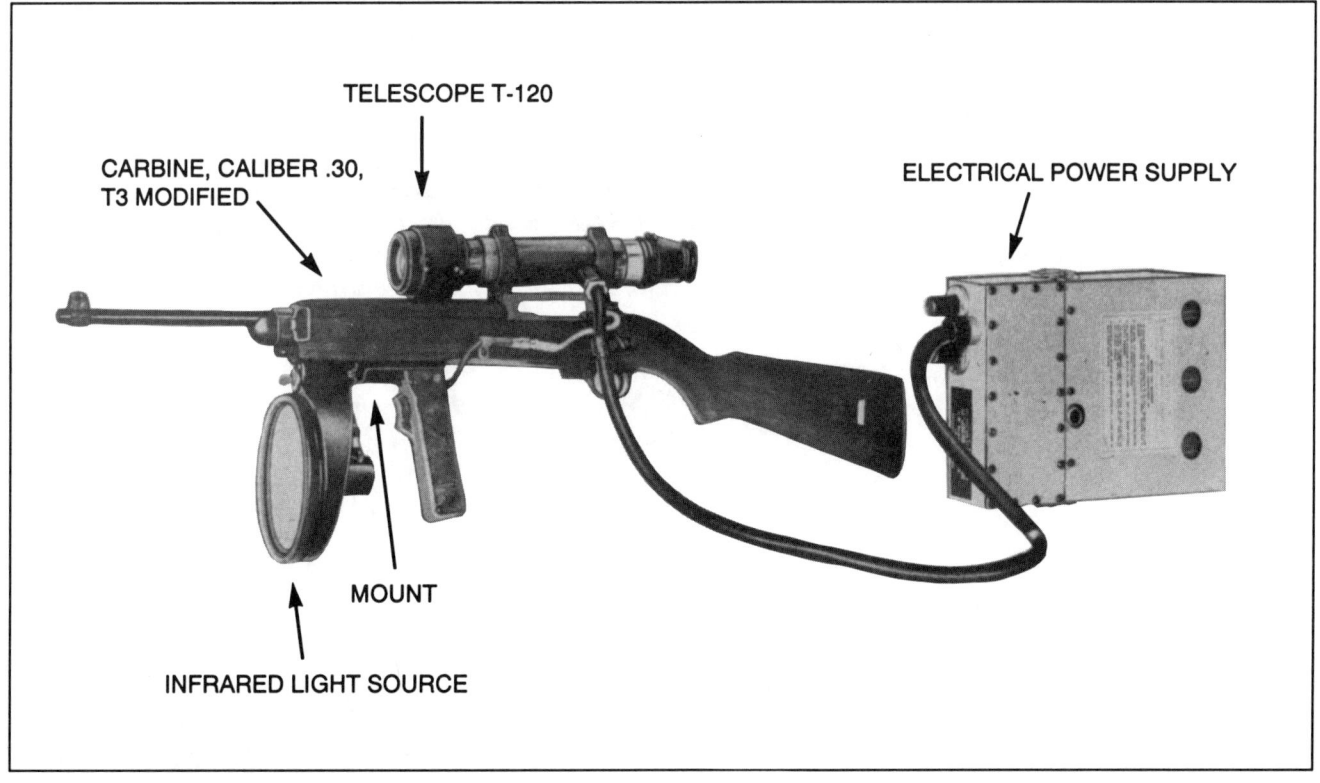

Infrared Sniperscope M1 with the .30-caliber Carbine T3, circa 1944. Operational infrared devices designated M1 utilized the service designed T-120 electronic telescope in original form. Subsequent development by Bell & Howell resulted in the introduction of Sniperscope M2 with a vastly improved T230 Telescope. (U.S. Army.)

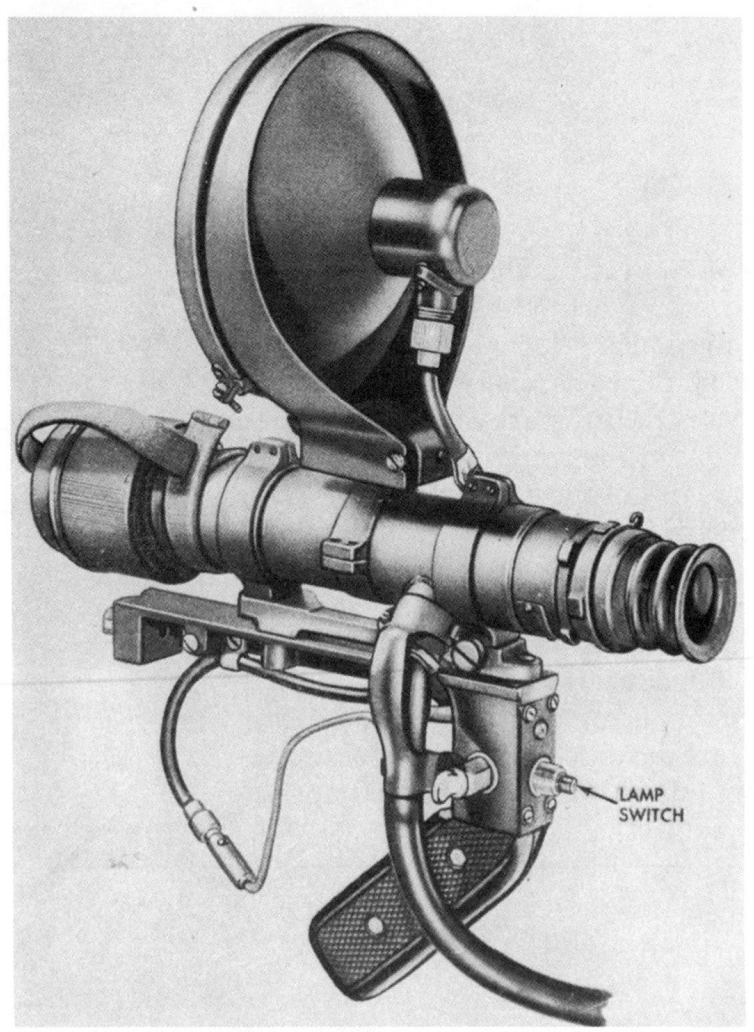

The original M1 infrared was designated "Sniperscope" when mounted on a carbine and "Snooperscope" when used with the hand-held mount for signaling or searching operations. A design progression in this case, an M1 unit has the infrared light source positioned above the electronic telescope. As originally fielded, the light source was mounted beneath the telescope. Though unconfirmed, the hand-held units are believed to have seen the first combat use during World War II. (U.S. Army.)

The T3 carbines developed for use with the infrared Sniperscope during World War II. The original pattern (bottom) had a "bridge-type" mount extending from the forward portion of the receiver rearward to the rear section, a system similar to that of the Redfield "Junior" telescope mounting base used with the M1903A4 sniper rifle. Subsequent models dispensed with the bridge mount altogether. The flat beneath the forward section of the T3 stock served as a mounting platform for the infrared hand grip assembly. An adaptor was eventually designed to mount the infrared units on any standard carbine. The T3 carbines were the only weapons manufactured especially for use with night vision instruments. (U.S. Army.)

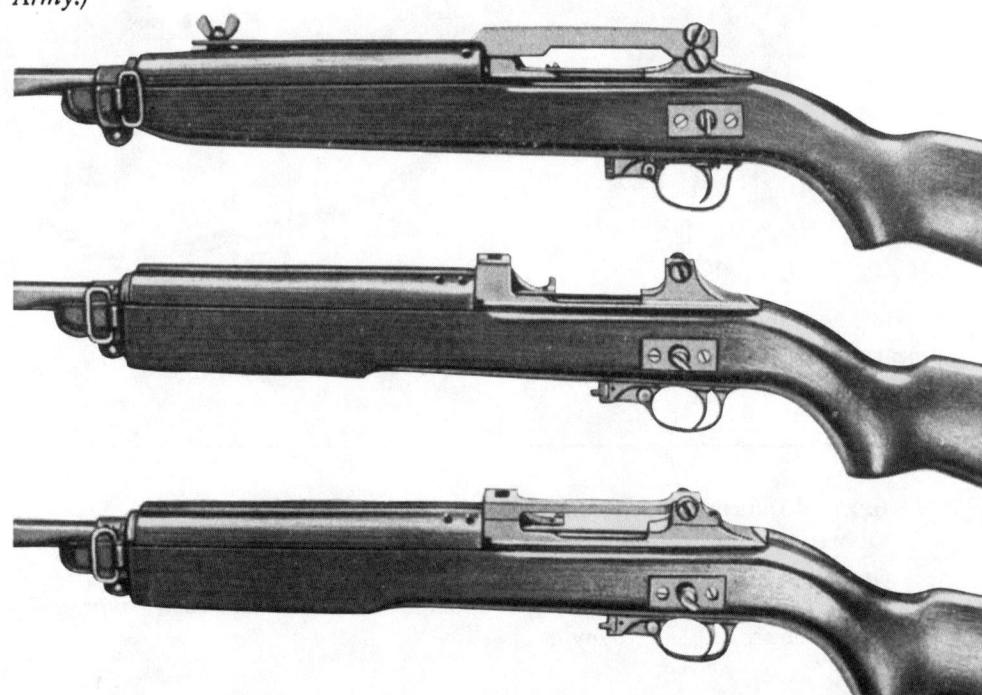

When introduced for combat use in 1944, the infrared units were available in two models: a carbine-mounted unit and a hand-held version

The carbine was provided with a special receiver to accommodate the infrared sight and a modified stock for attaching the infrared light source to the forend. As such, the carbine was designated Carbine, Caliber .30, T3 "Sniperscope." In addition to the Sniperscope, a companion device, the Snooperscope, was developed to supplement night observation and signaling. While similar in configuration to the Sniperscope, it was hand-held and not weapon-mounted.

An infrared design progression, a variant Sniperscope M2 is shown with supporting field equipment, carrying cases, and various accessories. Though similar to its predecessor, the improved M2 model differed in mechanical detail to the extent that most parts were not interchangeable with the earlier M1 units. Developed late in World War II, the M2 units did not see general combat use until the Korean War. (U.S. Army.)

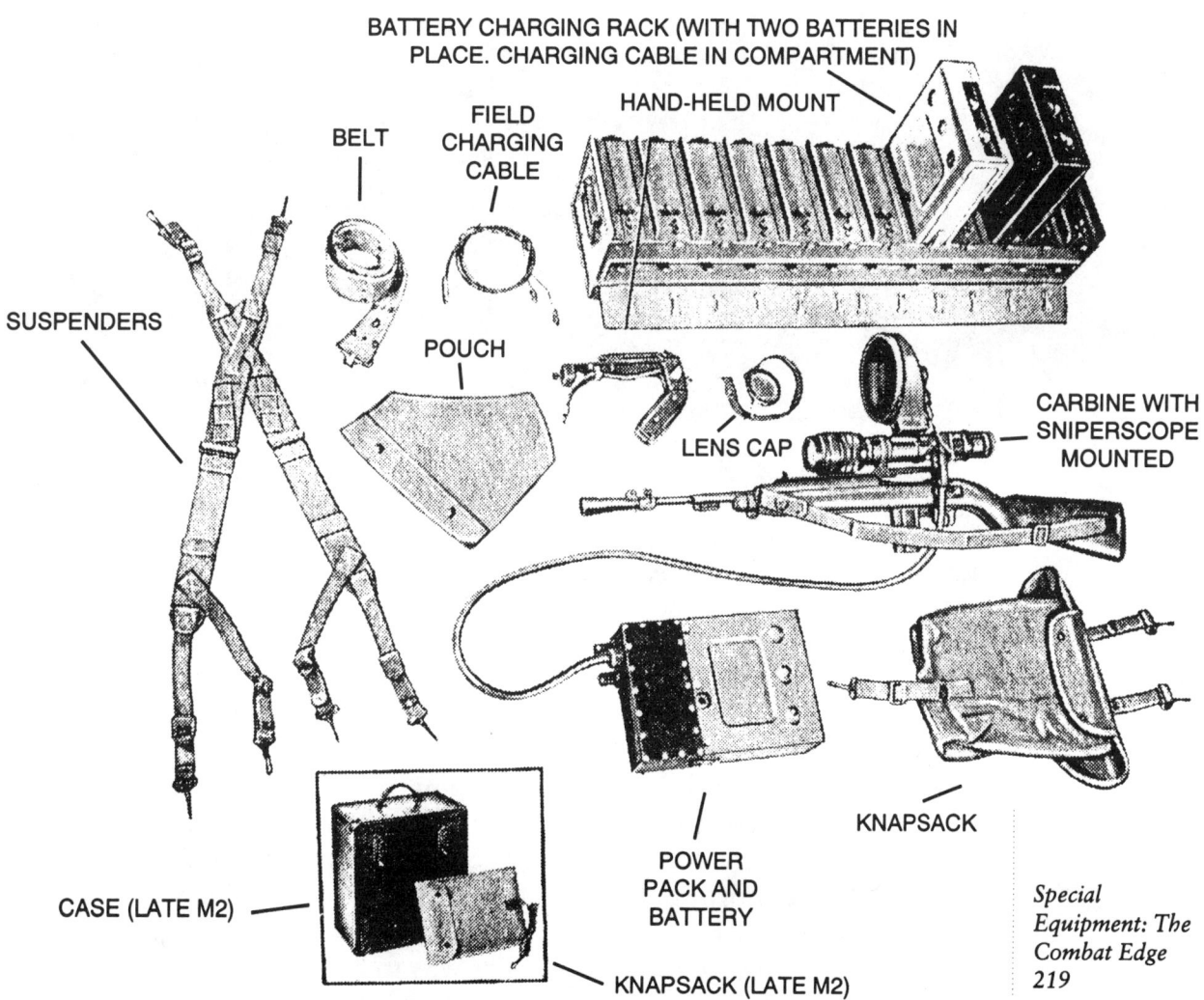

Though night vision equipment was previously believed to have been limited to Army use in the South Pacific, information provided by USMC combat personnel trained as scout-snipers during the last months of the war confirms that, at this level at least, the Marine Corps had been furnished with infrared equipment as well.

Designated Sniperscope M1 in original combat trim, subsequent modifications and improvements would result in the fielding of Sniperscope M2 and the last of the carbine-mounted units, the Sniperscope "Set No. 1/M3 20,000 volt."

Marine Corps riflemen receiving instruction in the use of the M1 infrared Sniperscope during the Korean War. According to the original caption, "First Marine Division's ordnance battalion holds school for members of the Fifth Marine Regiment somewhere in Korea. (U.S. Marine Corps.)

Developed and introduced at about the same time the United States was drawn into the conflict in Korea, the vastly improved M3 infrared devices extended the effective range to almost double that of the earlier units.

A night vision capability was to prove particularly effective in combating Japanese infiltration tactics during the later stages of the war in the Pacific. Combat reports cite approaching groups of Japanese being thoroughly decimated while attempting to pick their way through American lines. From that point forward, night activity of the average Japanese soldier was to be infinitely more hazardous. Although several thousand infrared units were reportedly manufactured during World War II, less than 500 were employed in the South Pacific. From all indications, the vast majority of these were used for training purposes rather than actual combat.

Classified "secret" at the time, information on the infrared units and their combat effectiveness was not disclosed until after the war. Interestingly, of all the "official" night vision information then circulated, the statement quoted most often by the media was: "The Sniperscope accounted for approximately 30 percent of the total Japanese casualties inflicted by small-arms fire during the first seven days of action on Okinawa."

Owing to the limits of actual infrared use, however, few among the Army and Marine Corps line troops involved in combat on Okinawa were in a position to offer their perspective on the matter.

In one case however, a combat veteran, Frank H. Booth, in a letter to the "Readers Comments" section of the August 1946 issue of *American Rifleman*, offered his views on the effectiveness of infrared on Okinawa:

> I served with a rifle company in the 77th Division during the Pacific War and contrary to popular belief, the value of the Sniperscope in the Ryukyus campaign was greatly overrated. We received our Sniperscopes and Snooperscopes and instruction in their use immediately after the close of the Leyte campaign. However, we found that they were of greater value in a jungle perimeter defense than in the comparatively open terrain encountered on Okinawa. Each night throughout the Okinawa campaign, the ground forces were supported by heavy mortars and Naval ships, supplying an endless stream of flares. These proved to be greater help in detecting the enemy than any other device.

In conjunction with an ongoing infrared weapon sight development program after the war, the requirement for a special stock was eliminated altogether. As then followed, the Carbine, Caliber .30, M3 was adopted and standardized for use with the night vision sight. While still utilizing a special receiver for mounting the electronic telescope, the M3 carbine was now fitted with a conventional stock typical of those employed with the selective fire M2 carbines.

In an effort to simplify the system, production of the special carbine receiver was eventually terminated. An adaptor mounting was designed to permit the use of a Sniperscope with any standard carbine.

Concurrent with standardization of the Carbine, M3, a flash hider (T23) was adopted for use with the Sniperscope units and selective fire carbines. The flash hider, supplied as an accessory with M2 Sniperscopes, was not supplied with the M1 variant as originally issued.

With active combat involvement in Korea, in addition to the newer M3 units, existing M1 and M2 infrared Sniperscopes stockpiled in ordnance depots after World War II were also employed in one form or another against the North Korean and Chinese Communist forces. Compared to the receptive attitude of American combat forces in the Pacific during World War II—when infrared could have weighed 100 pounds and still been most welcome—such devices were not popular in Korea. Objections to their use were manifold, and, as reports indicate, were centered on their bulk and susceptibility to damage during combat.

The last of the carbine-mounted infrared units, the M3 Sniperscope. Officially designated Sniperscope Infrared Set No. 1, 20,000 volts, the M3 system was manufactured beginning about 1951. While never in the quantities necessary to make a significant impact, night vision equipment was issued to all branches of the armed forces during the Korean War. (Sam Bases.)

As seems to be the case whenever "special equipment" is deployed in a combat zone, in some instances, infrared units were not available where they were needed most, or where they were available, combat personnel had not been trained to operate them properly.

In his *Weapons Usage in Korea*, S.L.A. Marshall stated:

> The Eighth Army is short on special equipment for the sniper, particularly the infrared scope needed for night work. . . . These were present in such limited numbers as to be hardly more than a novelty for the amusement of the command at a regimental headquarters. Infantry line comman-

Marines of the 1st Regiment, 1st Marine Division, "fire the carbine with the M3 20,000-volt Sniperscope" (Korea, 1953). The battery and power pack were strapped together and carried in a knapsack-type case. The Neoprene-coated case was water- and fungus-proofed. (U.S. Marine Corps.)

ders frequently expressed the view that if they could get the equipment in quantity, it would be a godsend in night defense.

Although carbine-mounted infrared was utilized with varying results, its most practical application came late in the conflict when activity was relegated to trench lines and bunkers with more frequent use of the night vision equipment in a defensive posture.

Infrared Sniperscopes were issued to all branches of the armed forces in Korea. Major use, other than by the Air Force for guarding aircraft installations, was by Army and Marine Corps combat troops. The designation "Sniperscope," actually a misnomer, did not require a specially trained marksman or sniper for satisfactory operation.

In reality, the use of snipers in Korea, other than the highly regarded Marine Corps scout-snipers, was an infrequent occur-

A Marine rifleman firing the carbine-mounted M3 infrared unit in Korea. Though reasonably effective in a combat environment, the cumbersome nature of the carbine-mounted infrared equipment limited its value as an attack weapon. The most practical application came with the use of night vision sights in fixed positions later in the war. The tool kit (left) was part of the issue field maintenance equipment for the M3 unit. (U.S. Marine Corps.)

Marine riflemen shown making necessary adjustments to the M3 electronic telescope after "sighting-in." Adjusting the telescope horizontally (azimuth) could be done during the day or at night. Adjusting the telescope vertically (reticle) was only done during periods of darkness. The small opening in the telescope lens cover simplified the sighting-in process. (U.S. Marine Corps.)

rence. Despite the use of infrared, few men participating in the Korean conflict were aware that American forces possessed a night-vision capability.

Without question, the most innovative application of sniping weapons in Korea involved the adaptation of .50-caliber Browning machine guns and modified World War II anti-tank rifles for extended long-range firing.

There has been some debate over which branch of the service (Army or Marine Corps) should be credited with first use of the "Big Fifty" for long-range sniping, and while it is difficult to determine beyond all question, experts tend to agree that the Army pioneered the use of .50-caliber machine guns in this capacity following the invasion of Europe, when long-range shooting requirements became greater than they were in the Pacific. Under favorable circumstances, and the right combination of gunner, telescopic sight, barrel quality, and ammunition, the .50-caliber Browning accounted for some phenomenal shooting at ranges of 2,000-plus yards during World War II.

The air-cooled infantry, or ground, .50 "M2 Heavy Barrel Flexible" machine gun, made use of a 45-inch barrel with no jacket of any kind beyond the short one incorporating a bearing surface which was firmly screwed into the receiver. Unlike most heavy machine guns, the M2 possessed both automatic and semiautomatic fire option.

Sight, Telescope, M1, manufactured by the Perfex Corp. in Milwaukee, Wisconsin (1942). Intended for "precise" long-range firing with the Browning machine gun, the 3.25-power prismatic sight weighed 1.68 pounds and was 6 5/8 inches in length with the eye guard in place. (Stephen M. Fleischman.)

Although original design had intended the use of semiautomatic action for sighting-in or targeting, unlocking the bolt latch release and alternately pressing the trigger and bolt latch release permitted semiautomatic or simply single-round firing. Fitted with conventional leaf and blade type sights, the rear sight base incorporated a dovetailed groove in which a telescope sight could be mounted.

Based on its single-shot capability in conjunction with telescopic sight, utilization of the air-cooled .50- Browning in a sniping capacity (to supplement long-range limitations of existing .30-caliber sniping rifles) was officially considered late in World War II and again when U.S. forces became involved in Korea a few years later. Unsuited as they were, ground .50s were employed in Korea with some success for sniping purposes. This depended, of course, on what constituted effective sniping, which in itself was a subject of considerable difference of opinion within the military establishment through the years.

The .50 Browning rear sight assembly was provided with a dovetail groove in which the M1 telescope sight was attached. Though later eliminated, the telescope mounting facilitated the use of various telescopic sights against Communist forces in Korea and in Vietnam as well. (Stephen M. Fleischman.)

Whereas the early prismatic machine gun telescopes originally intended for the .50 Browning had all but disappeared from ordnance stores when the war in Korea began, in place of the prismatic scope, imaginative ordnance personnel adapted Unertl and Lyman target scopes to the big fifties. Using what has been aptly

described as "double-dovetails," blocks of steel were machined to fit the existing dovetail groove on the Browning with a corresponding dovetail at the top of the block to match the target telescope mounts. Before making the target sights work, however, M81 and M82 telescopes were tried and found to be lacking the ranging capability demanded by the .50-caliber machine gun. The 2.5-power riflescopes were totally inadequate for long-range use.

A "driver's view" of the Browning machine gun illustrates the dovetail mounting of the prismatic telescopic sight. The range dial was graduated in yards and mils, the deflection dial in mils. While effective for single-shot firing, M1 sights saw limited use during World War II. (U.S. Army.)

Consequently, when a Marine sniper or sniper team "set up shop" by simply employing a telescope mounting block and a suitable target scope, an appropriately positioned Browning could be readily transformed into an effective long-range sniping weapon. As a matter of interest, the same concept was applied later in Vietnam by USMC scout-snipers as noted by Charles Henderson in his work, *Marine Sniper*:

> ... Snipers will go on missions and carry a set of mounts in their packs. When they get into the operational unit, it is a minor task to attach the mounts to any M-2, .50 caliber machine gun available. A sniper easily fastens the mounts to the big gun and removes his scope from his rifle and attaches it on the machine gun mounts. After that, it is a simple job of leveling the gun and zeroing the weapon to whatever distance that he expects to engage the majority of his targets.

For the record, however, though target scopes were employed effectively in Southeast Asia by both Army and USMC snipers, their use with the .50-caliber Browning machine gun originated during the Korean War.

A rear view of the "Big Fifty" with the prismatic sight removed. The telescope mounting groove (dovetail) is clearly visible. (Stephen M. Fleischman.)

An erstwhile Ordnance attempt to mount "effective telescopic sights" to the Browning machine gun in Korea. The 2.5-power M81 and M82 sights were tried and found totally inadequate for long-range firing with the "Big Fifty." In this case, an M1C telescope mounting was attached to a steel block machined to fit the dovetail groove on the Browning sight assembly. (U.S. Army.)

Even though .50-caliber ammunition was used "right out of the can" for the most part, with the quality being as marginal as it was in many instances, whenever a given lot of ammunition performed better than expected, every attempt was made to "set aside" as much as was practical when snipers were working from a static or fixed position. As one Marine combat veteran stated it, "Good ammunition was squirreled away whenever possible."

Browning machine gun, caliber .50, HB M2 with a 12-power Lyman Super Targetspot telescopic sight, circa 1952 (Korea), attached to the telescope mounting groove (dovetail) by means of a special steel block. In addition to Lyman target scopes, Unertl and Fecker sights were reportedly used in Korea as well. The concept of mounting target scopes to the .50-caliber Browning originated during the Korean War. (Max Crace illustration.)

In addition to the "Big Fifty," specially prepared anti-tank rifles, though used sparingly, were also brought to bear against Communist forces in Korea. Unlike the telescopic sighted .50-caliber machine guns, however, with exceptions possible, modified anti-tank rifles are not known to have been employed by Marine snipers for long-range sniping in Korea. Nevertheless, from the standpoint of their original combat application by American forces, while not intended for sniping purposes, the first use of anti-tank rifles in a "special weapons" capacity must be credited to the Marine Raiders of World War II.

An integral part of the Raider table of organization and equipment (TO&E) from the onset (1942), the choice of an anti-tank rifle had been influenced by the British Commandos. Referenced as "a light anti-tank weapon" by the British, the .55-caliber Boys anti-tank rifle served to supplement the firepower of the lightly equipped Raider assault units. Though originally intended for "taking out" lightly armored Japanese vehicles, the 36-pound "Elephant Guns," as the Raiders called them, were used against fortified positions, landing craft, and aircraft as well.

Special Equipment: The Combat Edge

Marine Raiders crossing a jungle stream during the campaign at New Georgia Island in July 1943. Two of the Raiders are carrying .55-caliber Boys antitank rifles. The 36-pound "elephant guns" served to enhance the firepower of the lightly armed Raider assault units. (U.S. Marine Corps.)

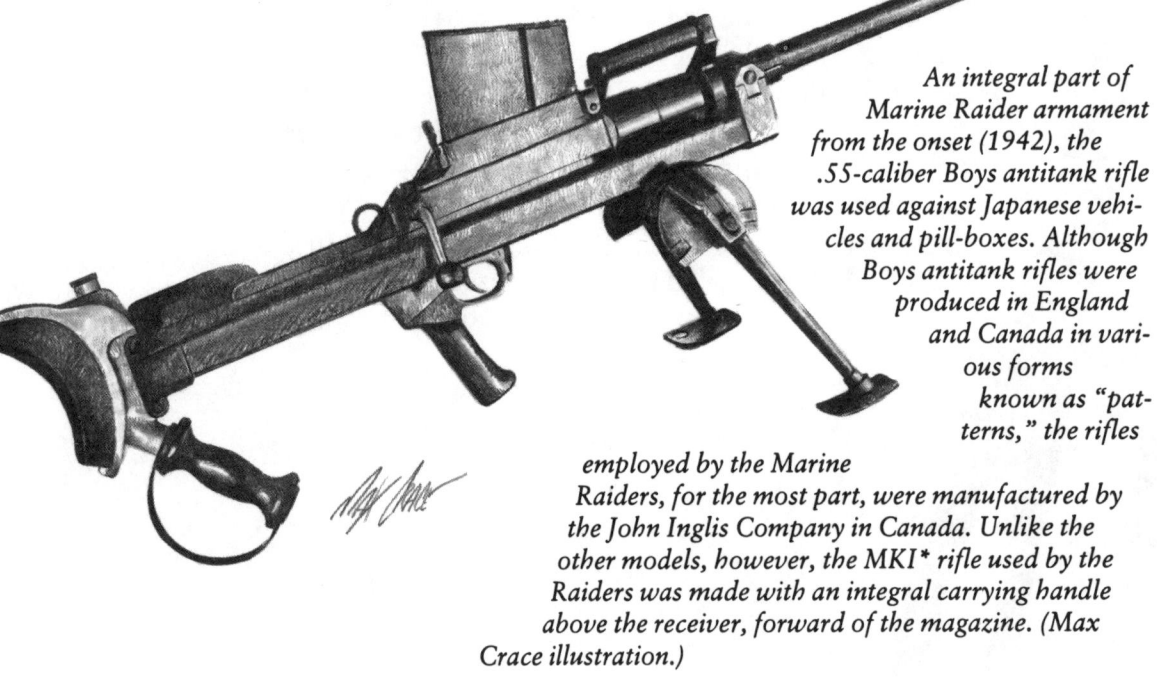

An integral part of Marine Raider armament from the onset (1942), the .55-caliber Boys antitank rifle was used against Japanese vehicles and pill-boxes. Although Boys antitank rifles were produced in England and Canada in various forms known as "patterns," the rifles employed by the Marine Raiders, for the most part, were manufactured by the John Inglis Company in Canada. Unlike the other models, however, the MKI* rifle used by the Raiders was made with an integral carrying handle above the receiver, forward of the magazine. (Max Crace illustration.)